Life-Study of Ephesians

Messages 64-97

Witness Lee

Living Stream Ministry
Anaheim, California

First Edition, October, 1991.

ISBN 978-0-7363-0962-2
(Complete set, softcover)
ISBN 978-0-87083-149-2
(Messages 64-97)

Published by

Living Stream Ministry
2431 W. La Palma Ave., Anaheim, CA 92801 U.S.A.
P. O. Box 2121, Anaheim, CA 92814 U.S.A.

Printed in the United States of America

10 11 12 13 14 15 / 10 9 8 7 6 5 4

CONTENTS

LIFE-STUDY OF EPHESIANS

MESSAGE SIXTY-FOUR

THE WHOLE ARMOR OF GOD

(1)

In this message and in the message following we shall consider the items that make up the whole armor of God. The first three items—the girdle, the breastplate, and the shoes—form a group. By means of these three things we are able to stand. Along with these three items, we need to take up the shield of faith and receive the helmet of salvation and the sword of the Spirit (6:16-17).

Soldiers in ancient times fought with a shield in one hand and a sword in the other. A shield is a defensive weapon, whereas a sword is an offensive weapon. Actually, of the six items of the whole armor of God, only the sword is an offensive weapon. All the other aspects of the armor are for defense. Let us first consider the girdle, the breastplate, and the shoes.

I. THE GIRDLE OF TRUTH

The first part of 6:14 says, "Stand therefore, having girded your loins with truth." For us to gird our loins is to strengthen our entire being. Our whole being needs to be strengthened with truth. This strengthening is not for sitting, but for standing.

According to the way the word truth is used in chapter four (vv. 15, 21, 24, 25), truth here refers to God in Christ as reality in our living, that is, God realized and experienced by us as our living. This is actually Christ Himself lived out by us (John 14:6). Such truth, such reality, is the girdle that strengthens our whole being for spiritual warfare. Our living must have a principle and a standard. This is nothing less than God Himself expressed in our living in a practical way. When such a truth girds our loins, we are made strong for the purpose of standing.

Suppose, however, that your daily living is far below the standard of the truth as it is in Jesus. Instead of being able to stand and to withstand in the evil day, you will flee. Because in your daily walk there is no testimony and no expression of God, you do not have the strength to stand against the stratagems of the Devil. If our daily living is loose, we are not able to stand against the powers of darkness. In order for us to stand, our daily living must be according to the principle of the truth and up to the standard of the truth. As we have pointed out, this truth is God Himself expressed as the principle of our daily walk, as the standard of our daily living, and as the pattern of our life.

Those who have such a living certainly have their loins girded with truth. These are the ones who are able to face attack and opposition. Because they are girded with truth, they can stand before the opposers. But if God is not expressed in our daily life and walk, we shall not have a girdle about our loins, and we shall have no strength to stand against the enemy. We shall not have the power to face opposition or controversy.

The truth with which we are girded for spiritual warfare is actually the very Christ we experience. In Philippians 1:21 Paul says, "To me to live is Christ." This Christ whom Paul lived was his girdle of truth. This Christ was God expressed and revealed in Paul's daily walk. Because Paul's daily living was conformed to the pattern of Christ, he had the strength to face all opposition and adverse circumstances. Because Paul had been girded about with truth, he had the strength to stand.

II. THE BREASTPLATE OF RIGHTEOUSNESS

In verse 14 Paul goes on to say, "Having put on the breastplate of righteousness." The breastplate of righteousness covers our conscience, signified by the breast. Satan is our accuser. In fighting against him we need a conscience void of offense. But no matter how good we may feel our conscience is, we need to have it covered with the breastplate of righteousness. Righteousness is to be right with both God and man. If we have just a little problem with either God or man, Satan will accuse us, and there will be holes in our conscience through which all of our faith and boldness will leak out. Hence, we need the covering of righteousness to protect us from the enemy's accusation. Such righteousness is Christ (1 Cor. 1:30).

If in any thing we are not righteous, our conscience will be a conscience with offense. But if we are to engage in spiritual warfare, we must have a conscience void of offense, a conscience without holes. When our conscience has holes in it, our faith will leak out through the holes. If accusations and offenses remain on our conscience, faith will disappear. Therefore, we need to deal with our conscience in order to have a good conscience, a conscience void of offense. In addition, we need to put on the breastplate of righteousness to cover our conscience.

Whenever we are about to fight the spiritual warfare, Satan, the accuser, attacks our conscience. He does not trouble us so much in this way at other times, Satan knows when there are offenses on our conscience. When he accuses us with respect to these offenses, we are immediately weakened.

Revelation 12:11 says, "They overcame him because of the blood of the Lamb." To be covered by the blood of the Lamb is mainly to have upon us the breastplate of righteousness. Righteousness is in the blood, and the covering of the blood is the breastplate. Although this may be difficult to explain doctrinally, we can understand it experientially. Whenever we intend to fight against the powers of darkness, Satan, through his accusations, causes our conscience to become very sensitive. These feelings actually are not the sensitivity of the conscience, but the result of Satan's accusations. Immediately our response should be, "I overcome Satan, the accuser, not by my perfection and not even by a conscience void of offense, but by the blood of the Lamb. I am defended against his accusations by the breastplate of righteousness."

The righteousness that covers our conscience and that guards us from Satan's accusations is Christ Himself. He is our righteousness. Thus, Christ is the truth that girds our loins and also the breastplate of righteousness that covers our conscience. We are covered not by our own righteousness, but by Christ as our righteousness. Some may wonder how the breastplate of righteousness can be related both to Christ and to the blood. In experience we cannot separate the blood from Christ. Apart from His blood, Christ could not cover us. Under the cleansing of His blood, He becomes our righteousness. Whenever we are about to take part in the spiritual warfare, we need to pray, "Lord, cover me with Yourself as my righteousness. Lord, I hide under Your blood." Furthermore, we must tell the accuser, "Satan, I overcome you, not by my merit, but by the prevailing blood of the Lamb."

III. THE FIRM FOUNDATION OF THE GOSPEL OF PEACE

Verse 15 says, "And having shod your feet with the firm foundation of the gospel of peace." Our feet must be shod in order to strengthen our stand in the battle. This is not for walking a way or running a course, but for fighting the battle.

The phrase "the firm foundation of the gospel of peace" means the establishment of the gospel of peace. Christ has made peace for us on the cross, both with God and with man, and this peace has become our gospel (2:13-17). This has been established as a firm foundation, as a readiness for our feet to be shod with. Thus, we shall have a firm footing that we may stand to fight the spiritual warfare. The peace for such a firm foundation is also Christ (2:14).

Most translations render the Greek here as readiness or preparation rather than firm foundation. Readiness or preparation indicates preparedness to put on shoes. Many readers of Ephesians think that in verse 15 Paul is charging us to be always ready and prepared to put on the shoes of the gospel. But this is an incorrect understanding derived from an inaccurate translation.

In order to understand Paul's thought in this verse, we need to see that here the gospel is not the gospel of grace, nor the gospel of the forgiveness of sins, nor even the gospel of the unsearchable riches of Christ. Here the gospel is the gospel of peace. According to 2:15 and 16, on the cross Christ accomplished peace so that the Gentiles can contact the Jewish believers and so that we all can contact God. This peace is glad tidings, good news. In other words, it is the gospel. For this reason, 2:17 says that Christ preached the gospel of peace.

We also must preach this peace as the gospel. The gospel of peace spoken of in 6:15 is the peace accomplished by Christ on the cross for us to be one with God and for the Gentile believers to be one with the Jewish believers. This peace is our gospel. With this peace there is preparation, readiness. The Greek word actually means a firm foundation. This firm foundation is a secure footing for our standing. Therefore, the peace accomplished by Christ on the cross is a firm footing, a firm foundation. As we fight against the evil powers, the peace Christ has accomplished is a firm foundation for our feet. To take part in the spiritual warfare, our feet must be shod with this firm foundation.

In the past most of us thought that the shoes of the gospel were for us to walk or to run in our preaching of the gospel. However, the firm foundation of the gospel of peace is not for running, but for standing. For running we may have a pair of lightweight shoes, but for standing we need a pair of sturdy shoes.

In fighting, the crucial thing is to stand. We must be able to stand and to withstand the attacks of the enemy. Those who are defeated will run, but those who are victorious will stand. As we wrestle against the enemy, we shall find that Satan does not run away. Even when we are victorious over him, he keeps on wrestling with us. Therefore we need to be able to stand. Spiritual warfare is not a boxing match, but a wrestling match. If we would wrestle against the enemy, we need a firm footing. Hallelujah, in the Lord's recovery we have such a foundation! Because there are those who have their feet shod with the firm foundation of the gospel of peace, they can withstand any attack of the enemy. Because they have such a firm footing, nothing can shake them. No matter what happens, they can stand and withstand in the evil day.

Usually peace is the opposite of warfare. When we have peace, we do not fight, and when we fight, we do not have peace. But here we fight with peace and in peace. We fight by standing in peace. If we lose the peace between us and God or between us and other believers, we lose the standing. Christ is the peace for us to be one with God and to be one with the saints. This peace is the firm foundation that enables us to stand fast against the enemy.

The three aspects of the armor of God covered in this message—the girdle of truth, the breastplate of righteousness, and the firm foundation of the gospel of peace—are all Christ. He is our truth, our righteousness, and our peace. Christ is God expressed and revealed, Christ is the righteous element that covers us, and Christ is the peace that enables us to stand. Therefore, we can stand in peace to fight the spiritual warfare. If we would be victorious in the spiritual warfare, we need Christ as our girdle of truth, as our breastplate of righteousness, and as our peace. By means of such a Christ we have the strength, the covering, and the firm footing. Then we are able to fight against the enemy.

LIFE-STUDY OF EPHESIANS

MESSAGE SIXTY-FIVE

THE WHOLE ARMOR OF GOD

(2)

In the foregoing message we considered the first three items of the armor of God: the girdle, the breastplate, and the shoes. The girdle is related to truth, the breastplate is related to righteousness, and the shoes are related to peace. We have seen that truth is God expressed in our living as our standard, pattern, and principle. Righteousness is Christ in our enjoyment and experience as the covering of our conscience. If we have truth in our living, we shall certainly have righteousness as our covering. The Bible reveals that righteousness issues in peace. This is peace both with God and with man. It is the very peace Christ accomplished on the cross for us. Therefore, to have the girdle, the breastplate, and the shoes is to have truth, righteousness, and peace. When we live out God in our daily living, we are covered with Christ as our righteousness, and we have peace as our firm foundation. Then we are prepared to fight against the enemy.

I. THE SHIELD OF FAITH

Verse 16 says, "With all these, having taken up the shield of faith, with which you shall be able to quench all the flaming darts of the evil one." We need truth to gird our loins, righteousness to cover our conscience, peace as the standing for our feet, and faith to shield our entire being. If we live by God as truth, we have righteousness (4:24), and righteousness issues in peace (Heb. 12:11; Isa. 32:17). With all these, we can easily have faith as a shield against the flaming darts of the evil one. Christ is the Author and Perfecter of such faith (Heb. 12:2). For us to stand firmly in the battle we need to be equipped with these four items of God's armor.

The shield of faith is not something that we put on, but something that we take up in order to protect ourselves against the attacks of the enemy. Faith comes after truth, righteousness, and peace. If we have truth in our living, righteousness as our covering, and peace as our standing, we shall spontaneously have faith. This faith is a safeguard against the fiery darts, the attacks, of the enemy.

We need now to consider the shield of faith in detail. We certainly are not to have faith in our own ability, strength, merit, or virtue. Our faith must be in God (Mark 11:22). God is real, living, present, and available. We need to have faith in Him.

We also should have faith in God's heart. Every Christian must know both God and the heart of God. God's heart toward us is always good. No matter what may happen to us or what kind of sufferings we may undergo, we must always believe in the goodness of God's heart. God has no intention to punish us, to injure us, or to cause us to suffer loss.

Along with faith in God's heart, we should have faith in God's faithfulness. We may change, but God does not change. As James 1:17 says, there is no shadow of turning with Him. Furthermore, He cannot lie (Titus 1:2), but is always faithful to His word.

God is not only faithful, but also able. Therefore, we need to have faith in God's ability. In 3:20 Paul declares that God "is able to do superabundantly above all that we ask or think."

Still another aspect of our faith is faith in God's word. God is bound to fulfill all that He has spoken. The more He speaks, the more responsible He becomes to fulfill His own word. We can tell Him, "God, You have spoken, and Your written Word is in our hand. Lord, You are bound to fulfill Your word." Hallelujah for God's faithful word!

We also need to have faith in God's will. Because God is a God of purpose, He has a will. His will with respect to us is always positive. Hence, no matter what befalls us, we should care not for our happiness or our environment, but for God's will. Our environment may change, but God's will never changes.

Furthermore, we must have faith in God's sovereignty. Because God is sovereign, God could never make a mistake. Under His sovereignty, even our mistakes work for good. If God did not sovereignly allow us to make mistakes, we could not possibly make them. (However, this does not mean that we should deliberately make mistakes.) When we are wrong, we need to repent. But there is no need for us to regret, for that means we are lacking in faith. After we repent for a mistake or shortcoming, we must still exercise faith in God's sovereignty. We could not have made that mistake if He had not sovereignly allowed us to do so. Hence, there is no need for regret.

We all need to have a full faith in God, in God's heart, in God's faithfulness, in God's ability, in God's word, in God's will, and in God's sovereignty. If we have such a faith, Satan's flaming darts will not be able to damage us.

The flaming darts are Satan's temptations, proposals, doubts, questions, lies, and attacks. Flaming darts were used by warriors in the apostle's time, and the apostle used this as an illustration of Satan's attacks on us. Every temptation is a deceit, a false promise. The flaming darts include the Devil's proposals that come to us. As we are waking up in the morning, often Satan will make proposals to us. For this reason, we need to get into the Word the first thing in the morning. If we are not in the Word, we shall have no covering against the Devil's proposals. Doubts and questions are also flaming darts of Satan. Have you ever noticed that a question mark looks very much like a serpent? It was Satan who asked Eve, "Hath God said?" (Gen. 3:1). When the Devil questions us in this way, our response should be to flee, without even talking to him. Many times Satan attacks us with lies. But the shield of faith also guards us against these flaming darts.

The Devil's flaming darts come as thoughts injected into our mind. These thoughts may seem to be our own thoughts, but they are actually Satan's. I used to believe that such thoughts were my own. Later I began to realize that they came from Satan. I discovered this after such thoughts persisted in coming after I had decided not to entertain them. I saw that these thoughts were not mine, but Satan's. Prior to that time, my practice was to confess all these thoughts to the Lord. Now I refuse to confess them. However, some may think that even though these thoughts come from Satan, they are injected into us because we are evil. Do not believe this. Rather, you should say, "Lord, I am fallen, but I am under Your cleansing. Satan, this thought is yours, and you must bear the responsibility for it. I will not share this responsibility." Nevertheless, due to an overly sensitive conscience some continually confess things that are caused by Satan. Never confess thoughts injected into you by Satan in his subtlety.

In order to have the faith to be defended against Satan's flaming darts, we need a proper spirit with a conscience void of offense. However, faith is not mainly in our spirit nor in our conscience, but in our will, the strongest part of our heart. The New Testament says that we believe with our heart (Rom. 10:10). According to our experience, this faith in our heart is related mainly to the exercise of our will. No one with a will like a jellyfish can have strong faith. In James 1:6 we are told that he who doubts is like a wave of the sea, driven by the wind. Such a person has a vacillating will. Hence, if we would have faith, we need to exercise our will.

II. THE HELMET OF SALVATION

In the first part of verse 17 Paul goes on to say, "And receive the helmet of salvation." This is for covering our mind, our mentality, against the negative thoughts directed at us by the evil one. Such a helmet, such a covering, is God's salvation. Satan injects into our mind threats, worries, anxieties, and other weakening thoughts. God's salvation is the covering we take up against all these. Such a salvation is the saving Christ we experience in our daily life (John 16:33).

Satan's darts come to us through our mind. Therefore, just as our conscience needs the breastplate of righteousness and our will needs the shield of faith, so our mind needs the helmet of salvation. We need truth, righteousness, peace, faith, and then salvation. Righteousness issues in peace, and peace gives us the ground to have faith. Then faith brings in salvation. Do not separate the helmet of salvation from the shield of faith. The shield protects the front of our being, but the helmet protects our head. The shield and the helmet work together.

III. THE SWORD OF THE SPIRIT

In verse 17 Paul also speaks of "the sword of the Spirit which is the word of God." Among the six items of God's armor, this is the only one for attacking the enemy. With the sword we cut the enemy to pieces. However, we do not take up the sword first. Rather, we must firstly put on the girdle, the breastplate, and the shoes, and then take up the shield of faith and the helmet of salvation. Then, when we are entirely protected and have salvation as our portion, we may receive the sword of the Spirit.

In verse 17 the antecedent of the word "which" is Spirit, not sword. This indicates that the Spirit is the word of God, both of which are Christ (2 Cor. 3:17; Rev. 19:13). If I were writing this verse, I would say, "the sword of the word of God." But Paul speaks of "the sword of the Spirit which is the word of God." Is the sword here the sword of the Spirit or the sword of the word? Most readers consider that Paul was saying that the sword is the word and that the Spirit wields the sword. I understood the verse this way for years. I thought that it was the Spirit, not I, who used the sword. In other words, according to this understanding, the sword is the word, and the One who uses the sword to slay the enemy is the Spirit. From my youth I was taught that the Spirit helps us to use the word of God as the sword. But this is not the meaning here. The correct meaning is that the Spirit is the sword itself, not the one who uses the sword. The Word of God is also a sword. The sword is the Spirit, and the Spirit is the Word. Here we have three that are one: the sword, the Spirit, and the Word.

My main burden in this message is on this matter. The Word is the Bible. But if this Word is only printed letters, it is neither the Spirit nor the sword. The Greek for word in verse 17 is *rhema,* the instant word spoken at the moment by the Spirit in any situation. When the *logos,* the constant word in the Bible, becomes the instant *rhema,* this *rhema* will be the Spirit. This *rhema,* which becomes the Spirit, is the sword that cuts the enemy to pieces. For example, we may read a particular verse again and again, only to have it remain the *logos*, a word in letters. Such a word cannot kill anything. But one day this verse becomes the *rhema* to us, the present, instant, living speaking. At that time this *rhema* becomes the Spirit. For this reason, in John 6:63 the Lord Jesus said, "The words which I have spoken unto you are spirit and are life." Here the Greek text also uses *rhema*. The instant, present word is the Spirit. This kind of word is the sword. Therefore, the sword, the Spirit, and the word are three that are one. Furthermore, we, not the Spirit, are the ones to use this sword to kill the enemy.

In our Christian experience, the Word and the Spirit must always be one. It is an utter falsehood to say that we take the Spirit without taking the Word. Without taking the Word, we cannot have the Spirit. In my experience, I receive the Spirit mostly through the Word. As I contact the Word in a living way, it becomes the Spirit to me. However, some take the Bible without the Spirit. This also is wrong. Those who wish to grow flowers need both the seeds and the life contained in the seeds. It is impossible to separate the life within the seeds from the seeds themselves. In order to have the life, we must take the seeds. The relationship between the Word and the Spirit is like that between the seeds and the life. We must have both. The Lord Jesus is both the Spirit and the Word. He is not the Spirit without being the Word, nor the Word without being the Spirit.

Because He is both the Word and the Spirit, He created us with a mind to understand and a spirit to receive. When we come to the Bible, we should exercise both our mind and our spirit. We exercise our mind by reading and our spirit by praying. Since we need both to read and to pray, we should pray-read the Word. I can testify that through pray-reading my spirit becomes strong and ready to devour the enemy. I not only exercise my spirit, but I also exercise my mind to consider the Word. For example, I may ask why grace and truth are mentioned in chapter four, whereas love and light are mentioned in chapter five. I also pray concerning this. The more my spirit is strengthened by pray-reading the Word, the more eager I am to use the sword of the Spirit to slay the enemy. In my speaking I have a sword with which to cut the enemy to pieces.

With the whole armor of God we have truth, righteousness, peace, faith, and salvation. Finally, we have the *rhema,* the Spirit, the sword. This is our offensive weapon to use in attacking the enemy. When we have the whole armor of God, including the sword, we are not only protected, but also prepared to wrestle against the enemy. By having truth, righteousness, peace, faith, and salvation we are equipped, qualified, strengthened, and empowered to use the sword in spiritual warfare. Then the enemy is subject to the cutting of our sword, and he is slaughtered by us.

As we engage in spiritual warfare against the enemy, we do not use gimmicks, skills, or politics. Our only weapon is the Spirit-Word, which is the sword. We do not employ cunning craftiness—we wield the sword of the Spirit. Our loins are girded with truth, and our conscience is covered by Christ as our righteousness. Then we have peace as our firm foundation. We can boast to the whole universe that we have no problems with God or man, for we are standing on the peace accomplished by Christ on the cross. Furthermore, we are protected by the shield of faith and guarded by the helmet of salvation. Therefore, when we pray-read the Word, every word becomes the *rhema,* the sword that cuts the enemy. In this way the victory is ours. We not only subdue the enemy and defeat him, but slay him and even cut him into pieces. This is what it means to fight the spiritual warfare with the whole armor of God. The church must be such an equipped, fighting, and victorious church to slay God's enemy.

LIFE-STUDY OF EPHESIANS

MESSAGE SIXTY-SIX

THE APPLICATION BY PRAYER

In this message we come to 6:18-20, which in particular covers the matter of prayer.

I. PRAYER AS THE APPLICATION OF THE ITEMS OF GOD'S ARMOR

We have seen that the armor of God is composed of six items: the girdle of truth, the breastplate of righteousness, the firm foundation of the gospel of peace, the shield of faith, the helmet of salvation, and the sword of the Spirit. When we are equipped with such a full armor, we can stand against the attack of the enemy and even take the offensive against him. After these items of the armor of God, Paul turns to prayer.

Verse 18 says, "By means of all prayer and petition, praying at every time in spirit, and watching unto this in all perseverance and petition concerning all the saints." The phrase "by means of all prayer and petition" modifies the word receive in verse 17. By prayer we receive both the helmet of salvation and the word of God. This indicates that we need to receive the word of God by means of all prayer and petition. We need to pray as we are receiving the word of God. We have seen that the whole armor of God is composed of six items. Prayer may be considered the seventh. It is the means by which we apply the other items.

The modifier "by means of all prayer and petition" in verse 18 is related to all six items of the armor covered in verses 14 through 17. It is by means of all prayer and petition that we gird our loins with truth, put on the breastplate of righteousness, and have our feet shod with the firm foundation of the gospel of peace. Furthermore, it is by prayer that we take up the shield of faith and receive the helmet of salvation and the sword of the Spirit, which is the word of God. Whenever we are about to put on the armor or to take up any item of the armor, we need to pray. We cannot and we should not attempt to use any part of God's armor without prayer. Prayer is the unique way to apply the armor of God. It is prayer that makes the armor available to us in a practical way. For example, we may have the helmet of salvation, but it is prayer that makes this helmet available and prevailing. Therefore, prayer is crucial and vital.

II. PRAYING

In verse 18 Paul speaks not just of one kind of prayer, but of all prayer and petition. Prayer is general, whereas petition is particular. We should pray both in an ordinary way and, when necessary, in an extraordinary way, perhaps giving up sleep or food in order to petition the Lord concerning a certain situation.

A. At Every Time

In verse 18 Paul speaks of "praying at every time." Some think the phrase "at every time" means simply every time we pray. To others it means all the time. To pray all the time corresponds to Paul's word in 1 Thessalonians 5:17 to pray without ceasing.

B. In Spirit

In verse 18 Paul says specifically that we are to pray in spirit. This refers to our regenerated spirit indwelt by the Spirit of God. It may be considered the mingled spirit—our spirit mingled with God's Spirit. Whenever we are in our spirit, we are also in the Holy Spirit, for our spirit is one with the Lord (1 Cor. 6:17). Therefore, Paul's charge to pray in spirit implies that we must also pray in the Spirit of God, for these two spirits are mingled in us.

In prayer, the main faculty we should use is our spirit. If our mind is overactive or if our emotion is not under control, we shall find it difficult to pray. When we pray, our mind should be at rest, and our emotion should be regulated, neither too hot nor too cold. According to my experience, I easily become distracted in prayer when my mind is preoccupied with other things. Likewise, when my emotion is not properly regulated, I find it difficult to utter something from my spirit in prayer. Hence, in order to pray in spirit, we need to be adjusted in our mind and balanced in our emotion. This requires a great deal of inward exercise.

Furthermore, if we would pray at every time in spirit, our will must be strong. A person with a will like a jellyfish cannot pray. It may seem that prayer is easy, but actually it is difficult. It is very easy to talk or read, but it is not easy to pray. This is the reason that prayer requires the exercise of our will.

A Christian must be a praying person. It is a sin not to pray. If you fail to pray for others, the saints or those in your family, you are sinning. However, not many Christians regard the lack of prayer as sin. We need to exercise our will to be people of prayer. For the sake of a proper prayer life, our mind must be sober, our emotion must be regulated, and our will must be strengthened. Then we shall be able to pray at every time in spirit.

III. WATCHING

A. For This Prayer

In verse 18 Paul goes on to speak of "watching unto this in all perseverance and petition concerning all the saints." This indicates that we need to be watchful, on the alert, for this prayer life. We need to be on guard lest we be robbed of time that should be devoted to prayer. To be watchful in a practical way, many in the churches set aside specific times to pray.

To watch unto prayer implies that we exercise our will, calm our mind, and regulate our emotion in order to pray properly. It takes a considerable amount of exercise to make our mind, emotion, and will submissive and obedient. Because many do not practice this, their mind is rebellious.

When they tell the mind to calm down, it becomes all the more active. Others have trouble with the emotion. We need to be those who exercise ourselves to such a degree that as soon as we have finished a long conversation we are able to pray. The need for such an exercise is implied in Paul's word about watching unto prayer.

If we do not watch unto our prayer life, we shall lose time. Here and there throughout the day, our time will be wasted. We may lose time because our time is neither scheduled nor controlled. When we are at work, our time may be closely regulated. But when it comes to prayer, many do not schedule their time. As a result, much time which could be devoted to prayer is lost. If we do not redeem our time and grasp every available opportunity, much time will be needlessly lost. Although you may be very busy, do not use this as an excuse for not praying. If you place a high value on your prayer life, you will watch unto it and arrange time for it. No matter how busy you may be, you will still have time to pray.

According to the examples in the Bible, it is better to have more than one time set aside for prayer daily. For example, Daniel prayed three times a day (Dan. 6:10). Also the psalmist spoke of praying in the morning, at noon, and in the evening (Psa. 55:17). If we build up the habit of praying at regular times every day, great blessing will be brought in. This blessing will affect not only our personal lives, but also the church, our neighborhood, and even our nation.

B. In All Perseverance

Paul charges us to watch unto prayer in all perseverance. To keep a prayer life we need all perseverance, a constant, persistent care. If you have set aside a certain time in the morning for prayer, then you need to persistently watch regarding this time. Do not allow any distractions. You may want to take the telephone off the hook for that period of time. If we are not persistent in watching unto prayer, the enemy will send in many distractions.

C. In All Petition

1. Concerning the Saints

In verse 18 Paul also speaks of "petition concerning all the saints." This indicates that we need to pray for the saints. In order to watch unto our prayer life, we need to pray in a particular way. This means that we should pray particularly for our watching unto prayer, that is, pray for our prayer life, for our prayer time. We also need to make petition concerning all the saints. Consider how much time is required to pray for the saints in your locality and for the saints in other cities and countries.

2. Concerning the Apostle

a. That Utterance May Be Given to Him

In verse 19 Paul continues, "And on my behalf, that utterance may be given to me in the opening of my mouth to make known in boldness the mystery of the gospel." The Greek word rendered utterance also means word, speech, expression. Paul was asking the believers to pray that the word would be given to him. He desired to open his mouth with boldness to make known the mystery of the gospel. Paul needed both the word and the boldness to declare it.

The mystery of the gospel is Christ and the church for the fulfillment of God's eternal purpose. Some Christians preach a gospel in which there is no mystery. But Paul declared the mystery of the gospel. This mystery implies the entire New Testament economy. Christ is the mystery of God, and the church is the mystery of Christ. Both Christ and the church are for God's economy, which also is a mystery. All these mysteries are related to the gospel.

I believe that the Lord intends for a gospel preaching atmosphere to be developed in all the local churches. Pray for such an atmosphere to become prevailing. In our gospel meetings we must do more than sing and tell others that Christ can meet their need for satisfaction. On the contrary, we need to give full messages on the high things concerning God's economy. Let us tell the unbelievers of God's eternal intention. Do not underestimate their ability to understand. They may understand much more than you expect. Surely this kind of gospel preaching will draw unbelievers to the Lord.

In our gospel meetings we need to both preach and teach. We should teach in a preaching atmosphere. Surely the saints will want to bring their relatives and friends to this kind of meeting. Our burden is to make known the mystery of the gospel. Pray about this. Pray that the Lord will give us utterance and open our mouths with boldness to teach and to preach the mystery of the gospel. We all need to declare the gospel in this uplifted way.

b. That He May Speak Boldly

In verse 20 Paul goes on to say, "On the behalf of which I am an ambassador in a chain, that in it I may speak boldly, as I ought to speak." Paul was an ambassador on behalf of the gospel. An ambassador is one sent by a particular authority to contact certain people. Paul considered himself an ambassador sent by God; he was one sent by the highest authority in the universe. However, he was an ambassador in a chain. The Greek word for chain is a term for the coupling chain, a chain which bound the prisoner to his guard. Paul's desire was that in this coupling chain he might speak boldly. Although Paul was chained to the one who guarded him, he nevertheless desired to speak boldly, as he ought to speak.

LIFE-STUDY OF EPHESIANS

MESSAGE SIXTY-SEVEN

CONCLUSION

In this message we come to the conclusion of Ephesians, 6:21-24.

I. RECOMMENDING TYCHICUS

In verses 19 and 20 Paul asks the saints to pray on his behalf. Then in verse 21 he goes on to say, "But that you also may know what concerns me, what I am doing, Tychicus, the beloved brother and faithful servant in the Lord, will make all things known to you." This indicates that, on the one hand, Paul needed the saints to pray for him, but, on the other hand, he had a real concern for the saints and sent Tychicus to them both to bring them information regarding him and also to comfort their hearts (v. 22).

This indicates that there was an excellent relationship with good fellowship between Paul and the saints in Ephesus. It also points out the need for a go-between such as Tychicus. The apostle, the believers, and Tychicus were one. Firstly, Paul set an example by asking the believers to pray for him. Then he sent Tychicus to them to bring them information concerning him and to comfort them. How sweet and beautiful this is! Although we rarely practice this today, we should endeavor to have such a practice. We need this kind of fellowship.

Tychicus was not sent to carry on a great work. On the contrary, his task was to inform the saints about Paul's situation and to comfort their hearts. Although in the time of Paul, there were no modern means of transportation, such as steamers or airplanes, he had Tychicus make the long journey from Rome to Asia Minor just to visit the saints on his behalf. The goal of this long journey was fellowship between the apostle and the saints. This is so important that it is recorded in the Word of God. The apostle was concerned for the church, and the church was concerned for the apostle. Therefore, Tychicus was sent from Rome to Asia Minor for the purpose of fellowship. In the Lord's recovery today, such a loving concern between the apostles and the churches needs to be restored. We need this concern, not to carry out a commission or do a work, but to have the necessary and proper fellowship. Today there also is the need for messengers to visit the churches to relay information and to encourage the saints.

In the Body of Christ we need much more traffic. The sending of Tychicus by the Apostle Paul to a local church created a kind of traffic. Traffic strengthens a country. Consider the impact of all the highways the federal government has built. These are the veins of the prosperity of the United States. Traffic, even across great stretches of open land, results in mutual supply and improvement. When I was growing up, just to travel the distance from our little village to Chefoo was a whole day's journey on foot. We had to make preparations the day before, then leave very early in the morning to get there by evening. It was such an effort to go just that distance that many people spent their whole lives in that village without ever going to Chefoo. It is traffic that has made the United States prosperous. In addition to the highways, the airlines with so many cross-country flights have increased the prosperity of this nation.

The more traffic among the churches, the better. Whenever we meet together, there is traffic. Without it, the churches are isolated. If we stay away from the meetings and meet together with just a few in our homes, the traffic is cut off. This is a subtlety of the enemy to cut the veins. When the blood flow is cut off, the result is death. However, by the proper traffic among the saints and between the churches, life multiplies. Therefore, we need to pay attention to Paul's word concerning this matter in the last chapter of Ephesians.

In speaking of Tychicus, Paul recommends him as a "beloved brother and faithful servant in the Lord." As a faithful servant in the Lord, Tychicus was a ministering servant. We have pointed out that he was sent to make all things known to the saints and to comfort their hearts. Once again I say that this reveals a sweet fellowship and intimate concern that need to be restored fully in the Lord's recovery today.

II. BLESSING

A. Peace and Love

Verses 23 and 24 are Paul's blessing: "Peace to the brothers, and love with faith, from God the Father and the Lord Jesus Christ. Grace be with all those who love our Lord Jesus Christ in incorruption." In the opening of the book, the apostle's greeting is with grace first as the enjoyment and then peace as the result of the enjoyment (1:2). But at the conclusion it is the other way around, from the result, which is in peace, to the enjoyment of grace.

In his opening word Paul spoke only of grace and peace. In his concluding word, he not only changes the order of grace and peace, but also mentions "love with faith." It is important to see why grace and peace are reversed and why love with faith was included. We have seen that grace is the enjoyment of the Lord and that peace is the result of this enjoyment. This book opens with grace, with the enjoyment of the Lord Himself as our life, life supply, and everything to us. But eventually this Epistle brings us into peace. However, after we have come into peace, we still need grace. We enter into peace through grace. Now as we are enjoying peace, we need more grace. This is grace upon grace. It also indicates that our experience is from grace to grace.

But why is love inserted between peace and grace? No other epistle written by Paul has such an insertion. The reason for this insertion is that the only way we can be kept in a situation of peace is by continually enjoying the Lord in love. The phrase "in love" is used six times in this book (1:4; 3:17; 4:2, 15, 16; 5:2). This connects this Epistle to Christ's word to the church in Ephesus in Revelation 2:1-7. There the Lord rebukes the church because she left her first love (v. 4). The problem with the church at Ephesus was not the lack of works or knowledge, but the loss of the first love. Because Paul realized that love is crucial, he spoke of love in relation to peace and grace, indicating thereby that love is needed to preserve us in a condition of peace.

This love is from God the Father and the Lord Jesus Christ. This indicates that love does not originate with us; it originates with God. Eventually, however, God's love becomes our love. This is the reason Paul speaks, in verse 24, of those who love our Lord Jesus Christ. God's love to us becomes our love for Him. Peace is maintained by this kind of love. By living in the intimacy of God's presence, love comes to us. Then this love returns to the Lord and becomes our love for Him. By this traffic of love, peace is maintained, and we are preserved in the enjoyment of grace. This is the reason Paul speaks of peace, love, and grace.

Notice that in verse 23 Paul uses the phrase "love with faith." Here, in contrast to 1 Timothy 1:14, he does not speak of love and faith. Love and faith are the two means by which we partake of Christ and experience Him. Faith is related to our receiving of Christ (John 1:12), and love is related to our enjoying Him (John 14:23). In the Gospel of John we are firstly told to believe in the Son in order to have eternal life (3:15). To believe in the Lord Jesus is to receive Him. The Gospel of John also emphasizes love. In chapter twenty-one the Lord asks Peter concerning his love for Him (vv. 15-17). Furthermore, in John 14:23 the Lord speaks of the Father and the Son making an abode with the one who loves the Lord Jesus. Therefore, by faith we receive the Lord Jesus and by love we enjoy Him. For this reason, in 1 Timothy 1:14 Paul puts faith and love together.

In 1 Thessalonians 5:8 Paul also speaks of faith and love. In this verse he encourages the saints to put on "the breastplate of faith and love." Comparing this verse to Ephesians 6:14, we see that there are two kinds of breastplates, the one for our daily living and the other for fighting. For our daily living we need the breastplate of faith and love. Faith and love are both tender; they are signified in the Bible by the breasts. Such tender parts of our being, our spiritual breasts, need to be covered with the breastplate. By means of the breastplate, our faith and love, which are necessary for a proper Christian life, are preserved. The breastplate of righteousness in 6:14, on the contrary, is for fighting. Whenever we take part in spiritual warfare, our conscience must be protected from Satan's accusation by the breastplate of righteousness.

The verses concerning faith and love in the Gospel of John, 1 Thessalonians, and 1 Timothy indicate that faith and love go together. But in 6:23 Paul does not say faith and love, nor love and faith, but love *with* faith. This indicates that we need faith to match, support, and serve our love. According to Galatians 5:6, faith operates through love. This operation is very delicate. In Galatians, a book that emphasizes justification by faith, we are told in 5:6 that "in Jesus Christ neither circumcision availeth any thing, nor uncircumcision; but faith which worketh by love." Have you ever realized that believing in the Lord Jesus is a matter of love? Do you know that your faith operates through love? A person who hears the gospel, repents, and then comes to appreciate the Lord Jesus and feels that He is altogether lovable, will have a strong faith. This faith operates through his love for the Lord. The more we love the Lord, the stronger will be our faith in Him. This is Paul's thought in Galatians.

Ephesians, however, emphasizes love, not faith. According to Galatians, the more we appreciate the Lord Jesus and love Him, the more we shall believe in Him. This is for salvation. But in Ephesians Paul's concern is not salvation, but continuation and fellowship. This requires love with faith. If our faith is weakened because we accept doubts and questions, we shall find it difficult to love the Lord. Whenever faith is damaged, love will be damaged also. In order to continue in fellowship with the Lord through loving Him, we need a strong faith. Therefore, we need both the faith that operates through love and the love that is with faith.

We have pointed out that love is from God. This means that love is on God's side. Faith, on the contrary, is on our side. Hence, the phrase "love with faith" implies traffic between God and us and between us and God. Love is from God to us, and faith is from us to God. God gives us love, and we respond with faith. This is the traffic between love and faith. Through this traffic peace remains our portion. We are kept in peace by God's love coming to us and by our faith going to Him.

B. Grace with All Those Who Love Our Lord Jesus Christ in Incorruption

This traffic will also keep us in grace, in the enjoyment of the Lord. In verse 24 Paul says, "Grace be with all those who love our Lord Jesus Christ in incorruption." Grace is needed for us to live a church life that fulfills God's eternal purpose and solves God's problem with His enemy. The enjoyment of the Lord as grace is to those who love Him. For the proper church life we need to love the Lord in incorruption, that is, in a condition which is incorruptible. Our love for the Lord must be incorruptible, immortal, and imperishable. Such a love is genuine and sincere.

The way Paul composed the writing of the blessing in these verses is significant. Here, at the conclusion of this Epistle, we have been brought into peace. We remain in this condition of peace by the love which is from God with the faith which is from us. By this traffic of love with faith we have a continual supply of grace. Hallelujah for peace, for love with faith, and for grace!

LIFE-STUDY OF EPHESIANS

MESSAGE SIXTY-EIGHT

THE CHURCH AS A HYBRID LIFE

God's eternal purpose is to have the church. His purpose is not just to create man, to rescue him from his fallen condition, and to bring him to heaven. Furthermore, God's purpose is not simply to have us be holy, spiritual, and victorious. Creation, salvation, sanctification, spirituality, and victory are all part of God's procedure to reach His goal, but they are not the goal itself.

GOD'S PURPOSE IN THE BEGINNING

In order to share in the recovery of the proper church life, we need to see what God's purpose was in the beginning. We need to understand that there are three different beginnings. John 1:1 says, "In the beginning was the Word." The beginning here is the beginning in eternity. Genesis 1:1 says, "In the beginning God created the heavens and the earth" (Heb.). In this verse the beginning denotes the time of creation. Finally, the beginning also refers to the start of the church life. Therefore, to go back to the beginning is to go back to the beginning in eternity, to the beginning in God's creation, or to the beginning of the church.

The book of Ephesians reveals that the church came into existence according to the eternal purpose which God purposed in Christ. Ephesians 3:11 says, "According to the purpose of the ages which He made in Christ Jesus our Lord." The purpose of the ages is the purpose of eternity, the eternal purpose, the eternal plan of God made in eternity past. This is the purpose made by God in eternity past for eternity future. God is a God of purpose. Before creation, before the foundation of the world, He made a plan. This plan is the purpose of the ages, or the eternal purpose.

In 1:9 Paul says, "Having made known to us the mystery of His will, according to His good pleasure which He purposed in Himself." This verse also speaks of God's purpose, but here Paul uses the word purpose as a verb instead of as a noun. A good pleasure according to God's will has been purposed by God in Himself. This will which He has purposed is a mystery. It was hidden in God; it was not revealed to the saints in the Old Testament. In 1:11 Paul also speaks of God's purpose: "In Whom also we were made an inheritance, having been predestinated according to the purpose of the One Who operates all things according to the counsel of His will." God's purpose in these verses refers to what God planned in the beginning, in eternity past.

In the beginning God planned to have the church. The Bible definitely reveals that this is God's intention. God created the heavens, the earth, and billions of items because He desired to have the church. The first two chapters of Genesis are apparently a record of God's creation. Actually these chapters reveal God's intention. The minerals are for the plants, the plants are for the animals, the animals are for man, and man is for God. In other words, all things are for us, and we are for God in order that He may fulfill His desire to have the church. Therefore, God created all things so that He could have the church.

Furthermore, God's redemption, regeneration, and calling are also for the church. God accomplished redemption so He could have the church. He also came to you, called you, and regenerated you for the church. Moreover, He dwells in you today for the sake of the church.

A DEFINITION OF THE CHURCH

Now we come to the crucial and difficult matter of giving a definition of the church. The church may be called a hybrid, because it is one entity produced by the mingling together of two lives. The two lives that are mingled to produce the church are the divine life and the human life. Therefore, the church is an entity constituted not just of the divine life or merely of the human life, but of the divine-human life. When the Lord Jesus was on earth, He lived a divine-human life. The church also has a divine-human life. We thank the Lord that although this has been hidden from the saints for centuries, He has revealed it to us in His recovery.

It is vital to see that the church is a hybrid produced by the mingling of the divine life with the human life. God desires to dispense Himself into man and to work Himself into man. In his book, *The Spirit of Christ,* Andrew Murray says that the divine life is interwoven with the human life. Although interwoven is a very good term, it is still not adequate. The divine life is not only interwoven with the human life, but the divine life and the human life are mingled to form one entity. Paul's word in Galatians 2:20 illustrates this. Here he says, "I have been crucified with Christ: nevertheless I live; yet not I, but Christ liveth in me" (Gk.). Paul says that it is he who lives; yet it is not he, but Christ. This indicates the mingling of Christ with Paul. The church is the product of such a mingling.

CHRISTIANS FOR THE CHURCH

Just as the members of our body are for the body, not for the members themselves, so we have become Christians for the church. Without the body, the members have no meaning. In the same principle, without the church, we Christians have no purpose. Therefore, as Christians we must be for the church.

ONE IN THE TRIUNE GOD

In Galatians 3:27 and 28 Paul says that as many as have been baptized into Christ have put on Christ and that we are all one in Christ Jesus. This oneness is the church. The church is the oneness in the Triune God of all those who are mingled with God.

The oneness in the Triune God is revealed in a full way in John 17. In John 17:21 the Lord Jesus prayed, "That they all may be one; even as You, Father, are in Me and I in You, that they also may be in Us." Here in this oneness there is no place for the flesh, sin, naturalness, or worldliness. In this oneness there is room only for the proper humanity mingled with the Triune God.

Some may say that we do not have the proper humanity because of the fall. I agree. But through the redemption of Christ God has recovered us and uplifted our fallen humanity. In Christ's resurrection our humanity has been uplifted. This resurrected and uplifted humanity is now mingled with the Triune God. This mingling is the very element of the church. In the proper church life there is no culture, religion, or worldliness. The church, on the contrary, is composed of the proper humanity, the humanity created by God and uplifted by Christ, mingled with the Triune God. This is the entity God planned to have in eternity past for eternity future.

A MINIATURE OF THE BIBLE

God's Creation

The book of Ephesians, which deals especially with the church, is a miniature of the whole Bible. This is proved by what this book includes. Firstly, as we have seen, this book speaks of the purpose of the ages, the eternal purpose of God. Secondly, it mentions God's creation. Ephesians 3:9 speaks of the "dispensation of the mystery, which from the ages has been hidden in God, Who created all things." There is a relationship between creation and the church, for God created all things for the church.

God's intention in His creation of all things, including man, was that man would be mingled with God to produce the church. Zechariah 12:1 says that the Lord stretched forth the heavens, laid the foundation of the earth, and formed the spirit of man within him. This indicates that the heavens are for the earth, that the earth is for man, and that man with the human spirit is for God. God's marvelous creation, focused on man, is for the purpose of producing the church. Therefore, Ephesians speaks of the creation of all things.

The Human Spirit

This book also refers a number of times to the human spirit. In 1:17, Paul prays that the Father of glory would give us a spirit of wisdom and revelation in the full knowledge of Him. What is needed for the church life is not a mind that is naturally keen, but a spirit of wisdom and revelation.

In 2:22 Paul speaks of the human spirit again: "In Whom you also are being built together into a dwelling place of God in spirit." This verse indicates that God's dwelling place is in our spirit. This dwelling place is God's building, the Body of Christ. Hence, the spirit is the very place to have the church life. If we would be in the church as God's building, we must be in our spirit.

In 3:5 Paul points out that the mystery of Christ "has now been revealed to His holy apostles and prophets in spirit." The hidden mystery is revealed to the apostles and prophets, not in the mind, but in their spirit, which has been regenerated and indwelt by the Holy Spirit of God. The inner man in verse 16 refers to this spirit. Our inner man, our spirit regenerated by the Spirit of God and indwelt by Him, needs to be strengthened with power through the Spirit so that Christ may make His home in our hearts.

In 4:23 Paul goes on to speak further about the human spirit: "And are renewed in the spirit of your mind." The spirit here is the human spirit mingled with the Holy Spirit. When this mingled spirit spreads into our mind, it becomes the spirit of our mind. Then our mind is under the control of our spirit. This renewing spirit is necessary for us to put off the old man and to put on the new man, which is the church life.

In 5:18 Paul gives the exhortation, "And do not be drunk with wine, in which is dissipation, but be filled in spirit." In our regenerated spirit we need to be filled with Christ unto all the fullness of God (3:19).

Finally, in 6:18 Paul speaks of "praying at every time in spirit." Whenever we pray, we need to pray in our spirit.

In every chapter of Ephesians there is mention of the

human spirit. This indicates that the human spirit is needed for the church life. The reason there is virtually no church life in Christianity today is that most Christians do not know the human spirit. Rather, most of today's Christian teachings are concerned with the mind. The book of Ephesians, however, is not focused on the mind, but on the spirit. Our spirit must be a spirit of wisdom and revelation, the place of God's building, the organ in which God reveals His mystery to us, and the inner man strengthened by the Spirit of God. Furthermore, we need to be renewed in the spirit of our mind and to pray in spirit. Through proper exercise, our spirit will eventually be filled unto all the fullness of God. This is the mingling of God and man that produces the church life.

Revealing the Triune God

Furthermore, the book of Ephesians reveals the Triune God more fully than any other book in the Bible. Ephesians 1:3 says, "Blessed be the God and Father of our Lord Jesus Christ, Who has blessed us with every spiritual blessing in the heavenlies in Christ." This verse speaks of God the Father and Christ the Son. The Spirit is not explicitly mentioned; however, the Spirit is implied in the spiritual blessings. These blessings are blessings of the Spirit and in the Spirit. Hence, in one verse we have the Father, the Son, and the Spirit. In 2:18 it says that through Him, the Son, we have access in one Spirit unto the Father. Here again we have in one verse the Triune God, the Son, the Spirit, and the Father. Through the Son and in the Spirit we have access to the Father. This is the experience of the Triune God for the church life.

In chapter three we also see the Triune God. Paul prayed to the Father to grant us to be strengthened through His Spirit into the inner man so that Christ may make His home in our hearts. Here we have the Father, the Spirit, and Christ the Son. Eventually, according to verse 19, we are filled unto all the fullness of God. Therefore, we have the Spirit strengthening us and Christ making His home in us;

then we are filled unto the fullness of God. Such a revelation of the Triune God is not found elsewhere in the Scriptures.

In 4:4-6 we also find the Triune God: the Spirit (v. 4), the Lord (v. 5), and God the Father (v. 6). The sequence here is significant. Firstly we have the Spirit, then the Son, and then the Father. In the Body life, the first Person of the Godhead we touch is the Spirit. When we touch the Spirit, we touch the Son. Then, by having the Son, we have the Father who is the origin and source of all. The Father is the source, the Son is the course, and the Spirit is the flow in the course. When we touch the flow, we are in the course, and when we are in the course, we are brought to the source. Here we have the reality of the one Body with the one Spirit, the one Lord, and the one God and Father.

The reason that Ephesians unfolds the Triune God to such a degree is that this book is on the church, the entity composed through the dispensing of the Triune God into humanity. The church comes into being only as the Triune God dispenses Himself into us and mingles Himself with us. In Ephesians we have not only the doctrine of the Trinity, but the practicality of the Trinity for the dispensing of God into man. The Triune God is not for teaching, but for imparting Himself into our being.

CHRIST MAKING HIS HOME IN OUR HEARTS

We have pointed out that, as the processed God, the Triune God today is the life-giving Spirit. As the Spirit, He can dispense Himself into our being. This makes it possible for us to be filled in our spirit unto all the fullness of God and for Christ to make His home in our heart. Christ is not simply dwelling within us, but is seeking the opportunity to make His home in our heart. This is to mingle Himself with every part of our being. Christ, the Son of God and the very embodiment of God, is the life-giving Spirit indwelling our spirit to spread into all of our inward parts. The result of this is not only holiness, spirituality, and victory, but the marvelous mingling of divinity with humanity to produce the church.

THE BODY AND THE NEW MAN

The church that is produced by the mingling of divinity with humanity is the Body of Christ. Certain Christian teachers think that the Body of Christ is merely an illustration. But this is not just an illustration—it is the very expression of Christ. Just as my physical body is the expression of myself, so Christ's spiritual Body is the expression of Himself. Hence, the church as the Body of Christ is a reality.

Furthermore, the church is the new man with Christ as the life and the person. A body must have life, but a man must have both life and a person. Trees have life, but they do not have a person with a mind, will, and emotion. Since the church is the Body and the new man, the church has Christ as both the life and the person. This understanding of the church is basic.

LIFE-STUDY OF EPHESIANS

MESSAGE SIXTY-NINE

THE MINGLED SPIRIT FOR THE CHURCH LIFE

In the foregoing message we pointed out that God's purpose is to obtain the church by dispensing Himself into man and making Himself one with man. In order to dispense Himself into man, God must be triune, the Father, the Son, and the Spirit. Furthermore, man must be in God's image and have a spirit to receive God and assimilate Him. One day, the Son of God, the embodiment of the Father, became a man. Passing through human living, crucifixion, and resurrection, He became the life-giving Spirit. As the Spirit, He comes into us and mingles with our spirit. Through this process there is brought into being a hybrid life, an entity composed of the mingling of the divine life with the human life. This is the church.

God is no longer the unprocessed God, but the processed God. He has accomplished everything necessary to come into us as the life-giving Spirit. Now we must believe in Him and call on the name of the Lord Jesus. When we do this, the life-giving Spirit comes into our spirit, and the mingling of the divine life and the human life takes place within us. This mingling produces the church.

THE FULLNESS OF GOD AND THE RICHES OF CHRIST

The book of Ephesians contains the fullest revelation of the Triune God in the Scriptures. For example, in chapter three Paul speaks of the fullness of God (v. 19), the riches of Christ (v. 8), and the power of the Spirit (v. 16). The fullness implies that the riches of all that God is become His expression. Colossians 2:9 says that the fullness of God dwells in Christ bodily. This means that Christ is the embodiment of the fullness of God, the embodiment of all that God is. When the fullness of God is embodied in Christ, there are the riches of Christ. The riches of Christ are realized through the power of the Spirit. Hence, Christ is the embodiment of God's fullness, and the Spirit is the realization of Christ's riches. To have the fullness of God, we must have Christ. Furthermore, to enjoy the riches of Christ, we must have the Spirit.

In the Gospel of John, the Spirit is called the Spirit of reality. The Spirit of reality makes real to the believers all that the Son is and has. Embodied in the Son is all that the Father is and has, and all that the Son is and has is revealed as reality to the believers through the Spirit (John 16:14-15). For example, Christ is life. However, if we do not touch the Spirit, we cannot have this life. But as we touch the Spirit, we experience the reality of Christ as life. In like manner, Christ is light. But if we do not contact the Spirit, we cannot be enlightened by Christ. When we contact the Spirit, we enjoy the reality of Christ as light.

Today our Triune God is the all-inclusive Spirit. Do not regard the Spirit as something other than Christ, nor think of Christ as separate from God the Father. No, the Father, the Son, and the Spirit are one. This is the reason that we refer to God as triune, as three in one. No one can adequately define the Trinity. God the Father is in God the Son, and God the Son has become the Spirit who gives life. For the sake of the church, the fullness of God is embodied in Christ that the riches of Christ may be made real to us through the Spirit. The more we contact the Spirit, the more we enjoy Christ's riches. Eventually we shall be filled unto all the fullness of God and be fully mingled with the Triune God.

ACCESS UNTO THE FATHER

In 2:18 all Three of the Triune God are mentioned: "For through Him we both have access in one Spirit unto the Father." Through Christ the Son we have access in one Spirit unto the Father. How wonderful! Notice that this verse does not say that we have access unto the Spirit. It speaks of access unto the Father. The Spirit is unto us, whereas we are unto the Father. The Father came to us in the Son, and the Son came into us as the Spirit. Now through the Son the Spirit brings us unto the Father. This is for the dispensing of the Triune God into us so that the church may come into existence. Once again we see that the church is produced by the mingling of the Triune God with humanity.

RESPONDING TO THE SPIRIT

The dispensing of the Triune God into man is altogether related to the Spirit. The processed God as the all-inclusive life-giving Spirit is waiting for our spirit to respond to Him and to cooperate with Him. To be saved is not merely to understand the gospel. It is to open ourselves from the depths of our being to respond to the Spirit. When we call on the name of the Lord Jesus, we must call from our spirit, from the depths of our being. If we do this, we shall be saved, even if we do not adequately understand the gospel.

Consider the case of Saul of Tarsus on the way to Damascus (Acts 9). He was saved by saying the words, "Who art Thou, Lord?" At the time he was saved, Saul was not so clear about the gospel, nor even about the Lord Jesus. However, simply by saying the words, "Who art Thou, Lord?" he was captured by the Lord. This shows that to be saved is not mainly a matter of understanding the gospel, but of contacting the life-giving Spirit, who is the processed God waiting for an opportunity to come into us. Contacting the life-giving Spirit is much like breathing. The important thing is not to understand the air, but to breathe the air into us. By breathing in the air, we receive all the benefits of the air.

This principle applies to our whole Christian life. Take holiness as an example. We become holy not by learning the doctrine of holiness, but by contacting the Spirit who Himself is the essence of holiness. The doctrine of holiness is not holiness itself. Holiness is a living Person, the processed God as the life-giving Spirit. It is possible to know the doctrine of holiness without having the reality of holiness. The way to be holy is to contact the life-giving Spirit. We may read a book on holiness, but have nothing of holiness as a result of our reading. However, if we spend the same amount of time calling on the name of the Lord as we would reading that book, we shall certainly experience God's holiness.

A SPIRIT OF WISDOM AND REVELATION

In the book of Ephesians there is great emphasis on the mingled spirit, the human spirit mingled with the divine Spirit. Ephesians 1:17 says, "That the God of our Lord Jesus Christ, the Father of glory, may give to you a spirit of wisdom and revelation in the full knowledge of Him." There is disagreement among scholars concerning the translation of the Greek word for spirit in this verse. Some insist on capitalizing the word spirit, because they think that the spirit here is the Holy Spirit. Others believe that the spirit here must refer to the human spirit. Actually, the spirit in this verse is our regenerated spirit indwelt by the Spirit of God. It is the human spirit mingled with the Holy Spirit. Such a spirit is given to us by God so that we may have wisdom and revelation to know Him and His economy. Without the Holy Spirit, our spirit cannot be a spirit of wisdom and revelation. But as soon as the Holy Spirit is mingled with our spirit, our spirit becomes a spirit of wisdom and revelation.

GOD'S DWELLING PLACE IN OUR SPIRIT

In 2:22 Paul again refers to the mingled spirit: "In Whom you also are being built together into a dwelling place of God in spirit." Translators differ about this verse also, with some arguing that the spirit here is the divine Spirit and others, that it is the human spirit. Actually, it is the mingled spirit, the believers' human spirit indwelt by God's Holy Spirit. God's Spirit is the indwelling One, not the dwelling place. The dwelling place is our spirit. God's Spirit dwells in our spirit. The Holy Spirit is, therefore, the indwelling One, not the indwelt One. The dwelling place of God is in our spirit, the human spirit mingled with the Holy Spirit.

THE MYSTERY OF CHRIST REVEALED IN SPIRIT

In 3:5 Paul says that the mystery of Christ "has now been revealed to His holy apostles and prophets in spirit." The spirit here is once again the mingled spirit. When our spirit is mingled with the divine Spirit, our spirit becomes the organ in which the mystery of Christ is revealed.

THE INNER MAN

In 3:16 Paul speaks of the inner man. The inner man is our regenerated spirit. The only way man's spirit can be regenerated is through having the Spirit of God come into it. Hence, the inner man in this verse also denotes the human spirit mingled with the Holy Spirit.

THE SPIRIT OF OUR MIND

Ephesians 4:23 says, "And are renewed in the spirit of your mind." Some say that the spirit here cannot be the human spirit because this is the renewing spirit. However, the spirit here must be the human spirit because it is the spirit of the mind. The spirit in this verse is the regenerated spirit of the believers mingled with the indwelling Spirit of God. Such a mingled spirit spreads into our mind and thus becomes the spirit of our mind. The human spirit can be the renewing spirit only by being mingled with the Holy Spirit. On the one hand, the spirit here is the spirit of the mind, but, on the other hand, it is the renewing spirit. This indicates that it is a matter of the mingled spirit. The human spirit, not the Holy Spirit, is the base.

FILLED IN SPIRIT

In 5:18 Paul exhorts us to be filled in spirit. Certainly he means that we should be filled in our spirit with the Holy Spirit.

PRAYING IN SPIRIT

In 6:18 Paul charges us to pray at every time in spirit. According to the context, the spirit here also refers to the human spirit mingled with the Holy Spirit. The Holy Spirit is the Word which we are to take in spirit by prayer.

NEAR, PRESENT, AND AVAILABLE

The Triune God has been fully processed to become the life-giving Spirit. As such a Spirit, He is near, present, and available. But He is holy, and we are sinful. How can this holy God be close to us? The answer is found in the fact that the element of redemption is included in the all-inclusive Spirit. The enemy, Satan, realizes this. If Satan would tell God that He has no right to be near sinful people, the blood of Jesus Christ would immediately testify against him. Before Christ's incarnation, the Spirit of God could not be so close to fallen mankind as now because there was not yet the element of redemption in the Spirit. The effectiveness of Christ's redemptive death, typified by the offerings in the Old Testament, is now in the life-giving Spirit. Perhaps not until we are in the New Jerusalem shall we fully understand what this Spirit means to us. Praise Him that this Spirit is the processed God, near, present, available, and ready for us to enjoy. Whenever we call on the name of the Lord Jesus, we receive the Spirit. The reason for this is that the Spirit is the reality of Christ.

THE SEAL AND THE PLEDGE

In 1:13 Paul says, "In Whom you also, hearing the word of the truth, the gospel of your salvation, in Whom also believing, you were sealed with the Holy Spirit of the promise." The seal here is the life-giving Spirit. By coming into us, the Spirit sealed us. According to 1:14, this seal is the pledge, the earnest, the guarantee, the foretaste, of our inheritance. The full taste will simply be the full portion of the Triune God. Today the life-giving Spirit gives us a foretaste of the Triune God as our portion.

NOT GRIEVING THE SPIRIT

In 4:30 we see that the crucial matter is for us not to grieve the Spirit. Rather, we must always please Him. If the

Spirit in us is not happy, we shall have difficulty. The most important thing in our Christian life is to take care that we do not grieve the Spirit. If you are faithful in this matter, you will be an outstanding Christian.

ONENESS IN THE TRIUNE GOD

According to 2:18, through Christ we have access in one Spirit unto the Father. When the Spirit comes into us, He spontaneously brings us back to the Father. In this Spirit we are truly one. This oneness is the proper church life. Hence, the church is the oneness in the Triune God of all those who have been mingled with the Triune God.

The depth of the book of Ephesians is in these verses that speak of the mingled spirit. The church is the mingling of the Holy Spirit as the processed God with humanity. This is greater than spirituality, holiness, or victory. As long as we are in this oneness, we are surely spiritual, holy, and victorious. Our goal should be nothing less than this oneness. If we are in this oneness, what need have we to seek spirituality or holiness or victory? By being in this marvelous oneness we have all this and much more.

LIFE-STUDY OF EPHESIANS

MESSAGE SEVENTY

ORDINANCES AND DOCTRINE

We have seen that the divine Spirit has been mingled with the human spirit to produce one entity. This oneness of the divine Spirit with the human spirit is the church life. Because the church is produced by the mingling of divinity with humanity, we may say that the church is a hybrid.

The book of Ephesians also deals with certain negative things that damage or hinder the church life. The reason these things are covered in this book is that Ephesians is focused on the church.

ABOLISHING THE ORDINANCES TO CREATE ONE NEW MAN

Those who have been Christians for years know that on the cross Christ died as the Lamb of God to take away the sin of the world (John 1:29). Furthermore, on the cross Christ crucified the old man, destroyed Satan, and dealt with the world. This means that on the cross Christ dealt with sin, with the old man including the old nature, with Satan, and with the world. However, not many Christians realize that on the cross Christ also dealt with the ordinances. Christ dealt with sins and with sin so that we might be saved. He dealt with our old nature in order to set us free from the old man. Moreover, Christ dealt with Satan so that we may be victorious and overcome the evil one. Finally, Christ dealt with the world, so that we may be holy, sanctified, separated from the world. But why did He deal with the ordinances? He dealt with them in order to create one new man. Christians do not see this point because they concentrate on personal salvation, sanctification, or victory, and pay no attention to the church. Even many Bible teachers fail to point out that in Ephesians Christ abolished the ordinances in order that the church might be produced. This is one of the most important revelations the Lord has given to the church in recent days. Christ's death was not only for our salvation, liberation, sanctification, and victory. His death was also to abolish the ordinances in order to create the church as the one new man.

Ordinances, commandments, and the law are in the same category. Apart from the law, we would not have any commandments. These commandments give rise to ordinances. On the cross Christ abolished the law of commandments in ordinances.

Ordinances are related both to religion and to culture and also to human nature. According to our nature, we have a strong tendency toward ordinances. Our ordinances match our culture. The more cultured we are, the more ordinances we have.

Christ abolished the ordinances in order to create in Himself one new man. He did not abolish them so that we may be holy, spiritual, or victorious. In a sense, He did not abolish the ordinances even that we may be saved. He abolished them so that the church might come into being.

DROPPING THE ORDINANCES FOR THE PROPER CHURCH LIFE

If we know the church, we shall reject all ordinances. The church is the mingling of the processed God with the proper humanity. Here in this mingling there are no ordinances, commandments, rules, or regulations. The more we are in the mingled spirit, in the mingling of the divine Spirit with the human spirit, the more we shall be set free from ordinances.

However, if we cling to ordinances, we shall be divisive. Christians have been divided mainly because of ordinances. Some denominations have been established because of ordinances. Do you have the confidence to say that you have no ordinances? Few of us can say this. The young people have their particular ordinances, and the older saints have theirs. Most of the problems among the leading ones in the churches are caused by ordinances.

Some Christians have an ordinance, for example, regarding speaking in tongues. After one meeting, a brother came to me very happy because he had not been bothered by a sister who had spoken in tongues in that meeting. I told this brother that even his happiness proved that he still had feelings about speaking in tongues. Hence, his reaction was not altogether positive. If he could be surrounded by those who spoke in tongues without having any feeling about it, that would prove that he had no ordinances concerning this matter.

If we would have the proper church life, we must drop all ordinances and concentrate on the mingling of the divine Spirit with the human spirit. Only in this mingling can we enjoy the genuine church life.

Ordinances are particularly related to religion. Without ordinances, it is impossible to have religion, for religion is composed of ordinances. But Christ does not want a religion. What He wants is the new man. Therefore, He abolished the ordinances on the cross. Some may prefer shouting in the meeting, whereas others prefer silence. But to be either for shouting or for silence is to have an ordinance. We should not be for either one or the other, but for the Spirit. However, according to our nature and upbringing, we are prone to have ordinances of one kind or another. But as long as there are ordinances, we do not have the reality of the church life. The church life does not consist of ordinances, but of the living Spirit.

THE CONTRAST BETWEEN ORDINANCES AND THE SPIRIT

In 2:13-22 we see a contrast between ordinances and the Spirit. Christ on the cross abolished the ordinances in order to produce the church. Now that the ordinances have been abolished, the Spirit comes in to replace them. If we have ordinances, we do not have the Spirit. But if we have the Spirit, we shall not have ordinances. The cross abolished the ordinances in order to give place to the Spirit in whom we have access unto the Father. Hence, the Spirit is the replacement of all ordinances. In the meetings we should not have an ordinance regarding shouting or quietness. As long as we are not in the Spirit, anything we do is an ordinance.

The church is neither an organization nor a religion, but the Body of Christ produced by the mingling of the divine Spirit with the human spirit. In the meetings we should not have rules and regulations; we should simply care to be in the Spirit. Do not be concerned about the arrangement of the chairs or about whether or not the sisters wear a head covering. To arrange the chairs in a particular way or to wear a head covering may be fine when done in the spirit. But to insist on these things is to make them ordinances. Anything we do in the meetings becomes an ordinance if we are not in the Spirit.

When Christ abolished the ordinances, He broke down the middle wall of partition (2:14). Now the separating wall of ordinances no longer exists. When I was young, I was strong in the matter of ordinances. But today I realize that God cares only for the divine Spirit in our human spirit. In 2:18 Paul speaks of the Holy Spirit and in verse 22, of the human spirit.

CARING FOR THE BUILDING UP OF THE BODY

Ephesians 2:22 says that God's dwelling place is in our spirit. For God to have such a dwelling place, there must be the practical building up of the Body. But if we still hold to certain ordinances, we cannot be built up with other believers. Ordinances are always divisive. If some sisters make an ordinance out of head coverings, they will be divided from the sisters who do not wear a head covering. Those who advocate head covering may be very strong, using 1 Corinthians 11 as their scriptural ground. But if they are strong in the way of ordinances, they will be divided from other sisters. However, if all the sisters are in the Spirit, not caring for ordinances about head covering, they will be built up together.

In today's Christianity seldom is a message given on the building. What most Christians care for is individual edification, not the building up of the Body. To edify someone usually means to educate him, to give him a spiritual education. Although many care for such education, they are not concerned about the building up of the Body of Christ. In the Lord's recovery we are not for personal edification, but for corporate building up. In 2:22 Paul says, "In Whom you also are being built together into a dwelling place of God in spirit." How can we be built up together in our locality if we still hold on to ordinances? It is impossible. Just as we all have different faces, so we all have different ordinances. We praise the Lord that no matter how different our background may be, we have one life and one Spirit! Therefore, in the church life today we do not care for ordinances, but we focus on the mingled spirit.

DOCTRINE AS A DAMAGE TO THE CHURCH LIFE

In 4:14 Paul speaks of a second negative thing that causes damage to the church life: "That we may be no longer babes tossed by waves and carried about by every wind of teaching in the sleight of men, in craftiness with a view to a system of error." Here Paul speaks of teaching or doctrine. In any religion there are not only ordinances, but also doctrines. Notice that in verse 14 Paul does not speak of heresy, but of doctrine, of teaching. Although doctrine seems good, it can cause us to be carried away from Christ and the church. No matter how positive a particular doctrine may seem to be, if it distracts you from Christ and the church, you must be careful about it and not take it in. Do not accept even the best doctrine if it distracts you from Christ and the church. It is the Spirit, not doctrine, that produces the church. Nevertheless, in today's Christianity there is doctrine upon doctrine. There sermon upon sermon is given on doctrine. However, the mere doctrine without life in the Spirit damages the church life.

In chapter four of Ephesians there is a contrast between doctrine and the reality of Christ. The reality of Christ is the Spirit of reality. If you cling to doctrine, you will automatically let go of the Spirit of reality. But if you take care of the Spirit of reality, you will let go of doctrine.

Christians today are divided either by ordinances or by doctrines. The denominations are established according to ordinances or doctrines. Without ordinances or doctrines, there would be no divisions. If ordinances and doctrines were removed, all genuine Christians would be one. We thank the Lord that no matter how diverse our backgrounds may be, we in the Lord's recovery are truly one. Even the evil angels recognize our oneness. The divisive elements of our backgrounds have been set aside, and we have come together to be one in the Lord.

Throughout the years we have learned to drop our opinions in order to keep the oneness. A number of times we have held different opinions, but by the Lord's mercy we have been willing to drop them for the sake of the oneness. The Body comes out of the Spirit. Certainly doctrinal dissension could never build up the Body. When we hold on to our doctrinal opinion, we are through with the reality of Christ, which is nothing less than the life-giving Spirit.

TAKING THE WORD AS NOURISHMENT

Since we emphasize the need to set aside doctrine for the building up of the church, you may wonder what we do with the Bible. We should not approach the Scriptures mainly for the purpose of gaining knowledge. On the contrary, we should use the Bible for spiritual nourishment. According to 6:17 and 18, we should take the Word of God by means of all prayer. In Matthew 4:4 the Lord Jesus said to the Devil who was tempting Him, "Man shall not live on bread alone, but on every word that proceeds out through the mouth of God." This indicates that the Lord Jesus took the word of God in the Scriptures as His bread and lived on it. The word that proceeds out through the mouth of God is for nourishment, not primarily for knowledge. Therefore, when we contact the

Word, we should exercise not only our mind but especially our spirit to take in the Word as nourishment.

Recently I turned once again to the book of Isaiah. In the past I acquired a good deal of knowledge of this book. But as I read Isaiah this time, I did not do so mainly for knowledge, but for nourishment. Isaiah 1:3 says, "The ox knoweth his owner, and the ass his master's crib." The fact that a crib is related to eating indicates that the book of Isaiah has the concept of nourishment. Once again I say that we should not take the Word of God just as knowledge; we should take it as food to nourish us. The best way to take the Word as nourishment is by pray-reading.

CARING FOR THE REALITY OF CHRIST

If we care for doctrine, we shall be divided. We in the Lord's recovery need to be clear that we are not for ordinances or for doctrine, but for the living Spirit, who is the reality of Christ. If we are faithful to care for the reality of Christ and not for doctrines or ordinances, we shall not be divided.

In the past certain divisive ones have been among us. They stayed for a while, but then began to insist on a particular doctrine. Because we refused to give place to their doctrine, they left. We have been and still are standing only for Christ and the church, not for any particular doctrine.

When we say that we are for the living Spirit and not for doctrine, this does not mean that we do not believe in the Bible. We believe the Bible at least as much as other Christians do, if not more. But we do not take the Bible as dead letters. To us, the Word is living. If through 1 Corinthians 11 some sisters are touched by the Lord to put on a head covering, we are thankful and appreciative, but we would not make this into a doctrine of head covering. In the same principle, if certain brothers and sisters feel that they are old and desire to be buried, we are willing to accommodate them. But we do not make a doctrine of being baptized more than once. The same holds true regarding the burning of things that are worldly or improper. If some are led of the

Lord to burn certain articles, they are free to do so. But they should not make this matter of burning into a doctrine. In fact, not even Christ and the church are mere doctrines to us. Rather, Christ and the church are a marvelous reality.

A CHARGE TO THE YOUNG PEOPLE

I realize that more and more the going on of the Lord in His recovery will be with the young people. No doubt the spread of the recovery in this country and elsewhere will be mainly with them. Therefore, in the presence of the Lord, I would charge the young people with the importance of realizing that in the recovery we are not for ordinances or for doctrine, but only for the life-giving Spirit as the reality of Christ. We do not take the Bible as a book of doctrine in letters. Rather, we take the Word as spirit and life. In Ephesians 2 there is the contrast between ordinances and the Spirit, and in chapter four there is the contrast between doctrine and the reality of Christ that produces the growth in life for the building up of the Body. Ordinances are a wall that separates, whereas doctrine is a wind that carries people away from the building up of the Body. In both chapter two and chapter four Paul is concerned with the building up of the church. When we are for the Spirit, we shall be built up as God's habitation in our spirit. In like manner, if we are for the reality of Christ, we shall have the growth in life for the building up of the Body in love. Therefore, we in the Lord's recovery must proclaim that we do not care for ordinances or for doctrine. We take the Word as revelation and nourishment, but we do not care for doctrine. We know that through the past several centuries God's people have been divided and even denominated by doctrine and ordinances. Therefore, we care only for the Spirit and for the reality of Christ.

LIFE-STUDY OF EPHESIANS

MESSAGE SEVENTY-ONE

THE OLD MAN AND THE NEW MAN

Scripture Reading: Eph. 4:22-24, 30; 5:18-21, 26-27; 6:17-18

Before we consider the matter of putting off the old man and putting on the new man, the church (4:22-24), we need to see that the abolishing of the ordinances for the creation of the new man is part of the gospel. Not many Christians realize that this matter must be proclaimed as part of the gospel. Speaking of Christ, 2:17 says, "He preached the gospel of peace." This indicates that what is covered by Paul in 2:12-22 is related to the gospel.

THE WHOLE GOSPEL

According to verse 12, we once were apart from Christ, alienated from the commonwealth of Israel, strangers from the covenants of promise, without hope, and without God in the world. But in Christ Jesus we have become near in the blood of Christ (v. 13). The context proves that we have been brought near to one another. The Gentiles were far off from the Jews, and the Jews were far off from the Gentiles. But on the cross Christ broke down the middle wall of partition between them. Therefore, now in the blood of Christ the Jews and the Gentiles are made near to one another. It is true that the blood has brought us to God. But in verse 13 Paul is not saying that we are brought near to God; he is saying that we are brought near to one another. This is part of the gospel.

Verse 14 says that Christ is our peace. The peace here is not that between us and God, but that between us and other believers. In particular, it is the peace between the Jewish believers and the Gentile believers. Christ, our peace, has made the Jews and the Gentiles one, having broken down the middle wall of partition that separated them. In His flesh He abolished the enmity, the law of commandments in ordinances, in order to create the two in Himself into one new man (vv. 14-15). In this way He made peace between the Gentiles and the Jews.

In verse 16 Paul goes on to say, "And might reconcile both in one Body to God through the cross, slaying the enmity by it." Christ reconciled the Jews and the Gentiles to God in one Body. This indicates that reconciliation is a corporate matter.

Verse 17 continues, "And coming, He preached the gospel of peace to you who were far off, and peace to those who were near." The subject of this verse is Christ. On the day we heard the gospel, Christ came as the Spirit to preach to us the good news of the peace which He had accomplished on the cross.

In verses 18 through 22 we see that we now have access unto the Father, that we are fellow-citizens of the saints and members of the household of God, that we are built upon the foundation of the apostles and prophets, that the whole building is growing together into a holy temple in the Lord, and that we also are being built together into a dwelling place of God in spirit. All these verses indicate that the abolishing of the ordinances for the producing of the church is part of the gospel.

Many of us can testify that without the church life our human life has no meaning. Although we have been saved and regenerated to become children of God, our daily life is meaningless without the church. Can you be satisfied simply with eating, sleeping, working, spending some time to pray and read the Bible, and then sometimes telling others about Christ? From my experience I can testify that if I do not have the church life, I have no desire to live. This indicates that even though we may be saved, we are lacking something vital if we do not have the church life in a practical way. The whole gospel, the perfect and ultimate gospel, must include the church life. Most Christians, however, do not have a complete gospel because they do not see that the gospel includes the abolishing of the ordinances for the creation of the new man. Today we in the Lord's recovery must preach not a partial gospel, but one that is complete, a whole gospel.

Many Christians preach only the first aspect of the gospel, redemption by the blood of Christ. Some also preach the second aspect, the matter of being saved by Christ's life (Rom. 5:10). Another aspect of the gospel is the enjoyment of the riches of Christ. In Ephesians 3:8 Paul said that grace had been given to him "to preach to the nations the unsearchable riches of Christ as the gospel." The final aspect of the gospel is what we have seen in Ephesians 2—the abolishing of the ordinances for the creation of the one new man, the church. Redemption, life, and the enjoyment of the riches of Christ are all for the church. Thus, the ultimate goal of the gospel is the church, the new man. We praise the Lord for showing us that, according to the book of Ephesians, the gospel includes the creation of the new man.

PUTTING OFF THE OLD MAN

We have considered two negative things that damage the church life: ordinances and doctrine. Now we come to a third negative thing—the old man. Some Christians interpret the old man in 4:22 as the old nature. It is true that the old man includes the old nature, but it also includes a great deal more. Ephesians 4:22 indicates that the old man is all-inclusive: "That you have put off, as regards your former manner of life, the old man, which is being corrupted according to the lusts of the deceit." Here Paul speaks of putting off, as regards our former manner of life, the old man. The former manner of life includes everything related to us: what we are, what we have, our family life, and our social life. Paul's meaning here is that we must put off whatever we are, whatever we do, and whatever we have. We are to put off our very way of living.

The old man with all it includes is a damage to the church life. Wherever the old man is, there can be no church. This means that what we are, what we have, and what we do make the church life an impossibility.

Ordinances, doctrine, and the old man are the three main negative things that damage the church life. If we have ordinances, the church life is gone. If we are occupied with doctrine, it will not be possible to have the proper church life. In addition, if we continue to live according to the old man, the church life will be seriously damaged, even terminated. However, if we have no ordinances or doctrines and if we put off the old man with his former manner of life, we shall have a marvelous church life, a church life that will be a miniature of the New Jerusalem in the new heaven and new earth. In such a church life it is impossible to have division.

I wish to say once again that in the Lord's recovery we are not for ordinances or for doctrine. However, we have deep respect for the Word of God. By the Lord's mercy, we would never break His Word. But we do not take the Bible as mere doctrine. To keep the Word in a living way is one thing, but to turn the revelations in the Word into doctrine is another. We need to take the Word as nourishment for growth in life. We should not take it as a book of doctrine and ordinances. Although I prefer to kneel down when I pray, I do not make this a formality or an ordinance that others are expected to follow. Rather, when I kneel to pray, I do so in spirit.

FLEXIBILITY FOR THE CHURCH LIFE

For the church life, we must have no ordinances, we must not be occupied with doctrine, and we must not have any oldness. If we would be free from oldness, we must lay aside what we are, what we do, and the way we live. Those who are released from oldness in this way are very flexible. When Paul was on the way to Damascus, he was altogether in the old man. He had strongly opposed Stephen and consented to his death. Being strong in the old man, Paul was for the temple, the priests, and for the religion of Judaism. He strongly reacted against those who opposed these things. However, after he came to the Lord and had been dealt with by Him, he became flexible, seemingly without opinion. In 1 Corinthians 9 he said that he could be all things to all men (v. 22). He could be flexible because he had put aside his old man.

During the early years of my ministry, I had much to say to those who came to me for advice. For example, if a brother consulted me about marriage, I had many points to share with him concerning married life. But now when the saints come to me for counsel, I do not have much to say. Mainly, I encourage them to contact the Lord in prayer. My desire is to be like Paul, to be one who has given up the old man and who has become flexible in dealing with people.

If we have truly put off the old man, others will have a difficult time describing us. However, if we can be described easily, we probably have not put off the old man. We should not be proud, and we should not be humble. Actually, we should be nothing. Then we shall be useful in the church life.

PUTTING ON THE NEW MAN

For the church life, we must not only put off the old man, but also put on the new man. The new man is the practical church life, which is Christ as the life-giving Spirit mingled with our spirit in a corporate way. To put on the church life as the new man is to put on this entity produced by the mingling of the divine Spirit with the human spirit. In this marvelous entity, the new man, there are no ordinances and there is nothing of the old man. There is only Christ as the all-inclusive, life-giving Spirit mingled with our spirit.

NOT GRIEVING THE SPIRIT

In 4:30 Paul charges us not to grieve the Holy Spirit of God. Not caring for the church life is one of the main ways we grieve the Spirit. For example, if you do not attend the meetings of the church, you may grieve the Spirit. Many grieve the Spirit by refusing to function in the meetings. Often they have the sense in their spirit to speak or to call on the name of the Lord, but they refuse to do so. At such times they grieve the Holy Spirit of God. Furthermore, we may grieve the Spirit in many ways in our daily life. Our daily living should be part of the new man, part of the church life. We are not to pretend that we are humble or well-behaved, but to put on the church life in a practical way. How marvelous it would be if day by day we all experienced Christ as the all-inclusive, life-giving Spirit mingling Himself with our spirit in a corporate way!

THE OVERFLOW OF THE INNER FILLING

In 5:18 Paul says, "And do not be drunk with wine, in which is dissipation, but be filled in spirit." In our regenerated spirit we need to be filled with the Triune God unto all the fullness of God. This will cause us to overflow with speaking, singing, praising, and submitting. This will not be the result of our efforts; it will come as the spontaneous overflow of the inner filling. If we are filled in spirit with all that God is, we shall certainly experience such an overflow.

THE WASHING OF WATER IN THE WORD

In 5:26 Paul goes on to speak of the cleansing that is by the washing of the water in the Word. Today the Lord Jesus is cleansing, purging, and purifying His church by the water in the Word. The water in the Word is the living Word with the divine life energized by the Spirit. The water in the Word is actually the life-giving Spirit Himself. In our experience the Word of God must not be letters, but spirit and life. In John 6:63 the Lord Jesus said, "The words which I have spoken unto you are spirit and are life." The Word as spirit and life is the water that cleanses us.

This cleansing does not wash away uncleanness; rather, it washes away all the spots and wrinkles. Wrinkles come from oldness, and spots come from wounds. The church needs to be washed both from oldness and from wounds. For this washing what is effective is not the blood of Christ, but the water in the Word. The blood deals with sin and uncleanness, whereas the water in the Word deals with wrinkles and spots, with oldness and hurts.

The way to have the washing of the water in the Word is presented in 6:17 and 18. In these verses Paul tells us to receive "the sword of the Spirit which is the word of God, by means of all prayer and petition, praying at every time in spirit." This indicates that we need to pray-read the Word. We need to take the living Word into the depths of our being by praying in spirit. This is to exercise our spirit to pray the Word into us. If we do this, the Word will not only be food to nourish us, but also water to wash us and to cleanse us from all oldness and wounds.

In the church life it is necessary to have frequent contact with one another. However, the more we contact one another, the more we hurt one another. If a brother would stay with me for several days, no doubt he would be hurt by me, and I would be hurt by him. The only way to remove the spots caused by this mutual wounding is to experience the washing of the water in the Word. If you are not cleansed of your wounds by the water in the Word, you may be offended and discouraged and even consider giving up the church life. However, if you exercise your spirit to pray-read the Word and thereby take the Word into the depths of your being, you will experience the washing of the water in the Word and you will be cleansed of all spots. Furthermore, the washing of water in the Word will cause you to grow, and by this growth you will be built up with others.

The entire book of Ephesians reveals in a consistent way that the church is the mingling of the divine Spirit with the human spirit. Today the divine Spirit is the Triune God in the holy Word. The Triune God is the all-inclusive, life-giving Spirit, and this Spirit is within the Word. Therefore, we should not only exercise our mind to study the Word, but also exercise our spirit to pray the Word. By pray-reading, we touch not only the Word, but also the Spirit. Then the Spirit will nourish us, water us, and wash us so that we may be purged of all wrinkles and spots. Eventually, through this washing, we shall be fully sanctified in a practical way. This is what the Lord is doing in the church today.

THE LIVING CHRIST WITH THE LIVING WORD

In the Lord's recovery, there is no place for ordinances, doctrines, or the old man. If we still hold on to these negative things, we shall be finished with the church life. We are here only for the living Christ with the living Word. Our way to approach the Word is not just to exercise our mind to study it and to gain knowledge of it, but also to exercise our spirit to pray the Word and to take it in as the life-giving Spirit for nourishment and washing. In this way we shall grow in a corporate way and be built up together. It is by this process that the Lord Jesus will fulfill the prophecy He uttered in Matthew 16:18: "I will build My church." Then we shall have the reality and the enjoyment of the full gospel, the gospel of Christ and the church.

LIFE-STUDY OF EPHESIANS

MESSAGE SEVENTY-TWO

GOD'S ACCOMPLISHED WORK CONCERNING THE CHURCH

Scripture Reading: Eph. 1:4-5, 7, 13-14, 17-18; 2:4-6, 8, 10, 13, 16; 3:16-17, 19; 4:4, 7, 12-13, 15-16, 23; 5:26, 29; 6:11-13

In this message we shall consider more than thirty points related to God's accomplished work concerning the church. Most of these points are expressed as verbs in various verses throughout the book of Ephesians.

CHOSEN

In 1:4 Paul says, "According as He chose us in Him before the foundation of the world that we should be holy and without blemish before Him, in love." God chose us in eternity past, when He was forming His plan to have the church. The fact that we were chosen in eternity means that our salvation began before the foundation of the world and before time. The word chosen implies that some were selected and that others were not selected. Praise the Lord that we are among the chosen ones! If we turn to our spirit and contact the Lord regarding this matter, we shall realize that just as God is eternal, so His choosing of us was also related to eternity.

PREDESTINATED

Ephesians 1:5 says that we have been predestinated unto sonship. The Greek word rendered predestinated means to be pre-marked, to be marked out beforehand. In eternity God, through His foresight, marked us out from among a vast number of people. Because we were marked out before the creation of the universe, we cannot escape from God. We may want to give Him up, but He will not give us up. What

God is doing with us was not initiated by us in time; it was initiated by God in eternity.

LOVED

After choosing and predestinating us, God created us in Adam. But the man created by God became fallen. Nevertheless, God still loved us. In 2:4 Paul speaks of the great love with which God loved us. He loved us even when we were dead in offenses and sins, when we were walking according to the age of this world, according to the ruler of the authority of the air (2:1-2). In 5:25 Paul says that Christ loved the church and gave Himself up for her. Therefore, we are not only the chosen and predestinated ones, but also the loved ones.

The Bible emphasizes God's love for us after the fall, not before the fall. Ephesians 2 is proof of this. Even after we had become sons of disobedience, God nevertheless loved us. Our fall gave opportunity for God's love.

CALLED

In 4:4 Paul says that we were called in one hope of our calling. Many of us know the exact time and place of our calling. I can still remember the afternoon I was called by God. God came to me and granted me a gracious visitation, and He called me. From the time I was called, I was caught by the Lord. As those who have been caught by Him, we cannot run away from Him. Try as we may, we simply cannot do this. If we run from Him temporarily, He will eventually bring us back to Himself. The fact that we cannot run from the Lord proves that we have been called by Him.

REDEEMED

In 1:7 Paul speaks of redemption, saying, "In Whom we have redemption through His blood, the forgiveness of offenses, according to the riches of His grace." As God was accomplishing His work concerning the church, He redeemed us.

RECONCILED

God has also reconciled us to Himself (2:16). We needed to be reconciled because we were God's enemies and were in rebellion against Him. There was enmity between us and God. But through the Lord's death on the cross, we have been saved from our fallen situation and reconciled to God. Praise the Lord that now there is nothing separating us from Him! We may still be weak, but we are in a reconciled condition. When we are in fellowship with the Lord, we are happy. But when we lose touch with the Lord, we are sad. But whatever our feelings, we nevertheless have been reconciled to Him.

SAVED

In 2:8 Paul tells us that "by grace you have been saved through faith." Before we were saved, we could enjoy certain worldly entertainments. But after we were saved, our tastes spontaneously changed. If you go back to those things you enjoyed before you were saved, you will find them very different. What a tremendous difference God's salvation makes!

GRACED

Using a verbal form of the Greek word for grace, in 1:6 Paul says that God has "graced us in the Beloved." He has put us into the position of grace that we may be the object of His grace and favor, that we may enjoy all that God is to us. Some versions say that God has favored us. We have been graced, favored, in the Beloved.

MADE ALIVE

In 2:5 we see that God has made us alive together with Christ. As those who were God's enemies, we needed to be reconciled. As those who were lost, we needed to be saved. Moreover, as those who were dead in trespasses and sins, we needed to be made alive. When we called on the name of the Lord Jesus, we were enlivened by receiving the Spirit of life. When Christ came into us, He came with the divine life. In this way, He made us alive. He enlivens us by being the life within us. The life with which we are enlivened includes the law of life, the sense of life, the fellowship of life, and every other aspect of the experience of life.

RAISED UP

In 2:6 we see that we have been raised up together in Christ. We were not only dead, but also buried. Therefore, God not only made us alive; He also raised us up from among the dead. Praise Him, we have been raised up from the grave!

SEATED

In 2:6 we also see that God has "seated us together in the heavenlies in Christ Jesus." Many Christians are waiting to go to heaven, but we are already in heaven. In Christ God has seated us all together, once for all, in the heavenlies. This was accomplished when Christ ascended to the heavens, and it is applied to us by the Spirit of Christ. Today we realize in experience this reality in our spirit through faith in the accomplished fact. If we exercise our spirit in a genuine way, we shall have the sense that we are sitting in the heavenlies looking down at the situation on earth. However, if we exercise our natural reason instead of our spirit, we shall have the sense that we are on earth. Nevertheless, according to the revelation of the Scriptures, we are seated with Christ in the heavenlies.

PURCHASED

In 1:14 Paul speaks of the redemption of the acquired or purchased possession. The New Testament reveals that God has purchased us with a great price, the precious blood of Christ. In order to acquire us, God had to pay such a high price.

SEALED

Ephesians 1:13 says that we "were sealed with the Holy Spirit of the promise." This verse indicates that God has sealed us; He has put His seal upon us. This seal is the Holy Spirit Himself. After we were purchased with the blood of

Christ, God sealed us. Because we have been sealed, we bear a mark, the image of God. Although we may fail and become unclean, this seal, this mark, cannot be removed.

POSSESSED

In 1:14 Paul says that we have become God's possession, His acquired possession. God possesses us. We should have the realization that we belong to Him.

GUARANTEED

On the one hand, we are God's. On the other hand, He is ours. Because we are His, we are sealed and possessed by Him. Because He is ours, we have received the guarantee that He is our portion, our inheritance. Our inheritance has nothing to do with material things; it is God Himself. We have the Holy Spirit as the guarantee, pledge, down payment, deposit, foretaste, and sample, of our inheritance.

CREATED

Ephesians 2:10 says, "For we are His workmanship, created in Christ Jesus for good works." This verse does not speak of the first creation, but of the second creation, the creation of the new man. We all have been created together as God's masterpiece, God's poem. The Greek word rendered masterpiece means something which has been made, a handiwork, or something which has been written or composed as a poem. The church is a poem written by God. In the universe nothing is more meaningful than the church. The church, the corporate new man, is God's masterpiece.

Concerning the church, the word created is used three times in Ephesians. In addition to 2:10, it is used in 2:15, which says that Christ abolished the law of the commandments in ordinances in order to create one new man. In 4:24 we are told that the new man was created according to God in righteousness and holiness of the truth. From a human point of view, there are many deficiencies and shortcomings in the church. But from God's perspective in eternity, the church is a finished product, something already accomplished by God. God is happy and can boast to His enemy, "Satan, no matter how much you try to do, I have already accomplished My work. I have created the one new man." In the eyes of God the church has already been built up.

BECOME NEAR

Ephesians 2:13 says, "But now in Christ Jesus you who once were far off have become near in the blood of Christ." Once we were far off from God and from one another, but in Christ Jesus God has caused us to become near. Before we were saved and brought near, we could not speak of one another as brothers and sisters. But now we have the deep sense that in Christ we are closer to one another than we are to our brothers and sisters in the flesh.

ENLIGHTENED

Now let us go on to consider certain items which from God's point of view have been accomplished, but from the standpoint of our experience are still in the process of being accomplished. The first is the matter of being enlightened. In 1:18 Paul speaks of the eyes of our heart being enlightened, and in 5:14, of Christ shining on us. In a sense, God has already enlightened us. But in another sense, we still need to be enlightened. We may be covered, veiled, by certain things, and need to turn to the light so that the light may shine on us.

If we would be enlightened, we need to turn to the spirit. According to 1:17 and 18, enlightenment is related to receiving a spirit of wisdom and revelation in the full knowledge of God. If we stay in our natural mind, we shall be in darkness. But if we turn to our regenerated spirit, we shall be enlightened.

I am concerned for those who do not open themselves up in the meetings. To be closed in this way is to be in darkness. We need to open ourselves by uttering something for the Lord in the meetings. When we turn from our reasonings to the spirit, we are enlightened. We rise up, and Christ shines on us. As we stand up to speak, the light shines on us, and we are enlightened. The more we are enlightened, the more we experience the work God has accomplished concerning us.

STRENGTHENED

In chapter three Paul prayed that our inner man, our regenerated spirit indwelt by the Holy Spirit, would be strengthened with power (v. 16). When we are enlightened, we realize the need for our inner man to be strengthened.

INDWELT

Our inner man needs to be strengthened so that Christ may make His home in our hearts (3:17). For Christ to make His home in us means that we are indwelt by Him. Christ, the living Person, desires to dwell in us, to fill every part of our inward being with Himself. All of our inward parts need to be a home for Christ so that we may be fully occupied by Him.

ROOTED AND GROUNDED

When Christ makes His home in us, we shall enjoy Him as unlimited love. In the words of 3:17, we shall be "rooted and grounded in love." We are rooted in Christ for growth, and we are grounded in Him for building.

FILLED

When we are strengthened into our inner man, when Christ makes His home in our hearts, and when we are rooted and grounded in love, we are filled unto all the fullness of God (3:19). It is in our spirit that we are filled unto all the fullness of the Triune God to become His expression.

GIFTED

In 4:7 Paul says, "But to each one of us was given grace according to the measure of the gift of Christ." Because every member has received grace, every member is a gift to the Body of Christ. No matter how insignificant we may be, we all are gifted. Do not think that Peter, James, John, and Paul were gifted and that you are not. Since we all are gifted, we should all function in the meetings. Many times it is not as helpful for an elder to say a certain thing as it is for one of the other saints to say the same thing. God has accomplished a complete work for us. In view of such a work, we should learn to function. All the points we have covered thus far leave us without any excuse for not functioning. Is it not true that all these wonderful things have been accomplished for us? We have been chosen, predestinated, loved, called, redeemed, reconciled, saved, graced, made alive, raised up, seated, purchased, sealed, possessed, guaranteed, created, made near, enlightened, strengthened, indwelt, rooted, grounded, and filled. Is it possible to have all this without being gifted? Surely it is not possible. Praise the Lord, we all are gifted!

We have pointed out a number of times that the Lord hates the deeds of the Nicolaitans (Rev. 2:6). This means that He hates the clergy-laity system, which is an abomination in His sight. Nevertheless, because of the influence of degraded Christianity, many still do not function in the meetings. In order to cast off this influence, we all must learn to function.

PERFECTED

In 4:12 Paul goes on to speak of the perfecting of the saints. The Greek word translated perfecting may also be rendered equipping. As those who are gifted, we perfect and equip one another with our gifts. Some may argue that only the apostles, prophets, evangelists, and shepherds and teachers can perfect the saints. Verse 16, however, speaks of every joint of supply and of the operation in the measure of each part. We all are parts of the Body. If we function, we shall help others to be perfected. In addition, as we function, we are the first to be perfected. Every time I minister the Word, I am the first to receive the benefit of my ministry. We all need to perfect others and to be perfected by functioning. If you have the sense that you have been perfected through functioning, that is an indication that others have been perfected also. May we all perfect one another.

GROWING UP

The result of being perfected is that we grow up into Christ (4:15-16). We perfect one another by helping one another grow in life. To perfect the saints is to nourish them by feeding them. I can testify that I have received much nourishment from the saints. This nourishment has helped me to grow.

FITTED TOGETHER

According to 4:16, the Body is fitted together. This is for building. How much we have been fitted together with others depends on our perfection and growth. Through nourishment we grow, and through growth we are fitted together with the saints.

KNIT TOGETHER

Furthermore, in 4:16 we see that we are knit together. This is closely related to the matter of fitting. However, it emphasizes the aspect of attachment. We need to be attached to one another. As we are fitted and knit together, we are built up. Once we have been built up in the church life, it will be very difficult for us to leave the church. This is altogether different from joining a denomination. We do not join the church; we are built into it. Those who have been built into the church can be neither pulled out nor pushed out.

RENEWED

Ephesians 4:23 speaks of being "renewed in the spirit of your mind." We all need to be renewed. We need to have the old element discharged, and a new element wrought into us. The old element, the element of Adam, is discharged, and the eternal element, the element of Christ, is added to take its place.

SANCTIFIED

According to 5:26, Christ is sanctifying the church. To be sanctified is to have the divine nature wrought into our human nature. Once again we may use the illustration of making tea. When tea is added to water, the water is "tea-ified." In the same principle, when the divine element is added to us, we are sanctified. Christ as the heavenly "tea" is wrought into us. To be sanctified does not mean that we wear certain kinds of clothes or style our hair in a particular way. That is mere outward correction or adjustment. I am not for long hair or for short hair, but for sanctified hair. When the element of God is worked into our being, we are truly sanctified.

CLEANSED

In 5:26 we see that Christ is cleansing the church by the washing of the water in the Word. Such a washing cleanses us from wrinkles caused by oldness and from spots caused by wounds. This cleansing is a metabolic cleansing, a cleansing in which a new element is added to replace the old element that is being discharged.

NOURISHED AND CHERISHED

In 5:29 Paul points out that Christ is also nourishing and cherishing the church. To nourish is to feed, and to cherish is to nurture with tender love and foster with tender care. A mother nourishes her child by feeding the child healthy food. She also cherishes her child by embracing the little one in love. As we are cherished by Christ, we are warmed, softened, and comforted, just as a child is soothed by the loving embrace of the mother.

ARMORED

Finally, according to 6:11 and 13, we need to be armored. This means that we put on the armor of God in order to stand against the stratagems of the Devil. To be armored is to be armed for warfare. As we are armed with the whole armor of God, we become God's army to fight the battle for God's purpose and for His kingdom.

If we would have the proper church life, we need to experience every aspect of God's work covered in this message. We need to pray concerning all these items, pray-reading the verses that speak of them, until they become our reality. May we exercise our spirit to apply all the aspects of God's work concerning the church.

LIFE-STUDY OF EPHESIANS

MESSAGE SEVENTY-THREE

THREE ITEMS THAT DAMAGE THE CHURCH

Scripture Reading: Eph. 1:5-7, 13, 17, 22-23; 2:4, 5, 15, 18, 22; 3:8, 16-17, 19, 21; 4:4-6, 15; 5:18, 26-27; 6:11, 18

In this message we shall consider how the church became degraded. Before we do this, let us look at some of the key verses in each chapter of Ephesians.

GOD'S ULTIMATE GOAL

In 1:5 Paul says that we have been predestinated to sonship, that is, predestinated to become sons of God. In creation, God is our Creator, not our Father. None of us were born of Him in creation. The fact that God has predestinated us, or marked us out beforehand, to be His sons means that we have been predestinated to be born of Him. This implies that God must come into us and that we must receive His life and have a relationship with Him in life. Therefore, to be predestinated to sonship is to be predestinated to be born of God so that He may become our Father and that we may become His sons.

In 1:6 and 7 we see that God has graced us in the Beloved and redeemed us in Him. Having become the object of God's grace, we have been favored in Christ, and we have redemption through the blood of Christ.

Ephesians 1:13 says that we have been sealed with the Holy Spirit of the promise. On the day we believed in the Lord Jesus, God sealed us with Himself as the Spirit.

In 1:17 Paul speaks of our need for a spirit of wisdom and revelation. This spirit denotes our regenerated spirit indwelt by the Spirit of God.

The closing word in the first chapter of Ephesians concerns

the church, which is Christ's Body, the fullness of the One who fills all in all (vv. 22-23).

By putting these verses together we can see Ephesians 1 in a new way. We have been predestinated, we have been sealed, and we have received a spirit of wisdom and revelation so that we may know the Body. Selection, predestination, redemption, and sealing are not ends in themselves. All this is for the Body. We were chosen, predestinated, favored, graced, redeemed, and sealed for the Body. Furthermore, for the Body we have been given a spirit of wisdom and revelation. In Ephesians 1 the Body is God's ultimate goal.

In the past many of us heard sermons on predestination and redemption. We have also heard about being graced and sealed with the Spirit. But had you ever heard that God's selection, predestination, favor, redemption, and sealing are all for the Body?

THE DWELLING PLACE OF GOD

In 2:4 and 5 we see that even when we were dead in offenses, God made us alive together with Christ. Not only were we sinful, we were also dead. But God came in to enliven us. If He had redeemed us and forgiven us without enlivening us, God would have had a great many redeemed ones who were still in death. Praise Him that in addition to redeeming us He made us alive!

He also created us into one new man (2:15). Furthermore, we have been given access to the Father in the Spirit (v. 18). Finally, we are being built up into a dwelling place of God in our spirit (v. 22). Just as chapter one ends with the Body, so chapter two concludes with the building up of God's dwelling place. This indicates that we have been enlivened not just for the sake of being enlivened, but for the building up of God's dwelling place. In other words, God made us alive for the church. His final word both in chapter one and in chapter two concerns the church. At the end of chapter one, we have the church as Christ's Body, the fullness of Him who fills all in all. At the end of chapter two, we have the church as the dwelling place of God in our spirit.

NOT INDIVIDUAL SPIRITUALITY, BUT THE CHURCH

In 3:8 Paul said that he preached the unsearchable riches of Christ as the gospel. Paul did not preach doctrine, not even the doctrine of the riches of Christ. What he preached was the riches of Christ themselves. Furthermore, in this chapter Paul prayed that we would be strengthened by the Spirit into our inner man so that Christ may make His home in our hearts (vv. 16-17). The goal of this strengthening and indwelling is that we may be filled unto all the fullness of God (v. 19). The result of this is glory to God in the church (v. 21). Therefore, chapter three, like the preceding chapters, ends with the church. This means that the preaching of the unsearchable riches of Christ, the strengthening of our inner man, Christ making His home in our heart, and being filled unto all the fullness of God are not for our individual spirituality, but for the church.

GROWING FOR THE BODY

In 4:4-6 we have the Triune God—the Father, the Son, and the Spirit—with the Body. According to 4:15, we need to grow up into Christ in all things. This growth is for the sake of the Body, the church.

FILLED AND WASHED FOR THE CHURCH

In 5:18 Paul charges us to be filled in spirit. This filling surely is related to being filled unto all the fullness of God. Through the infilling we have the water in the Word to wash away our spots and wrinkles (vv. 26-27). The result of this washing is that we are corporately sanctified. Sanctification is not primarily an individual matter, but a corporate matter, a matter for the Body. Moreover, in this chapter we see that Christ is nourishing and cherishing the Body (v. 29).

PUTTING ON THE ARMOR TO BE GOD'S WARRIOR

Finally, in chapter six Paul tells us to put on the whole armor of God (v. 11). We need to receive the sword of the

Spirit, which is the Word of God, by means of all prayer, praying at every time in spirit (v. 18). This is for the church to be God's warrior.

SEEING THE VISION OF THE CHURCH

As we consider all these verses, we see that in the genuine church there is no religion, tradition, regulations, forms, or rituals. Instead, there is just the Triune God as the all-inclusive Spirit working in our spirit to produce the Body, the new man. I hope that we all shall pray-read these verses until we see this vision of the church. Then we shall realize that God has predestinated us for this. We have been made alive for God's dwelling place, and we enjoy the riches of Christ that we may be part of the church. The church is produced by the mingling of the Triune God with redeemed mankind. The church life is thus the corporate mingling of the divine Spirit with the human spirit. If we have Christ as our reality, we shall not have ordinances or forms, but we shall have only the experience of the living Christ in our spirit.

JUDAISM AS A CAUSE OF DEGRADATION

If we study church history, we can learn how the church became degraded. Firstly, Satan used Judaism, a religion founded and formed according to God's oracle, to corrupt the church. In his subtlety, Satan caused Judaism to creep into the church. We have seen that the church is an entity produced by the mingling of the Holy Spirit with the human spirit. In this entity there is no room for regulations, organization, forms, or doctrines. There is room only for the Triune God as the all-inclusive Spirit mingled with our spirit in a corporate way. The church on the day of Pentecost was like this. At that time, there were no so-called services or methods of worship. The saints were not preoccupied with doctrinal knowledge, and they were not under any kind of organization. On the day of Pentecost, there was no religion. There was only a group of people living in the mingled spirit and experiencing the genuine church life.

Later, however, Judaism crept in with its forms and ordinances, especially the ordinances concerning circumcision, the Sabbath, and eating. Paul wrote the book of Galatians in order to deal with the damage caused by Judaism, by religion.

KNOWLEDGE AS A SOURCE OF CORRUPTION

Secondly, Satan used philosophy, especially a mixture of various philosophies called Gnosticism, to damage the church. Certain forms of Gnosticism included elements of Judaism and Christianity. The point here is that Satan used knowledge and the exercise of the natural mind to corrupt the church. The Epistle to the Colossians was written to deal with this, just as Galatians was written to deal with religion. The subtlety of the enemy is to turn the church from the mingled spirit to the natural mind, that is, to turn the saints from the tree of life to the tree of knowledge. In the beginning, those in the church life were feeding on the tree of life. Then Satan came in to distract the saints from the tree of life to the tree of knowledge. William Law, a contemporary of John Wesley, saw this. In a book entitled *The Power of the Spirit* Law is quoted as saying the following:

> ...A trust in the wisdom of men and the letter of Scripture has caused the church to fall from its first gospel state in much the way that Adam fell through eating of the same tree of knowledge. The Bible teacher and religious leader who gain and hold a church position through intellectual attainments and oratorical skills can be said to differ from lesser men only as the serpent differed from the other beasts of the field—in that it was more subtle.

Furthermore, speaking of the turn from the tree of life to the tree of knowledge, Law said:

> In the first apostolic church, the wisdom of words was no more sought after than friendship with the world which is enmity with God. In that new-born

> church, the tree of life, which grew in the midst of Paradise, took root and grew up again, spreading glory and virtue as men fed upon it. In the present church, the tree of life is hissed at as the visionary food of extremists, and the tree of death, called the tree of knowledge, has the eyes and hearts of priests and people, and is thought to do as much good to Christians as it did evil to the first inhabitants of Paradise.

At the end of Genesis 3, the way to the tree of life was closed to fallen man. But through the redemption of Christ, the church was brought back to the tree of life. However Satan intervened and turned the church from the tree of life to the tree of knowledge.

THE DISPUTES CONCERNING THE PERSON OF CHRIST

This turn to the tree of knowledge was expressed in the controversies concerning Christology that were common during the first several centuries in the history of the church. These debates and disputations were related to the Person of Christ. Much of this debate was brought about by the threat of Gnosticism, which taught heresy concerning the Person of Christ, saying that He was not actually God incarnated as a man. A number of sound Christian teachers rose up to refute the Gnostic heresy. However, the result was that various opinions concerning Christ were put forth and debated. Some said that Christ was only God and not man, whereas others argued that Christ was only a man and not God. Others taught that Christ had a human nature, but that this nature was not real or complete. Some who held this view said that Christ had a soul and a body, but not a spirit. Still others taught that Christ was a man who eventually became God. Others claimed that Christ had not only two natures, but also two persons. Another view was that Christ's natures were mingled together in such a way as to produce a third nature. All these different opinions caused considerable argument among the early church fathers. It was largely due to these debates that the church was divided. This is an illustration of how the enemy in his subtlety turned the saints from the spirit to the exercise of the natural mind to analyze doctrine and to systematize it.

We need to learn from this simply to take the pure Word of God without any attempt to systematize it. We should believe whatever the Bible says and say amen to it. For example, John 1:1 says, "In the beginning was the Word, and the Word was with God, and the Word was God." This verse says that the Word was with God; it also says that the Word was God. We say amen to both statements. The New Testament also reveals that Christ is both the Son of God and the Son of man. We believe both of these facts and say amen.

NOT DISPUTATION BUT ENJOYMENT

How foolish it is to presume to analyze Christ! We cannot even adequately or thoroughly analyze ourselves, much less the Lord Jesus Christ. If Christ were altogether understandable to us, He would not be Christ. We simply cannot fully comprehend who Christ is and what Christ is. Instead of engaging in disputes over the Person of Christ, let us receive in simplicity whatever the Scriptures reveal concerning Him. For us, the age of disputation is over. We just care to enjoy the wonderful Christ.

Today's Christianity is preoccupied with doctrine, but is short of the enjoyment of the all-inclusive Christ. Nearly every sect or denomination has been established according to a particular doctrine. For example, the Baptist denomination is built upon the doctrine of baptism by immersion. Certain Baptist groups go so far as to insist that people be baptized only in their water. No other baptism is recognized. Hence, the Baptist denomination is a division caused by adhering to a teaching concerning baptism. By this we see that even today the church is being corrupted and damaged by knowledge. Many who care for a particular doctrine have no concern for the Body.

KEEPING THE ONENESS

Because Satan has used religion and knowledge to damage the church, we in the Lord's recovery must strongly testify that we are not for religion or for knowledge. Satan is subtle. Firstly he used the tree of knowledge to corrupt the old creation. Then he used the same tree to corrupt the church as God's new creation. Today his work is the same. Therefore, we must not take the way of knowledge, not even of biblical knowledge in letters. If we are distracted from the tree of life to doctrinal knowledge, we shall lose the oneness.

Many who have visited the church in Los Angeles have been impressed with the oneness. To them this has been the most convincing aspect of the church life. The reason for the oneness among us is that we condemn and despise the tree of knowledge. From the very beginning, when the foundation of the church life was laid in this locality, we had nothing to do with the tree of knowledge. This is the reason we have been kept and preserved in oneness.

ORGANIZATION AS A CAUSE OF DAMAGE

The third item that has damaged the church throughout its history is organization. This damaging and corrupting element began to appear in the second century, largely through the influence of a certain spiritual leader, Ignatius, who taught that bishops were different from elders. According to the Scriptures, however, elders and bishops refer to the same people. The term elder denotes the person, whereas the term bishop, or overseer, denotes the function. In the New Testament the elders oversee the various aspects of the church life. The teaching that bishops are above elders prepared the way for the development of a hierarchy, with an elaborate organization that included bishops, archbishops, cardinals, and the pope. The result was that the Holy Spirit was given no place in the so-called church. In order for organization to be maintained, there is the need for regulations, forms, and rituals. This is the reason these things have been prevailing in the so-called church.

Religion, knowledge, and organization have surely damaged the church. Even nominal Christians have some form of religion, although they have no experience of the living Christ. Furthermore, nearly all Christians, whether genuine believers or false professors, have some knowledge of doctrine. Moreover, organization abounds in today's Christianity. But very few Christians know the life-giving Spirit or the reality of the Body of Christ. It seems that the lexicon used by most Christians does not include these terms, but includes only terms related to religion, knowledge, organization, regulations, forms, and rituals.

Praise the Lord that we have escaped from all this! If we are clear about the factors that have damaged and corrupted the church, we shall be kept from taking the old way of Christianity. We shall give no place to religion, the tree of knowledge, or organization.

THE SEVENFOLD SPIRIT

In the church life in the Lord's recovery we are not for organization with its emphasis on position or rank. It is not wrong to speak of elders and deacons. However, in the book of Revelation there is no mention of these terms. This book speaks, on the contrary, of the seven Spirits, the sevenfold intensified Spirit that deals with the fallen, degraded church. We are not for doctrines, rituals, or rank—we are for the sevenfold Spirit. Everything apart from this all-inclusive Spirit is dung (Phil. 3:8).

Recently, in a time of fellowship with the Lord, I had the sense that I was immersed in the Spirit. Inwardly I was filled with the Spirit, and outwardly I was clothed with Him. The church life consists in the corporate experience of the mingled Spirit, not in religion, doctrine, or organization with its titles, ranks, and positions. Like Paul in Philippians 3, we count as dung everything other than Christ, who is the all-inclusive life-giving Spirit.

UNLOADED AND RELEASED

Before the Lord, I know what my burden is today. I am

not interested in teaching the saints. My burden is that we all be "wrecked" for Christ and the church, and that we be unloaded of the old things of Christianity. In the Lord's recovery we must go all the way back to the beginning, where there was the eating of the tree of life. In the beginning there was just the Word to feed us; there was no religion, no tree of knowledge, and no organization. How we need to be unloaded of these three devilish factors of corruption and damage in the church! By the Lord's mercy, many of us have been unloaded, and others are being unloaded meeting after meeting. As I contact the saints, I realize that many have been fully released from religion, knowledge, and organization. Because we have been unloaded and released, we can be living and aggressive for Christ and the church wherever we may go. Having been unloaded, we are one, and we have brotherly love not as a doctrine, but as a reality.

Sometimes people ask us if we speak in tongues or if we exercise the gifts of the Spirit. We can testify that we are filled, saturated, and possessed by the Spirit. In this experience of the Spirit we have the church life.

THE CHURCH LIFE IN THE ALL-INCLUSIVE SPIRIT

May we all be deeply impressed that the church life has nothing to do with religion, knowledge, or organization. In the church there is no room for regulations, forms, or rituals. We do not care even for the knowledge of the Bible in mere letters. To us, every word of the Bible must be spirit and life (John 6:63). Then the church will be living and preserved in the oneness. The life-giving Spirit is our oneness. Everything we need for the church life is in the all-inclusive Spirit. As we come to the Holy Word, we need to exercise our spirit to pray. Then the Word will become the Spirit in our experience, and we shall have the genuine and proper church life. As long as we have the church life, we have everything: salvation, redemption, sanctification, the overcoming life, the rapture, and the kingdom. In the church life everything in time and eternity is ours.

LIFE-STUDY OF EPHESIANS

MESSAGE SEVENTY-FOUR

SEVEN ASPECTS OF THE CHURCH

Scripture Reading: Eph. 1:23; 2:15-16, 19, 21-22; 4:4, 12-13, 16, 24; 5:5, 25, 31-32; 6:11, 13

Throughout history, Satan has damaged the church by religion, knowledge, and organization. Satan's goal is to divide the Body of Christ through knowledge and doctrine and to destroy the functions of the members of the Body through organization, especially organization that issues in the clergy-laity system. This system has replaced the functions of the members of the Body. If Satan cannot keep people from the Lord, then he will seek to damage and corrupt the Body of Christ. God's intention is not simply to save millions of people and then transport them into heaven. God's intention in His eternal purpose is to have the Body to express Christ. He desires to have a number of genuine believers built up together in the life of Christ.

THE BUILDING OF THE CHURCH TODAY

Due to the subtlety of Satan, many think that such a building can take place only in the future. According to this concept, all we can do today is preach the gospel, bring people to the Lord, and help them to know the Bible, to love the Lord, and to seek spirituality. Some Christian teachers say that, according to the type in the Old Testament, we are living in the age of David, in the time of fighting the battle and of making preparations for the building of the temple. Later, in the age of Solomon, the temple will be built up. However, this teaching annuls the book of Ephesians. In 2:22 Paul says, "In Whom you also are being built together into a dwelling place of God in spirit." This verse does not say that we shall be built up some day in the future; it says plainly that we are being built even today. Hence, the building of the church is for today.

In 4:11 and 12 we see that the Lord has given apostles, prophets, evangelists, and shepherds and teachers for the perfecting of the saints unto the building up of the Body of Christ. This also indicates that the building of the church is taking place today.

Ephesians 4:16 offers further proof of this. Here we see the growth that is unto the building up of the Body. The operation in the measure of each part causes the growth of the Body unto the building up of itself in love. Paul's word clearly indicates that the growth which is unto building is taking place today.

Certain Christian teachers evade the issue of the present building up of the Body because they know that they are in a situation in which it is impossible to have the church life. They are in division. They can merely shake hands over the denominational fences and say to one another that they are one in Christ. This, however, is a false oneness, a oneness in pretense. Therefore, they excuse their situation by saying that it is impossible for the church to be built up today. They follow the teaching that the building of the church will be only in the future. This is the subtlety of Satan.

THE LORD'S PROMISE TO BUILD HIS CHURCH

No matter how many souls we may bring to the Lord, how many saints we may edify, and how much we help others to study the Bible and to be spiritual, God's purpose is not fulfilled. I believe that the main reason for the delay of the Lord's coming back is that His church has not yet been built up. In Matthew 16:18 the Lord Jesus promised and prophesied, "I will build My church." This word must be fulfilled before the Lord comes back. Otherwise, concerning the building of the church, He would be put to shame. Satan would be able to boast of defeating the Lord. Then Satan would be able to say to the Lord Jesus, "For nearly two thousand years You have been trying to build the church, but You have not been successful. Your work on the cross, in resurrection, in ascension, and as the life-giving Spirit has not been sufficient to defeat me. You have not reached Your goal." The Lord Jesus will not allow Satan to boast in this way. He will put him to shame through the building up of the church, even in the midst of this dark age. Then the Lord will be able to boast to Satan, "Satan, even in such a dark and evil age, I have built My church."

The Lord is doing a marvelous work of recovery. He will show His enemy that He is well able to build His church. No matter what the situation may be on earth, we have the assurance that the Lord is carrying on the work of His recovery.

STANDING AGAINST DEGRADATION

Today's Christianity is filled with religion, doctrine, organization, forms, rituals, and regulations. People are helped to be saved, to become religious, to pursue spirituality, and to desire a closer walk with the Lord. But where is the Body? It seems that so many Christians do not see that in the book of Ephesians the church is emphasized. In his subtlety the enemy, Satan, has used various good things such as fundamental doctrine to damage the church. We must stand against the degradation of today's Christianity. In doing this, we do not fight against people, but against the Devil, the subtle one.

Because the Lord is sovereign, He cannot be defeated. Even today He is fulfilling His purpose. In the Lord's recovery we are not for religion, knowledge, organization, rituals, forms, or regulations; we are only for the all-inclusive Christ as the life-giving Spirit in our spirit. As we enjoy the mingled spirit in a corporate way, we have the church life.

The book of Ephesians reveals various aspects of the church. In this message we shall consider seven of these aspects: the Body, the new man, the Bride, the family, the kingdom, the dwelling place of God, and the warrior.

THE BODY

According to 1:22 and 23, the church is Christ's Body, the

fullness of the One who fills all in all. It was in this one Body that both the Jews and the Gentiles were reconciled to God through the cross (2:16). We, the believers, were reconciled not only *for* the Body of Christ, but also *in* the Body of Christ. We all have been reconciled in the one Body. As we have seen, the gifted persons are for the building up of the Body, and the Body is growing unto the building up of itself in love.

THE NEW MAN

In 2:15 we see that Christ created the Jews and the Gentiles in Himself into one new man. This new man is corporate and universal. There are many believers, but there is only one new man in the universe. All the believers are components of this corporate and universal new man. According to 4:13, we are to grow up until we arrive at a full-grown man, and in 4:24 we see that, in a practical way, we need to put on the new man.

THE BRIDE

In Ephesians 5 we see the church as the Bride of Christ. This aspect reveals that the church comes out of Christ, as Eve came out of Adam (Gen. 2:21-22). The church has the same life and nature as Christ and becomes one with Him to be His counterpart, as Eve became one flesh with Adam (Gen. 2:24). Eventually, as Eve went back to Adam and was presented to him, so the church will go back to Christ and be presented to Him as His Bride.

THE FAMILY

In 2:19 Paul says, "So then you are no longer strangers and sojourners, but you are fellow-citizens of the saints and members of the household of God." As members of the household of God, we are God's family, even God's house. Both the Jewish and Gentile believers are members of God's house, which is a matter of life and enjoyment. All believers were born of God into His house to enjoy His riches.

THE KINGDOM

The house of God leads to the kingdom of God, indicated by the term "fellow-citizens of the saints." All the believers are citizens in God's kingdom. His kingdom is a sphere for Him to exercise His authority. In 5:5 Paul says that "every fornicator or unclean person or person of unbridled greedy lust, who is an idolater, has no inheritance in the kingdom of Christ and of God." This refers not only to the millennium, but also to the church life today. The believers have been regenerated into the kingdom of God (John 3:5) and are in the church life, living in the kingdom of God today (Rom. 14:17).

THE DWELLING PLACE

In 2:22 we see that the church is God's dwelling place. God's Spirit dwells in our spirit. Therefore, the dwelling place of God is in our spirit.

THE WARRIOR

Finally, in chapter six we see that the church is a warrior to defeat God's enemy, the Devil. In order to fight the spiritual warfare, we need both the power of the Lord and also the whole armor of God. The church is a corporate warrior, and the believers are parts of this unique warrior. We must fight the spiritual warfare in the Body, not individually.

In his subtlety, Satan will allow Christians to do things that are scriptural and spiritual, as long as they do not have the Body or the new man. Most Christians do not even realize that the church is the new man, a corporate man. They may speak a little regarding the church as the Bride of Christ or as God's family, but they have no concept that the church is God's present kingdom or God's dwelling place.

WHY WE ARE HERE

Can you find these seven aspects of the church in Christianity? Concerning the church, Christianity has missed the mark. We in the Lord's recovery are not here for soul-winning, for Bible study, or for spirituality. We are here for the expression of the Body on earth. We are also here to be the new man and the Bride.

At present, Christ is preparing us to be His Bride. One day the wedding will come. That will be the fulfillment of Revelation 19. As we are preparing for that day, we are the church in the aspects of the family, the kingdom, the dwelling place, and the warrior. Praise the Lord that we are His family! When we came into the church life, we had the sense that we had come home. Furthermore, the church is God's kingdom, for here we are under God's authority. Moreover, as God's warrior we are fighting against His enemy. We are here for the Body, the new man, the Bride, the family, the kingdom, and the warrior.

EXPRESSING CHRIST AS LIFE

As the Body, the church needs life. Without life, our physical body would become a corpse. The same is true of the Body of Christ.

Some opposers argue that the Body is just a symbol, a figure, not a divine reality. It is utterly wrong to say that the Body of Christ is merely a symbol. Our body is a symbol and a figure, but the Body of Christ is a reality, for our body symbolizes Christ's Body. To say that the Body of Christ is merely a symbol indicates a lack of a proper understanding of the church. Those who hold this view do not see that the church is actually the Body of Christ. Surely Christ is real. How can such a real One be expressed through a symbolic Body? How ridiculous! In order for Christ to be expressed, He must have a real and living Body.

We do not express Christ by endeavoring to correct or improve ourselves. Through such efforts we can express only our own character. If we would express Christ, we need the life of Christ. We need Christ as the living Spirit to live Himself out from within us. This is not outward correction or improvement; it is the experience of Christ as our inner life. Christ is the life-giving Spirit living within us and lived out from within us. This makes us His Body for His expression.

What we express as the Body of Christ is not our character, but Christ Himself as life.

TAKING CHRIST AS OUR PERSON

As the new man, the church needs not only life, but also Christ as the person. A tree has only life, not a person. But a man must have a person as well as life. The church not only possesses Christ as life, but also holds Christ as the person. Hence, today the Lord Jesus is not only the life of the church, but also the person of the church. In order to have the church life, we all must take Christ as our person. But if we each hold to our own person, we shall be through with the church life.

Colossians 3:10 and 11 reveal that in the new man "there cannot be Greek and Jew, circumcision and uncircumcision, barbarian, Scythian, slave, freeman, but Christ is all and in all." This indicates that in the new man there is just one person—Christ. There is no room for Chinese, Japanese, American, British, German, or any other nationality. This should not be a mere doctrine, but should be our practical experience in the spirit. As a part of the new man, we all have Christ as our person. We need to pray, "Lord, make this real to us. We cannot be satisfied with knowledge or with the doctrine that the church is the new man with Christ as the person. We want this to be experienced in our daily life. O Lord, help us to take You as our person." If we do this, the church will be truly one, and the enemy will be subdued. Whoever comes into the meetings of the church will see a number of people who take Christ as their person. How marvelous!

A MATTER OF LOVE

Eve typifies the church as Christ's Bride. Eve was built with a rib taken out of Adam. After building this rib into a woman, God presented her to Adam. What came out of Adam went back to him and became one with him. In the same principle, the church comes out of Christ and will go back to Christ to be one with Him.

The aspect of the church as the Bride implies love. Marriage is a matter of love, and the life of a marriage depends on love. If a husband and wife do not love each other, it will be very difficult for them to remain together. No doubt, Adam and Eve loved each other. Because of this love, they became one. Today there is a mutual love between Christ and the church. Not only do we have Him as our life and as our person, but we also enjoy this mutual love. Christ desires to make known His love to the church, and the church responds by telling the Lord how much she loves Him. Whatever we do for the Lord we do joyfully and willingly out of love for Him. When you love someone, you are happy to serve him. You serve not out of necessity, but out of love. As the church, we must bear the testimony that we love the Lord. Whoever contacts us should receive an impression that we love the Lord and, out of our love for Him, serve Him willingly. This is the aspect of the church as Christ's Bride.

OUR REAL FAMILY

If we have a genuine love for the Lord, we shall spontaneously be the church in the aspect of God's family. So many worldly people today are either orphans or wanderers. They are homeless. We in the church life are members of God's family. Therefore, we are at home. The church is our real family. We appreciate the natural family life created by God. But we can testify that this family life is not as sweet as the family life in the church. How pleasant is the church as God's family! If you stay away from the church life for a period of time, you will realize how precious the church is in the aspect of God's family. Oh, we in the church are God's family!

UNDER GOD'S RULE

As we have pointed out, we are also God's kingdom. In the church we all are under God's government, God's authority and rule. We are not lawless. On the contrary, we are governed spontaneously in a pleasant and loving way. Although there are elders in the churches, they do not exercise control over the saints. Rather, all the saints are willingly under God's rule. This is the church as the kingdom of God. If all the people in this country lived like this, the enemy would be completely subdued.

In the church we are under divine government. Because of an inward ruling, we cannot cheat others or take advantage of them. This inner ruling is the reality of the kingdom. Today in the church Jesus Christ is King. He is the King on the throne within us and among us.

GOD'S DWELLING PLACE IN OUR SPIRIT

Furthermore, the church is the dwelling place of God in spirit. When we are not in our spirit, we do not have the church as God's dwelling place in a practical way. But whenever we turn to our spirit, we sense that God has a dwelling place in our spirit. This dwelling place is for God's rest.

DEFEATING THE ENEMY AND PREPARING THE WAY FOR THE LORD TO COME BACK

Not only is the church the Body, the new man, the Bride, the family, the kingdom, and the dwelling place; the church is also the warrior to fight against God's enemy. God's enemy, Satan, is terrified of such a church. Satan is not afraid of individualistic Christians, not even if they number in the thousands. But whenever the believers come together as the church in the aspect of the Body and in these other aspects, Satan trembles. By the church in these seven aspects Christ is expressed, the Father has rest, and the enemy is defeated. May we all see the vision that the church is not a matter of individual holiness or spirituality. On the contrary, it is a matter of being built up together as the Body, the new man, the Bride, the family, the kingdom, the dwelling place, and the warrior. As such a church, we defeat the enemy and prepare the way for the Lord Jesus to come back.

LIFE-STUDY OF EPHESIANS

MESSAGE SEVENTY-FIVE

GOD'S ECONOMY—CHRIST WITH THE CHURCH

Scripture Reading: Eph. 1:5, 9-11, 22-23; 3:2-4, 9-11; John 15:1, 5

God's economy is Christ with the church. As we consider God's economy as revealed in the book of Ephesians, we need to pray that the Lord will give us an open heaven with a clear sky. If we would know God's economy, not only must we have the knowledge of the book of Ephesians; we must also touch the reality contained in this book. We are not for mere knowledge—we are for reality. The reality in the book of Ephesians is God's economy concerning Christ with the church.

SOME IMPORTANT TERMS

Economy

In relation to God's purpose, the word economy is unfamiliar to many Christians. The Greek word for economy, *oikonomia*, is used three times in Ephesians. In 1:10 Paul speaks of a dispensation, or economy, of the fullness of the times, in which all things will be headed up in Christ. In 3:2 he speaks of the stewardship of the grace of God, and in 3:9, of the dispensation of the mystery. The English word economy is an anglicized form of *oikonomia,* which means administration, stewardship, arrangement, or dispensation. In particular, in this sense economy denotes dispensing. God's economy is to dispense Himself into His chosen people. Apart from Himself, God has nothing to dispense into His chosen ones. Hence, His economy is to dispense Himself into us. This is altogether related to Christ with the church.

Will

Besides the term economy, a number of other important terms are used by Paul in Ephesians. Three times in chapter one Paul mentions God's will: the good pleasure of His will (v. 5), the mystery of His will (v. 9), and the counsel of His will (v. 11). God has an economy because He has a will. In eternity God planned a will. This will was hidden in Him. Hence, it was a mystery. In His wisdom and prudence He has made this hidden mystery known to us through His revelation in Christ, that is, through Christ's incarnation, crucifixion, resurrection, and ascension.

Good Pleasure

Another important term is "good pleasure" (1:5, 9). God has a will in which is His good pleasure. This good pleasure refers to the delight of God's heart. The book of Ephesians speaks from the standpoint of the good pleasure of God's heart. According to 1:9 and 10, God's good pleasure is what He has purposed in Himself for an administration. In human terms, God's good pleasure is that which makes Him happy. There is something within God's heart that pleases Him and makes Him happy. This is God's good pleasure. Do not think that the term "good pleasure" is insignificant. On the contrary, it is a very important term in Ephesians.

Purpose

In Ephesians the word purpose is used three times, twice as a noun and once as a verb. In 1:11 Paul says that we have been predestinated according to the purpose of the One who operates all things according to the counsel of His will. In 3:11 Paul speaks of the purpose of the ages. The purpose of the ages is the purpose of eternity, the eternal purpose, the eternal plan of God made in eternity past. In 1:9 the word purpose is used as a verb: "Having made known to us the mystery of His will, according to His good pleasure which He purposed in Himself." God has a purpose. Here the word purpose is the equivalent of the English word plan. God has a plan which He made in eternity. God has a plan because He has a will, a good pleasure, and an economy. According to His economy, He made a plan, a purpose.

Counsel

In 1:11 Paul uses the word counsel, saying that God operates all things according to the counsel of His will. When God created man, a conference was held within the Godhead. For this reason, Genesis 1:26 says, "And God said, Let us make man in our image." God took counsel with Himself. This counsel is related to His will.

Mystery

Still another crucial word in Ephesians is mystery. As we have seen, 1:9 mentions the mystery of God's will. In 3:3 Paul says, "That by revelation the mystery was made known to me." God's hidden purpose is the mystery, and the unveiling of this mystery is revelation. In 3:4 Paul goes on to speak of the "mystery of Christ." The mystery of God in Colossians 2:2 is Christ, whereas the mystery of Christ here is the church. God is a mystery, and Christ, as the embodiment of God to express Him, is the mystery of God. Christ is also a mystery, and the church, as the Body of Christ to express Him, is the mystery of Christ.

In 3:9 Paul speaks of bringing to light the "dispensation of the mystery." God's mystery is His hidden purpose. His purpose is to dispense Himself into His chosen people. Hence, there is a dispensation of the mystery of God. This mystery was hidden in God from the ages (that is, from eternity) and through all past ages, but now it has been brought to light to the New Testament believers. God's intention is to make known the dispensation, the economy, of His mystery.

Ephesians 5:32 and 6:19 also use the term mystery. In 5:32 Paul says, "This mystery is great, but I speak with regard to Christ and the church." The fact that Christ and the church are one spirit (1 Cor. 6:17), as typified by the husband and wife who are one flesh, is the great mystery. In 6:19 Paul speaks of making known in boldness the "mystery of the gospel." This mystery is Christ and the church for the fulfillment of God's eternal purpose.

A SECRET

It is important that we remember these crucial terms: will, good pleasure, purpose, counsel, economy, and mystery. On the one hand, these terms are deep and profound, and it would take years to understand them adequately. On the other hand, there is a simple secret to grasping their significance. This secret is Christ with the church. God's will is to have Christ with the church. Likewise, God's good pleasure and God's purpose are to have Christ with the church. We have already pointed out that Christ with the church is God's economy. Furthermore, God counseled with Himself to have Christ with the church. God's mystery is also related to Christ with the church. Therefore, Christ with the church is the secret to understanding these crucial terms. What is God's will? It is Christ with the church. What is God's good pleasure? Christ with the church is His good pleasure, the delight of His heart. Furthermore, God's purpose in eternity and for eternity is Christ with the church. Likewise, God's counsel, economy, and mystery are all related to Christ with the church.

HOW GOD FULFILLS HIS ECONOMY

Since God's economy is Christ with the church, we need to consider how He carries out this economy and fulfills it. Oh, may the Lord blow away all the clouds and give us a clear sky concerning this! Regarding the accomplishment of God's economy, the sky over all the saints in all the local churches needs to be crystal clear.

Selection

The first step in the working out of God's economy was God's selection. Ephesians 1:4 says, "According as He chose us in Him before the foundation of the world that we should be holy and without blemish before Him, in love." In eternity past, before the foundation of the world, God selected us. His choosing is His selection. From among innumerable people, He selected us. This He did in Christ. Christ was the sphere in which we were selected by God. Outside of Christ we are not God's choice. This took place in eternity past. God chose us according to His infinite foresight before He created us.

Have you ever been impressed with the fact that God chose you in Christ before the foundation of the world? Whenever I think of God choosing me in eternity past, I am filled with worship and praise to Him. I do not need to be chosen by man, for I have been chosen by the Triune God.

Christians often say to the Lord, "O Lord, we did not first love You. You were the One who first loved us." However, concerning God's selection, we need to say, "Lord, we didn't choose You—You chose us." We all need to thank the Lord for His eternal selection, the selection made in eternity past for eternity future. We have been selected not to occupy a position of prominence in the world, but to be in the church. God's selection was for the church.

Predestination

The second step God took in working out His economy was predestination. Ephesians 1:5 says, "Having predestinated us unto sonship through Jesus Christ to Himself, according to the good pleasure of His will." The Greek word rendered predestinated can also be translated "marked out beforehand." Marking out beforehand is the process, while predestination is the purpose to determine a destiny beforehand. God firstly selected us and then marked us out beforehand, that is, before the foundation of the world, unto a certain destiny. This destiny is sonship. We were predestinated to be sons of God even before we were created. Hence, as God's creatures we need to be regenerated by Him that we may participate in His life to be His sons. Sonship implies not only the life, but also the position of the son. God's marked-out ones have the life to be His sons and the position to inherit God Himself.

We all need to have the realization that we have been

marked out by God for the accomplishment of His economy. Because God has put His mark on us, we cannot run away from Him. We were marked out by God before we were born, even before the foundation of the world. Since we have been pre-marked, we have no choice except to give ourselves to the Lord for His recovery and even to be beside ourselves for the church life.

Other human beings cannot see God's mark on us, but all the beings in the spiritual world can see it. The angels, the demons, and Satan himself know that we have been marked out by God.

This mark is not merely outward, but something very inward. Because of this inward mark, we have no peace unless we give ourselves to the church life. We are a selected and marked-out people. This was accomplished by God in eternity past.

Redemption

In 1:7 Paul speaks of redemption through the blood of Christ. We were chosen and predestinated. But after creation we became fallen. Hence, we need redemption, which God has accomplished for us in Christ through His blood. Redemption is the third step God took in carrying out His economy.

Redemption is not only for our personal and individual salvation; it is for the church. In fact, God did not redeem us individually; He redeemed us corporately. This means that He redeemed His chosen church. Therefore, selection, predestination, and redemption are all for the church.

Salvation

The fourth step, closely related to redemption, is God's salvation. When Paul speaks of salvation in 2:5 and 8, he speaks of a corporate salvation. We have been saved not as individuals, but as a corporate entity. Consider the type of the children of Israel in the Old Testament. They were not saved from the tyranny of the Egyptians one by one. On the contrary, the entire nation of Israel was saved at the same time. Yes, each of the children of Israel had an individual experience of this salvation, but they were saved corporately, all at the same time. This indicates that God's salvation is not for individuals, but for the church.

Sanctification

In chapter five Paul deals with sanctification, another step in the carrying out of God's economy concerning Christ with the church. Although we have been redeemed, we are still in the process of sanctification. This process involves a change both of our position and of our disposition. As this change takes place, we are transformed.

Growth

Still another step in the carrying out of God's economy is growth. We need to grow up into Christ, the Head, in all things until we arrive at a full-grown man (4:15, 13). I can testify that many who have been with us for some years have truly grown in the Lord. I praise Him that the saints are growing. This growth is for the accomplishment of God's economy.

Building Up

Along with the growth, we have the building up. In 2:22 Paul says that we are being built together into a dwelling place of God in spirit. In 4:12 he speaks of the building up of the Body of Christ, and in 4:16 he indicates that, according to the operation in the measure of each part, the Body grows and builds itself up in love.

We have been selected, predestinated, redeemed, and saved. Now we are being sanctified and are gradually growing in Christ. As we grow, we are being built up as the Body of Christ. These are the steps God takes in carrying out His economy.

THE VINE WITH THE BRANCHES

God's economy is revealed not only in Ephesians, but also in chapter fifteen of John. This chapter is the unique chapter in the Gospels revealing God's economy. John 15:1 says, "I am the true vine, and My Father is the husbandman," and in verse 5 the Lord says, "I am the vine, you are the branches." This true vine, which is the Son, with its branches, which are the believers in the Son, is the organism of the Triune God in God's economy to grow with His riches and to express His divine life. The Father as the husbandman is the source, the author, the planner, the planter, the life, the substance, the soil, the water, the air, the sunshine, and everything to the vine. The Son as the vine is the center of God's economy and the embodiment of all the riches of the Father. The Father, by cultivating the Son, works Himself with all His riches into the vine. Eventually, the vine expresses the Father through its branches in a corporate way. This is the Father's economy in the universe.

God's economy is the vine with the branches, Christ with the church. God's intention is to care for this vine and the branches until we grow to maturity. Regarding His economy, may God bless us and grant us a clear vision.

LIFE-STUDY OF EPHESIANS

MESSAGE SEVENTY-SIX

GOD'S ECONOMY—TO WORK CHRIST INTO US

Scripture Reading: Eph. 1:19-20; 2:10; 3:8; 4:13-15; 5:29-30, 32

We have seen that God's economy is Christ with the church and that the word economy denotes a dispensation. God's intention is to dispense Himself into His chosen people. To be saved is not merely to have our sins forgiven, to be justified, and to be made ready for heaven. To be saved is for God to begin dispensing Himself into us.

WHAT GOD IS SEEKING TODAY

God's dispensation is altogether related to Christ. According to the natural concept, we think that after salvation we need to improve our behavior, seek power, or carry on a fruitful work for the Lord. Some Christians believe that they need to pursue such gifts as speaking in tongues, prophecy, and healing. Others feel that the most important thing for a saved one is to gain the proper knowledge of the Bible. However, if we view salvation from the perspective of God's economy, we shall see the Christian life in a different way.

The New Testament does speak of proper conduct, power, gifts, and knowledge. Nevertheless, the crucial point is how much of Christ has been wrought into us. God is seeking to work Christ into us. We all need to be enlightened to see what God is doing today. God's intention is not to improve us. Whatever we are in ourselves means nothing to God. What matters to Him is that Christ is wrought into us.

In 1:19 and 20 Paul speaks of the "surpassing greatness of His power toward us who believe." This power was wrought in Christ when God raised Him from among the dead and seated Him at His right hand in the heavenlies. Today God's main activity is to work this Christ into us.

OUR NEED FOR CHRIST TO LIVE IN US

Suppose one day you are unpleasant with another brother or sister. Surely you would repent and ask the Lord to forgive you for your poor attitude. You may even pray that the Lord will make you better. Even if you do not make this request specifically, deep within this is your feeling as you pray about your failure. This kind of prayer is religious. You may have read the book *Christ versus Religion,* but you are still very religious in your daily practice. If you see God's economy, you will pray like this, "Lord, the Devil within me caused me to behave in that way. But, Lord, even if my behavior had been good, it still would not have been You living within me. Lord, You do not want me to be good—You want to live in me. Lord, in one sense, I do repent and ask You to forgive me. But I also put the blame on Satan and command him to get away from me. Lord, I will not try to be better. I just need You to live in me."

Galatians 2:20 says that we have been crucified with Christ and that Christ now lives within us. We may have some knowledge of this verse and declare, "It is no longer I, but Christ." However, in our daily living it is no longer Christ, but I. To recite Galatians 2:20 is one thing, but to live out Christ in a practical way is another.

Suppose you are very kind to the brothers and sisters. You may not sense any need to repent or ask the Lord to forgive you. Nevertheless, according to God's evaluation, it makes little difference whether you are kind or unkind toward others as long as you are the one living and not Christ. Whether our behavior is good or bad, we still do not live out Christ. God's economy is focused on Christ. His economy is not a matter of ethics, morality, or good character. In His economy God desires to work Christ into us. In our relationships with the brothers and sisters in the church, we need to live out Christ.

Some books have been written about Christ as life. However, it is difficult to find a group of Christians who genuinely live by Christ. God's intention is not to improve us; it is to work the living Christ into us, into our mind, emotion, and will. God's desire is to replace us with Christ. He wants to see that Christ is being lived out of the brothers and sisters in the churches. Oh, may the Father of glory give us a spirit of wisdom and revelation so that we may be enlightened to know what God is seeking to accomplish today. I repeat, God is not seeking to improve us—He is endeavoring to work Christ into us.

The Christ God is seeking to work into us is the crucified, resurrected, and ascended Christ. Satan put Christ on the cross. But God raised Him from the dead and seated Him at His right hand in the heavenlies. Now God intends to work this crucified, resurrected, and ascended Christ into us. There is a great difference between ethics, conduct, and behavior, on the one hand, and such a Christ wrought into our being, on the other.

GOD'S CONCERN

Throughout the centuries, Christians have argued about doctrines and practices. For example, there has been much disputation about baptism, head covering, foot-washing, and about loudness or quietness in Christian meetings. In Galatians 6:15 Paul says, "For in Christ Jesus neither circumcision availeth any thing, nor uncircumcision, but a new creation" (Gk.). Forms and regulations do not avail anything, because they are not Christ. Neither circumcision nor uncircumcision is the new creation that is in Christ Jesus. The new creation that Paul refers to is Christ wrought into our being. When Christ is wrought into us, a new creation takes place within us. Furthermore, this new creation is not merely an individual matter; it is a corporate matter involving the corporate entity of the new man, the Body of Christ.

God's concern is not foot-washing, the length of our hair, or how many times we have been baptized. God cares about how much of Christ has been wrought into us. God is not concerned whether or not we are humble or proud, crude or gentle. He cares only that Christ is wrought into our being. Again and again I wish to proclaim that God cares only for Christ. Morality, ethics, forms, and regulations cannot produce a church that matches Christ. Only Christ Himself wrought into us can produce a church to match Himself.

The church is the Body of Christ. Only what comes out of Christ can be part of the Body of Christ. This means that mere gifts, teachings, and power cannot produce the Body. Nothing other than Christ wrought into the saints can produce the Body of Christ. Our eyes need to be enlightened to see this vision. In Ephesians 1 Paul prayed in a specific way, asking that our inner eyes be enlightened so that we may see that God's intention is to work Christ into us. God does not desire to adjust us or to improve us. His intention is to work Christ into us.

In a very real sense, we need to repent more of our goodness than of our evil. When you are good to your wife in a natural way, you need to repent and say, "Lord, forgive me. This is not Christ. In myself I may be good, but I am not living by Christ. Lord, I am good in a natural way, but I do not give You the opportunity to live out of me." We all are full of regret when we do things that are bad, but we may not realize that we need to be even more repentant when we do good things apart from Christ.

GOD'S WORKMANSHIP

In 2:10 Paul says, "For we are His workmanship, created in Christ Jesus for good works, which God before prepared that we should walk in them." We should not think that we are able to work for God or to do God's work. We are God's workmanship. This indicates that God does not expect us to work for Him. On the contrary, He is seeking the opportunity to work upon us. If we consider our situation, we shall realize how much work remains to be done on us. God does not need us to work for Him. Rather, He will work on us until we become His masterpiece. We, the church, are the masterpiece of God's work, expressing God's infinite wisdom and divine design. The reason we are God's masterpiece is that Christ is being wrought into us. We can boast to God's creation that we have Christ in us. The more Christ is wrought into us, the more we become part of God's workmanship, God's masterpiece.

THE DIFFERENCE BETWEEN NATURAL GOODNESS AND CHRIST

In 1934 I met a certain brother in Shanghai. Before I met him, I heard many good things about him. At that time, I was not able to discern between Christ and good behavior. Eventually, through the help of Brother Nee, I realized that although this particular brother was good, not much of Christ was lived out of him. We all need to learn the difference between natural goodness and Christ. A person may be good in certain aspects, but these good things may have nothing to do with Christ. Our desire should not be to become a good brother or sister; we should desire to become a "Christ" brother or a "Christ" sister. If we would be God's masterpiece, Christ must be wrought into us. This should be not only a revelation, but also a revolution that takes place within our being. Oh, may we all see clearly that God does not desire us to be good Christians, but to be "Christ" Christians, those who have Christ wrought into them and lived out of them.

THE UNSEARCHABLE RICHES OF CHRIST

In 3:8 Paul says that he preached the unsearchable riches of Christ as the gospel. What Paul preached was not doctrine, gifts, knowledge, or power. He preached the riches of Christ. This means that Paul ministered these riches to others. The unsearchable riches of Christ include all the aspects of what Christ is to us. In a gradual way, Christ's riches need to be wrought into us. For example, we are not the ones who should be patient, kind, gentle, or loving. Rather, Christ must be wrought into us to be our patience, kindness, gentleness, and love. This means that we need to participate in the riches of Christ and to have these riches daily, even hourly, wrought into us in a specific way. In our daily experience we should be able to itemize Christ's riches. Christ must become our patience, our love, our everything.

CHRIST MAKING HIS HOME IN OUR HEARTS

Christ must be wrought into our being to such an extent that He makes His home in our hearts (3:17). I am concerned that for many of us the matter of Christ making His home in our hearts is simply a doctrine. Is Christ actually making His home in your heart? Who is presently at home in your heart—you or Christ? If you are honest, you will have to say that, for the most part, your heart is your home, not Christ's home. You are the one living there, not Christ. We may hear a message about Christ making His home in us and shout that our heart is Christ's home. But there may be no reality to support what we proclaim. In order for Christ to make His home in our heart, we need to take Him both as our person and as our life. In such a case, we shall be able to testify that the person living in our heart is no longer the self, but Christ.

The crucial issue is not whether we are humble or proud, weak or powerful, gifted or not gifted. The question concerns who is living in our heart. Who is the person taking up residence in your heart? You may be unusually gifted, but your heart may not yet be Christ's home. Rather, it may be the home of the self, as long as you are still the person living in your heart.

Today's Christianity is a religion of behavior, doctrine, work, power, gifts, and knowledge. However, it is virtually devoid of the reality of Christ. Most Christians are veiled by natural and religious concepts. This is the reason that we need a heavenly vision to know what is in God's heart and to see what He planned in eternity.

God desires to have a people who care only for Christ. He wants a people who are not occupied with knowledge, work, behavior, or power, but who simply care for Christ in a very practical way. The experience of the riches of Christ and the reality of Christ making His home in our hearts should not be mere doctrines. They must be the reality of our daily Christian experience.

In the past, quite often husbands and wives have come to me with problems. Usually the husband would accuse the wife, and then the wife would accuse the husband. Then they would say, "Since you are a servant of the Lord and have spiritual understanding, you can discern who is right and render a fair judgment." My practice was not to judge according to right and wrong. Instead, I would ask them whether or not Christ was making His home in their hearts. I would then go on to ask if Christ was living in them while they were accusing each other. Usually, they had nothing further to say, and eventually the word went out not to bring such problems to me.

Sometimes people come to me with the intention to argue about doctrine. But instead of answering them in a doctrinal way, I ask them to what extent Christ is making His home in their heart. What good does it do to be right in doctrine if we do not have Christ living in us? The Pharisees were apparently correct as far as doctrine was concerned. However, the Lord Jesus still rebuked them because they did not have any reality.

In a very practical way, our hearts need to become Christ's home. He must be able to live in us and to settle down in us. He, not the self, must be the One who occupies our hearts. This is our need today.

Apart from this, it does not matter very much whether husbands love their wives or wives submit to their husbands. In the book of Ephesians the matter of Christ making His home in our hearts is more strategic than love for wives or submission to husbands. However, I am fully assured that if a brother allows Christ to make His home in his heart, he will certainly love his wife in a proper way. Moreover, if a wife allows Christ to dwell in her heart, she will no doubt be submissive to her husband.

What we need more than anything else is for Christ to make His home in our hearts. The Lord's recovery is not a matter of doctrine, biblical interpretation, or conduct.

Furthermore, it is not a matter of knowledge, gifts, power, or work. In contrast to all this, the Lord's recovery is altogether a matter of Christ wrought into us and making His home in our hearts.

ARRIVING AT A FULL-GROWN MAN

In 4:13 Paul says that we all need to arrive "at a full-grown man, at the measure of the stature of the fullness of Christ." We need to become not only a perfect man, complete man, or whole man, but a full-grown man, one who has the measure of the stature of the fullness of Christ. The fullness of Christ is the Body of Christ (1:23), which has the stature with the measure.

In 4:15 Paul goes on to say that we need to hold to truth in love so that we may grow up into Christ in all things. To grow up into Christ in all things is to have Christ increase in us in all things until we attain to a full-grown man.

PARTS OF CHRIST

In 5:30 Paul says that we are members of Christ's Body. This indicates that we are members of Christ, parts of Christ. According to our natural constitution, we cannot be members of Christ's Body. Christ Himself is the element, the factor, that makes us part of Him. Hence, in order to be parts of Christ as members of His Body, we must have Christ wrought into our very being.

In 5:32 Paul says that the great mystery is Christ and the church. In the Lord's recovery we should devote our attention to the matter of Christ being wrought into us to make us a proper church for the expression of Christ. This is God's economy.

LIFE-STUDY OF EPHESIANS

MESSAGE SEVENTY-SEVEN

CHRIST IN GOD'S ECONOMY

Scripture Reading: Eph. 1:20-23; 3:8, 16-19; 4:8-10

God's economy is Christ with the church. May the Lord grant us a clear sky so that we may see the vision of Christ and the church. Although Ephesians is a short book, no other book in the Bible reveals Christ in His all-inclusiveness, both vertically and horizontally, as the book of Ephesians does.

FAR ABOVE ALL AND FILLING ALL

Many students of the Word realize that Colossians reveals Christ as the Head and Ephesians reveals the church as the Body. However, not even the book of Colossians reveals Christ in such a vertical and horizontal way as He is revealed in Ephesians. Ephesians 1:21 says that Christ is "far above all." Such a word cannot be found in Colossians. Colossians says that Christ must have the preeminence, the first place, in all things, but it does not say that Christ is far above all. Some may regard the third heaven as the highest point in the universe. But in 4:10 Paul says that Christ has "ascended far above all the heavens that He might fill all things."

Ephesians 1:23 says that Christ "fills all in all." Colossians 3:11 says that Christ is all and in all. However, Christ's filling all in all in Ephesians 1:23 surpasses His being all and in all in Colossians 3:11. Colossians 3:11 refers to the sphere of the new man. Hence, in the new man Christ is all and in all. But Ephesians 1:23 refers to the universe, which includes time and space. Christ is not only all and in all with respect to the new man, but He fills all in all with respect to the universe. Universally, Christ is above all and fills all in all.

In 3:8 Paul refers to the unsearchable riches of Christ. This term is not found in Colossians. The riches of Christ are what Christ is to us, such as light, life, righteousness, and holiness. These riches are unsearchable and past our tracing out.

In 3:18 Paul speaks of the "breadth and length and height and depth." The breadth, length, height, and depth are the dimensions of Christ. Christ is not only higher than all things—He is the height. He is not only deeper and broader and longer than all things—He is the breadth, the length, and the depth.

This very Christ who is all-inclusive both vertically and horizontally is making His home in our hearts in a very intimate way. Oh, may we see that the all-inclusive Christ is now making His home in our hearts!

RAISED FROM AMONG THE DEAD

Christ is far above all because He has been raised from among the dead (1:20-21). Apart from Christ, no one has been able to overcome death and come out from among the dead. For Christ to be raised up out of death indicates that nothing can hold Him down. When death comes to visit us, we cannot refuse it, for death has the power to hold us. But it did not have the power to hold Christ (Acts 2:24). After visiting the realm of the dead for three days, Christ came forth in resurrection. Although death did everything possible to hold Him, Christ could have said, "Death, is this all you can do to Me? If this is all, then it is time for Me to walk away from you in resurrection."

Just as nothing can hold Christ down, so nothing negative can hold us down, because we have Christ in us. We who believe in Christ must be the raised-up ones. Christ has been raised from the dead, and nothing can hold Him down. This is the reason that He is now far above all. He has been resurrected to be far above all. This is our Christ.

All Christians know that Christ is the Redeemer and the Savior. Some realize that Christ is the Giver of all gifts and that He Himself is our life. But Christ is even more than this. In Ephesians, a book concerned with God's economy, we see that Christ is far above all. I can testify that the Christ I enjoy is the One who is far above all.

A DIFFERENT CHRIST

In a number of respects the Christ we enjoy in the Lord's recovery is different from the Christ in Christianity. When some hear this, they may accuse us of heresy. But consider the typology in the book of Leviticus. In this book five main offerings are described: the burnt offering, the meal offering, the peace offering, the sin offering, and the trespass offering. These offerings typify Christ in various aspects. Even with one kind of offering, such as the burnt offering, there are different types of sacrifices. One could offer as a burnt offering a bullock, a lamb, or a bird. All these are types of Christ. This gives us the ground to say that in our experience the Christ we enjoy may be different from the Christ enjoyed by others. The Christ I experience may be different from the Christ you experience, and the Christ you enjoy may differ from the Christ enjoyed by others.

THE IMMEASURABLE CHRIST MAKING HIS HOME IN OUR HEARTS

Chapter three of Ephesians reveals three important things regarding Christ: that His riches are unsearchable, that He is making His home in our heart, and that His dimensions are universal. As we have pointed out, Christ is the breadth, the length, the height, and the depth. Who can say how broad is the breadth or how high is the height? Oh, we may experience the unsearchable riches of the immeasurable Christ! Christ is the breadth, length, height, and depth of the universe. Hallelujah for Christ in His immeasurable dimensions! We need to ask ourselves whether or not we know such a Christ.

Although Christ is immeasurable, He is still making His home in our hearts. The immeasurable Christ is a wonderful Person who makes His home in our hearts in a very intimate way. In order for Christ to make His home in our hearts, we need to be strengthened with power through the Spirit into our inner man. Then we shall be filled unto all the fullness of God (v. 19).

The immeasurable Christ who is making home in us is the Spirit, on the one hand, and the very God of fullness, on the other hand. If we are strengthened by the Spirit and Christ makes His home in us, we shall be filled unto all the fullness of God. Do not say that Christ is only the Son, but not the Spirit and not God the Father. Be careful that you are not under the influence of the systematized doctrine of Christianity. Christ is too wonderful to be systematized in doctrine. When He makes His home in us, the Spirit is strengthening us, and we are being filled unto the fullness of God.

Have you noticed that in Ephesians 3 Paul speaks of the Spirit, Christ, and God? The Spirit strengthens us, Christ makes home in us, and we are filled unto the fullness of God. Christ is the all-inclusive One. He is the Spirit who strengthens us, the Christ who makes His home in us, and the God who fills us unto His fullness. Many of us have read the book of Ephesians without ever seeing the vision of such a Christ. May we all see that the Christ whom we have received is the Spirit who strengthens and the God who fills us unto His fullness. I can testify that the Christ I enjoy is such a wonderful One.

THE DESCENDING AND ASCENDING CHRIST

In 4:9 and 10 Paul says, "Now this, He ascended, what is it except that He also descended into the lower parts of the earth? He Who descended is the same Who also ascended far above all the heavens that He might fill all things." Christ has done a great deal of traveling in the universe. Firstly, He descended from heaven to earth in His incarnation. Then He descended further, from earth to Hades, the lower parts of the earth, in His death. Eventually, He ascended from Hades to earth in His resurrection, and from earth to heaven in His ascension. Through such a journey, He cut the way that He might fill all things. When Christ ascended up on high, to the third heaven, that was not the end of His traveling. After He ascended, He descended into our spirit. Therefore, Christ is the One who descends, ascends, travels, and comes to us in gracious visitations.

Today Christ is still traveling. He is still ascending and descending. However, His traveling takes place mainly within us. In our experience we may be up or down. When we are down, Christ comes down to where we are and brings us up to God. Many times during the course of a day we may be brought by Christ into the heavens. From our experience we can testify that within us Christ descends and ascends; He goes up and down. Although He is always steady, He does not stand still. On the contrary, He does a great deal of traveling within us.

It is difficult to say where Christ is. Is He in heaven or on earth? If you say that He is on earth, you may have the sense that He is in heaven. But if you say that He is in heaven, you may soon realize that He is on earth. Actually, Christ is everywhere. According to 4:9 and 10, He descended and ascended in order to fill all things. Do you think that Christ will fill all things in the universe without also filling you? Through His descending and ascending, Christ will fill us with Himself.

CONSTITUTED GIFTS

It is by His descending and ascending that Christ constitutes us gifts to the Body. The more He descends and ascends within us, the more we become gifts. Many brothers and sisters have very little function in the church because they have not yet been constituted as gifts. They may be good brothers and sisters, but they are not gifts to the church. But as Christ descends and ascends within them, He captures them, vanquishes them, and constitutes them into gifts to His Body. As a result of Christ's traveling, they become useful gifts. I am concerned, however, that within some of the saints Christ's traveling may have ceased. He no longer goes up and down within them.

I can testify that I have been constituted as a gift to the church through Christ's descending and ascending within me. Christ has had many ups and downs within me. If we try to hold Christ as the Head without allowing Him to descend and ascend within us, we damage the process by which we are constituted gifts. The Lord will constitute us as gifts only through His descending and ascending within us. After such experiences of Christ's inward traveling over a period of time, we become useful in the church.

Allow me to give a word of testimony on behalf of a certain brother whom I met more than twenty years ago. At that time, he had not experienced very much of Christ's descending and ascending. But this brother's situation is much different today. Through Christ's descending and ascending within him, he has been constituted into a useful gift to the Lord's recovery. He could tell you that especially on the days he is used by the Lord, Christ goes down and up within him. Christ comes down to where he is and ascends with him into the heavenlies. Christ truly is a descending and ascending Christ.

OUR CHRIST

If you consider the verses we have covered in this message, you will see that the Christ we experience in the Lord's recovery is different from the Christ we heard about in religion. What a Christ we have! He is the embodiment of God and the content of the church. Our Christ is the all-inclusive, universal Christ. He is far above all, He is unsearchable and immeasurable, and yet He is intimately making His home in our hearts. Furthermore, our Christ is continually descending and ascending within us. Because all the fullness of God is in Him, He is the very embodiment of God. Therefore, as He makes home in our heart, we are filled unto all the fullness of God. This Christ who is the embodiment of God is also the very content of the church. Furthermore, through His descending and ascending He fills all things, universally, vertically, and horizontally.

We should not focus our attention on ourselves, but on the all-inclusive Christ. Do not consider how weak or how poor you are. Rather, think of Christ, speak of Christ, and look away to Christ. Praise the Lord for the revelation of Christ in God's economy found in the book of Ephesians! This book says little of Christ as the Redeemer or Savior. But it does reveal that Christ is far above all and that He is now filling all in all. Nevertheless, this Christ is available to us. He is making His home in our heart, and He is imparting into us His unsearchable riches so that we may be filled unto all the fullness of God. Eventually, we as the church shall have Christ fully wrought into us as our unique content.

LIFE-STUDY OF EPHESIANS

MESSAGE SEVENTY-EIGHT

TAKING CHRIST AS OUR PERSON FOR THE CHURCH LIFE

Scripture Reading: Eph. 2:15-16; 3:17a; 4:13-15, 22-24

The book of Ephesians reveals that the church is not only the Body, but also the new man. As the new man, the church must have Christ both as the life and as the person. Only in recent years has the aspect of the church as the new man been recovered. We thank the Lord that He has shown us clearly through the book of Ephesians that the church is the new man.

During the past two centuries, many Christians have seen that the church is the Body of Christ. In particular, the Brethren speak of this aspect of the church. Furthermore, since the end of World War II, many in this country have begun to talk about the Body. Today it is common to hear terms such as Body ministry. However, although the church is the Body of Christ, this is not the highest revelation of the church. We must go on to see the church as the new man.

ABOLISHING THE ORDINANCES FOR THE CREATION OF THE NEW MAN

Ephesians 2:15 says that Christ abolished in His flesh the law of commandments in ordinances in order to create the Jews and the Gentiles into one new man. Through His death on the cross, not only did Christ deal with sin, the old man, the flesh, the world, and the Devil; He also dealt with the law of the commandments in ordinances. Many good messages have been given on how the cross of Christ has dealt with sin, the old man, the flesh, the world, and the Devil. But have you ever heard that on the cross Christ abolished the law of commandments in ordinances? Christ did this not for salvation, sanctification, or even victory. He abolished the ordinances in order to create the new man. We freely admit that sin, the old man, the flesh, the world, and the Devil all needed the dealing of the cross, and we praise the Lord that all these negative things have been crucified. But we must go on to see the crucial importance of Christ's abolishing the law of the commandments in ordinances in order to create us into one new man.

The fact that the Jews and the Gentiles have been created into one new man indicates that the new man is an entity that is corporate and universal. There are many believers, but there is just one new man. All the believers are part of this one corporate and universal new man. The highest revelation of the church given in the book of Ephesians is that of the new man.

To be regenerated is not only to be saved; it is also to be created anew. On the cross Christ abolished the ordinances so that a re-creation could take place. The Jews and the Gentiles were separated by ordinances. But the two peoples have been created in Christ with the divine essence into one new entity, the corporate new man.

Ordinances are the various forms or ways of living and worship. For example, the Jews have their particular way of worshipping God. Based upon this way of worship, they have ordinances that govern their daily living. Other peoples also have their own ways of living and worship. This is true among the denominations in today's Christianity. The Baptists, Presbyterians, Methodists, Lutherans, and Episcopalians all have different ways of worship. How widespread is this matter of ordinances, and how all-pervading!

God's intention is not to have a certain kind of worship. His desire is to have the one new man. However, in his subtlety, Satan, the enemy of God, uses ordinances to damage the new man and to keep believers from realizing the new man in a practical way. Satan's goal is not to keep Christians from heaven or from pursuing spirituality; it is to keep them from seeing and experiencing the church as the one new man.

We thank the Lord that He has made us very clear regarding the ground of the church. But it is not adequate simply to know the church ground. Although the ground of the church is necessary, God's desire is not merely to have the church ground. He desires to have the church as the new man. Ordinances are the main obstacles to the fulfillment of this desire of God. If we would have the church in the aspect of the new man, we need to lay aside our ways of living. On the cross, Christ abolished all the ordinances. However, He did so not merely for the purpose of eliminating ordinances; He abolished the ordinances in order to create the one new man.

In His wisdom God has chosen us out of every tribe, tongue, people, and nation (Rev. 5:9). In the local churches today there are believers from many races and nationalities. Surely the greatest test of whether or not we take Christ as our life and as our person is related to ordinances. For example, it is difficult for the Chinese who have moved to this country from the Far East to realize the church as the new man because it is not easy to set aside their Chinese way of living. When certain Chinese brothers and sisters were in the Far East, they were more useful in the church life than they are now because now they hold on to their Chinese ordinances. To be fair, we need to point out that all of us have the problem of holding on to our ordinances. In the new man there is no room for Jew, Greek, barbarian, Scythian, circumcision or uncircumcision. This means that in the church as the new man there can be no Chinese, American, British, German, or any other nationality. There is room only for Christ. It is crucial for us all to see that more than nineteen hundred years ago all our ordinances were abolished by Christ on the cross.

THE NEED FOR PRACTICAL EXPERIENCE

If we sincerely desire to take Christ as our life and as our person, we must let go of our ordinances. For example, we should not have an ordinance about hair styles. Rather, we should contact the Lord concerning this and pray, "Lord

Jesus, I am one of Your members. What kind of haircut do You want to have? I don't care for any way of worship or living, and I am not concerned about customs or habits. Lord, I only care that You be my life and my person." Spontaneously the living Lord Jesus will let you know how you should cut your hair. Then you simply act according to what He shows you. This is not an ordinance; it is a practical experience of taking Christ as your person.

Our need today is not doctrinal knowledge, but the practical and daily experience of taking Christ as our person. In 1970 we first began to speak of the church as the new man. At that time we pointed out that in order to have the church in the aspect of the new man, we need to take Christ as our person. Since that time, there has been much talk about the new man and about taking Christ as our person. Even some good hymns have been written along this line. But according to my observation, there is little reality among us of actually taking Christ as our person. We should not be satisfied if others regard us as good people. We must be those who take Christ as our person. May we all go to the Lord and have a thorough transaction with Him concerning all the details of our daily living.

RECEIVING CHRIST

In many respects we are still quite religious. Even the way we preach the gospel and help others to be saved may be carried out in a religious way. We may tell people that they are sinful and that Christ died on the cross for their sins. We may go on to say that if they believe in Him, they will be forgiven, justified, saved, and made ready for heaven. In a sense such gospel preaching is good, fundamental, and even scriptural. However, it may be religious. The important factor in the preaching of the gospel is to help people open to the Lord Jesus and take Him into them. Even if a person has no concept of forgiveness, justification, or heaven, he will have the reality of all these if he takes Christ into him. When we have Christ, we have forgiveness, redemption, justification, salvation, and sanctification.

God's purpose is not simply to forgive our sins, to justify us, and then to carry us away to heaven. His intention is to work Christ into us. Before the foundation of the world, He chose us in Christ and put a mark on us. Then, in time, He called us. When God called us, His desire was that we focus our attention not on forgiveness or justification, but on receiving His dear Son into us. As long as Christ is living in us, we shall have no problem with forgiveness, justification, salvation, or heaven.

Only by having Christ in us can we become part of the Body of Christ. It is Christ alone who constitutes us a part of Himself. For this, forgiveness, justification, and sanctification are not sufficient. May the Lord grant that we may see that we have not only been forgiven, justified, saved, and sanctified, but also re-created in Christ and with Christ.

Because I have had experience with various kinds of Christianity, including fundamental, Pentecostal, and inner life Christianity, I am familiar with many different religious practices. I can testify that today I am not for any practice, but only for taking Christ as my person in a genuine and living way. My desire is to help others receive and experience the living Christ. He is not a form, religion, regulation, ordinance, or practice—He is the living Spirit. Our need is simply to open to Him and to take Him into us.

ALLOWING CHRIST TO MAKE HIS HOME IN OUR HEARTS

Without Ephesians 3, Ephesians 2 would only be doctrine to us. It is a fact that Christ has abolished the ordinances in order to create the Jews and the Gentiles into one new man. But for this to be practical in our daily experience, we must allow Christ to make His home in our hearts (3:17). One way to tell whether or not you still have ordinances is to check whether or not Christ is making His home in your heart. Are you allowing Him to make His home in your heart? If we are honest, most of us would have to say that we do not give Him much opportunity to do this. The reason for this is that we do not care firstly for Christ, but for our own way.

Consider the experience of Peter in Acts 10. As he was praying on the housetop, he "saw heaven opened, and a certain vessel descending unto him, as it had been a great sheet knit at the four corners, and let down to the earth" (v. 11). In this sheet were "all manner of four-footed beasts of the earth, and wild beasts, and creeping things, and fowls of the air" (v. 12). Then a voice said to Peter, "Rise, Peter; kill and eat" (v. 13). However, Peter's response was, "Not so, Lord; for I have never eaten any thing that is common or unclean" (v. 14). On this occasion, Peter did not take Christ as His person. Instead, Peter was his own person.

We should not think that we are more spiritual than Peter. Most of the time we also fail to take Christ as our person. When the Lord speaks something to us, we often respond, "Not so, Lord." We may say, "Lord, I don't believe that You would ask me to do such a thing." Our experience testifies that whenever we refuse to go along with the Lord, we lose His presence and His anointing. However, when we agree with the Lord, we enjoy His presence and experience the inner anointing in a fresh way. We may even be beside ourselves with joy in the Lord.

Let us forget religion, regulations, ordinances, all the different practices of worshipping God, and our own ways of living in order that we may simply allow Christ to make His home in our hearts. Christ has come into us to be our life and our person, and He will not be satisfied until we take Him as our person in a practical way. If we do not take Him as our person, we shall have the sense deep within that, no matter how much we love Christ and the church and no matter how much we are for the Lord's recovery, we are lacking something. This sense of lack comes from the shortage of Christ as our person.

Our heart should not be the dwelling place of the self, but the dwelling place of Christ. Again I ask, who is the person living within you, you or Christ? In this matter I do not care for doctrine; I care only for reality. Christ has not abolished the ordinances so that we may have other kinds of ordinances. His intention is to make His home in our hearts.

Many married sisters are reluctant to read Ephesians 5 because it speaks about wives submitting to their own husbands. When they read this chapter, they are exposed and realize that they are not submissive. Some may blame their husband or environment for their lack of submission. They may even blame the Lord and tell Him that if He had given them a different husband, they would surely be submissive to him. Sisters, do not try to submit to your husband but let Christ make His home in your heart. If you take Him as your person and allow Him to make His home in your heart, you will surely submit to your husband.

We need to forget about everything religious and simply take Christ as our person. If we do this, we shall have the growth spoken of in chapter four, and we shall put on the new man. This is the proper church life.

God does not want us to try in a religious way to submit to our husbands or to love our wives. His concern is that we take Christ as our person and set aside all ordinances. God wants a people in whose heart Christ is making His home. This is our need in the church life today.

THE UNIQUE FACTOR IN THE LORD'S RECOVERY

The Lord's recovery is not a recovery of teaching. In the recovery the unique factor is Christ. To be sure, we honor, respect, and apply the Bible. We keep the Word as much as other Christians do, if not more. Nevertheless, we must be clear that the Lord's recovery is not simply a matter of following the teaching of the Bible. It is altogether a matter of Christ living and making His home in our hearts, so that in all things we may grow up into Him as the Head. The more we grow up into Christ, the more we put on the new man, the proper and practical church life. Our unique need today is to take Christ as our person for the church life.

LIFE-STUDY OF EPHESIANS

MESSAGE SEVENTY-NINE

FIVE ASPECTS OF CHRIST

Scripture Reading: Eph. 5:25-27; 2:15-16; 1:20-23; 4:7-8, 11, 12; 3:17a

Christ is the embodiment of God and the content of the church. Although all genuine Christians recognize that Christ is the Son of God, not many have an adequate realization that He is the embodiment of God. To say that Christ is the embodiment of God means that in Christ is embodied all that God is. In eternity past, God in Christ made a plan, selected us, and predestinated us, or marked us out. Then in Christ and through Christ God created all things. Eventually, Christ was incarnated, accomplished redemption through crucifixion, was buried, resurrected, and then ascended to the third heaven. Furthermore, He has descended as the Spirit upon His Body. Now He is waiting for people to open to Him and call upon Him so that He may come into them, regenerate them, and make His home in their hearts. One day, He will come back from the heavens by coming out from within His people. Then He will be the King over all the earth, and His chosen people will be co-kings with Him in His kingdom. For eternity, He will be the centrality of the New Jerusalem. It is impossible to exhaust all that God is and all that He has done and will do in Christ.

When I was young, I heard about Jesus, but what I was told was far short of the revelation of Christ as the embodiment of God. Many of us can testify that, before coming into the Lord's recovery, we did not know Christ adequately as the embodiment of God. However, after we came into the church life, we began to realize that our Christ is the embodiment of all that God is.

THE CONTENT OF THE CHURCH

As the embodiment of God, Christ is the content of the church. Ephesians 3 says that the Spirit strengthens us into our inner man so that Christ can make His home in our hearts (vv. 16-17). Eventually, we shall be filled unto all the fullness of God (v. 19). This indicates that the content of the church is the embodiment of God.

The church is not simply a group of people who have been saved out of hell, who are waiting to go to heaven, and who beg the Lord to give them peace, joy, and a good life. The church in the Lord's recovery does not beg God for things. Rather, we in the local churches praise the Lord for all He is to us. Praise Him that the church has the embodiment of God as her content! How we thank the Lord for revealing this to us!

The church is the one new man with Christ as the person. As the person of the new man, Christ is the embodiment of God. Do you realize that the One you are to take as your person is the very embodiment of God? If we see this vision, we shall be beside ourselves with joy. Oh, what a Person we have within us! It is crucial for us all to see that the church is a vessel with the living Christ as its unique content.

SEEING CHRIST IN A FULL WAY

In this message we shall consider five aspects of Christ. If we would see these five aspects clearly, we need to ask the Lord to blow away all the clouds that for centuries have kept Christians from seeing Christ in a full way. In previous messages we have pointed out that Christ is unlimited, immeasurable, and unsearchable. He is the all-inclusive One that fills all in all (1:23). He is even the very dimensions of the universe: the breadth, and length, and height, and depth (3:18). What a Christ He is!

THE CHURCH-LOVING CHRIST

Ephesians 5:25 says that Christ "loved the church and gave Himself up for her." This verse indicates that Christ is a church-loving Christ. Galatians 2:20 says that Christ loved me and gave Himself for me. Although Christians pay attention to this verse, they may not also pay attention to Ephesians 5:25, where we are told that Christ loved the church and gave Himself up for the church.

Sanctifying the Church

In 5:25-27 we see that Christ gave Himself up for the church, not merely to save the church from hell and bring her into heaven, but to sanctify her and to cleanse her by the washing of the water in the Word. Through this washing He will present the church to Himself glorious, not having spot or wrinkle or any such thing. The church Christ will present to Himself will be holy and without blemish.

Christ's purpose in giving Himself up for the church was to sanctify her. He will not only separate the church to Himself from everything common, but will also saturate her with Himself so that she may be His counterpart. This is accomplished by the washing of water in the Word. How Christ loves the church! The Christ who dwells within us is the Christ who loves the church. Having given Himself up for the church and to the church, He is now sanctifying her. In His love for the church, He is cleansing and purifying her to make her holy and without blemish.

According to 5:27, the day is coming when the church will not have spot or wrinkle. Spots come from wounds, and wrinkles come from oldness. Through Christ's sanctifying work, the church will eventually be without spot or wrinkle. She will be holy and without blemish. To be holy is to be saturated and transformed with Christ, and to be without blemish is to be spotless and without wrinkle. One day the church will be fully transformed. Only Christ can bring the church to such a condition. The Christ who is the embodiment of God is the Christ who loves the church and is cleansing her by the washing of the water in the Word.

A Full Recovery of the Church Life

I have the assurance that before the Lord comes back, He will fully recover the proper church life. Many Christian teachers, however, do not believe that this is possible. According to them, we cannot have the church life in this age; they say the church life is possible only in the age to come. Those who hold this view say that we should not talk about the church, but simply love the Lord, preach the gospel, and help the believers to be spiritual. Many of those who take such a position are opposed to the Lord's present recovery. But in spite of all opposition, we have the assurance that the church life will be recovered in full in this age, not in the age to come.

It is contrary to the Scriptures to say that the church life will be in the coming age. The next age will not be the age of the church; it will be the age of the kingdom. In this present age, before His coming back, the Lord must have the church life to shame the enemy. I believe that for centuries Satan, the enemy of God, has been challenging Christ concerning the church. Perhaps Satan has said to Him, "Where is Your church? Show me the church You have promised to build. Some of Your servants even teach that it is not possible to have the church life in this age." Perhaps Christ is saying to Satan, "Satan, look at the local churches on earth today. Consider how many of My people are testifying that it is possible to have the church life in this age. They are not only for the church life, but are in the church life in a practical way."

Back to Jerusalem

I believe that in the coming years the Lord will spread the church life to England, Germany, France, and Italy. Furthermore, I believe that one day there will be a church in Rome and even in Jerusalem, where the church life began more than nineteen centuries ago. Acts 1:9-12 tells us that Christ ascended from the Mount of Olives, and Zechariah 14:4 reveals that Christ will return also to the Mount of Olives. In the same principle, the Lord began His church in Jerusalem and, I believe, will send the recovery of His church back to Jerusalem.

For years I was deeply troubled by the loss of mainland China. After more than twenty years of labor, in 1948 there were churches in all the leading cities of China. Then suddenly everything was lost. One day, after many years had passed, I saw something encouraging about this. I realized that in the 1920s the Lord desired to have the proper church life. However, because Europe and the United States had been spoiled by religion, the Lord was forced to go to a heathen country in the Far East for the recovery of the church life. Brother Nee once told us that the Lord went to China because it was virgin soil for the cultivation of the church life. However, the Lord knew that, primarily because of language, China was not the best place for the spread of His recovery. Much of what the Lord had revealed to us was buried in the Chinese language. Nevertheless, God used the virgin soil of China as a nursery. Watchman Nee was sown as a seed into this soil, and the church life began to grow. Then, through the loss of mainland China, the recovery was transplanted to the United States. However, the United States is not the goal; it is a stepping-stone for the spread of the recovery to Europe and eventually to Jerusalem. The Lord began from Jerusalem and then spread the church to Greece and Italy. I believe that He will also go back to Jerusalem by way of Italy and Greece. I long for there to be a church in Jerusalem waiting for the Lord Jesus when He returns.

Concerning the recovery of the church life, the Lord Jesus cannot be defeated. When the Japanese army took over the Philippines during World War II, General MacArthur was forced to withdraw. But he vowed to return. As we all know, General MacArthur did return to the Philippines. In like manner, no matter what Satan does to damage the church, the Lord Jesus will return, and His church will be waiting for Him. There may be a church in the city of Jerusalem. Perhaps the meeting hall will not be far from the Mount of Olives, the place from which He ascended and to which He will descend in His coming back. It would be a shame to the Lord Jesus to come back without having a church in

Jerusalem ready for Him. The Lord will not suffer such a shame. For this reason, He is waiting for His recovery to spread to Europe and, ultimately, to Jerusalem.

May the Lord inspire us concerning His move in His recovery! May He spread the church life throughout Europe, the Middle East, and to Jerusalem. Perhaps one day we shall hold a prayer meeting in the garden of Gethsemane, which is located at the foot of the Mount of Olives, and pray fervently to the Lord for His coming back!

We all need to enjoy Christ and to experience Him as the church-loving Christ. Because we also love the church, we are one with Him for the spread of His recovery throughout the world and back to Jerusalem. Oh, how Christ loves the church! He is in us as the church-loving Christ. His love for the church makes us willing to give our all for the recovery of the church life.

THE NEW-MAN-CREATING CHRIST

In 2:15 and 16 we see that Christ is also the new-man-creating Christ. For centuries, Christians have spoken about Christ's death on the cross without seeing the consummate point that He died for the creation of the new man. He abolished in His flesh the ordinances in order to create in Himself one new man. The cross is not only for salvation, release, and victory; it is also for the creation of the new man. The creation of the new man required that all ordinances be abolished. Praise the Lord that He is the new-man-creating Christ! By abolishing the ordinances on the cross, He has created the Jews and the Gentiles into one new man.

THE ALL-THINGS-HEADING-UP CHRIST

In 1:20-23 we see that Christ is also the all-things-heading-up Christ. God has seated Him at His right hand in the heavenlies and has subjected all things under His feet. Furthermore, Christ has been made Head over all things to the church. The headship over all things has been given to Christ as a gift from God.

THE GIFT-MAKING AND GIFT-GIVING CHRIST

Chapter four reveals that Christ is the gift-making and gift-giving Christ (4:7-8, 11-12). Because Christ is the Head over all things to the church, He is able to make gifts and to present them to the church. Ephesians 1:22 says that Christ is the Head over all things *to* the church. The little word *to* is crucial. It implies transmission. Whatever Christ, the Head, attained and obtained is transmitted to the church, His Body. In this transmission the church shares with Christ in all His attainments. Because all that Christ is and has is transmitted to the church, He is able to constitute us as gifts to the Body.

We have pointed out that it is through His descending and ascending that Christ constitutes us into gifts to the church. By His traveling, by His descending and ascending within us, we are made useful gifts to the church.

When the church life first began in Los Angeles, we all had the sense that we were weak and useless. We wondered how we could possibly take care of the church. However, by Christ's descending and ascending, many have been constituted into useful gifts. The leadership needed for the spread of the church life is produced in this way. As brothers experience the descending and ascending Christ, they become proper leaders to take care of the churches that are raised up by the Lord. This leadership is not produced by man's education or training; it is constituted by the descending and ascending Christ. We need to praise the Lord for His traveling, for the marvelous two-way traffic between heaven and earth and between earth and heaven. It is through such traffic that the gift-making and gift-giving Christ produces gifts for His Body.

THE HOME-MAKING CHRIST

Finally, as 3:17 reveals, Christ is the home-making Christ. He is no longer homeless, for He is making His home in our hearts. The more Christ settles down in our hearts, the more He can boast to Satan that He has a home in His believers.

May we all be impressed with these five aspects of Christ. He is the church-loving Christ, the new-man-creating Christ, the all-things-heading-up-Christ, the gift-making and gift-giving Christ, and the home-making Christ. What a Christ we have!

LIFE-STUDY OF EPHESIANS

MESSAGE EIGHTY

PUTTING ON THE NEW MAN BY GROWING UP INTO CHRIST

Scripture Reading: Eph. 4:12-16, 22-24

We have pointed out that the church is not only the Body, but also the new man. As the Body, the church needs Christ as life. But as the new man, the church needs Christ as the person. For example, trees have life, but they do not have a person and therefore have no personality. As human beings, however, we have both life and personality, for we are persons.

CHRIST BECOMING THE PERSON IN OUR HEARTS

Because the church is not only the Body with Christ as life but also the new man with Christ as the person, Paul in 3:17 emphasizes the importance of Christ making His home in our hearts. Although our spirit is a vessel to contain God, the spirit is not the center of personality. The center of personality is the heart. The various functions of our personality—our mind, emotion, and will—are directly related to our heart, not to our spirit. Because all the functions of personality are concentrated in the heart, it is the place where Christ desires to make His home. Christ as the life-giving Spirit is now in our spirit. However, He wants to spread into our hearts and make His home there.

Through regeneration we have Christ as the Spirit in our spirit. But through transformation Christ will spread from our spirit into our heart. Every regenerated person has Christ in his spirit, but not many have allowed Christ to spread into their hearts. This is the reason Paul prayed that we would be strengthened into our inner man so that Christ may make His home in our hearts (3:16). It seems as if Paul wanted to tell the Ephesians, "Because you have been saved and regenerated, you have Christ in your spirit. But I'm concerned that you have not allowed Christ to spread into your hearts. Therefore, I pray for you that you may be strengthened in your spirit by the Spirit so that Christ may make His home in your hearts."

We need to take Christ not only as the life in our spirit, but also as the person in our heart. When Christ is in our spirit, He is our life. However, when He spreads into our heart, He also becomes our person. We all have Christ in our spirit, but I wonder how much Christ has spread into our heart.

Sisters, do you take Christ as your person when you go shopping? Do you allow Him to make home in your heart as you are deciding what to buy? For the most part, you are the one who makes these decisions, not Christ. You have Christ in your spirit as life. The problem is that you confine Him to your spirit. Deep within I am afraid that you say, "Lord Jesus, You are my life in my spirit. But when it comes to shopping, I want You to stay in my spirit. Let me shop according to what is in my heart. I want to buy the things I like. Lord, my spirit is Your sphere. But my heart is reserved for me." When you pray, you may contact the Lord in your spirit, only to leave Him and go shopping according to your own desire and choice. Of course, the sisters may not put this into words, but this may be their attitude. I doubt that many sisters consult the Lord about their shopping. This indicates that in the practical matter of shopping they do not take Christ as their person in their hearts.

Simply having Christ as life does not produce the church life. In order to have the proper church life, we must take Christ as our person. Remember that the church is the new man as well as the Body. As the new man, the church needs Christ as the person. The main problem is not with the life, but with the person. There is no need to adjust the life, but there is the need for a change of person. Our mind, emotion, and will all need to be adjusted. With the church life, the problem is not only with our taking Christ as life; it is also with our taking Christ as our person. Very few saints take Christ as their person in an adequate way. To have Christ as our person is deeper, higher, and fuller than to have Him as our life. In Ephesians 3 Paul did not pray that the saints would have Christ as life. He prayed that they would take Him as their person by allowing Him to make His home in their hearts. This is our need today.

Whatever we do, we should do by taking Christ as our person. The question is not what we do, but who is doing it. Are we the ones, or is it Christ? Concerning shopping, it is not a matter of what we intend to buy; it is a matter of who is buying that particular item. Are we the ones buying it, or is it Christ? If we do not take Christ as our person, it may even be wrong in the eyes of the Lord to purchase a Bible. Hence, the question is not what we do or what we buy; it is who is doing that thing or buying that item.

CHRIST EXPRESSED IN THE CHURCH

The only way for Christ to be our person is for Him to make His home in our hearts. The need in all the local churches is for the saints to take Christ both as their life and as their person by allowing Him to make His home in their hearts. The churches are the Lord's testimony on earth. But this testimony must have an inward reality. I am sorry to say that it is possible for the church to be an empty shell, a shell without content. The content of the church must be the very Christ whom we take as life and as our person. If we take Christ as our person, then as we come together in the meetings Christ will be expressed from our spirit and through our heart. All those who come will sense that Christ is present both as our life and as our person.

The meetings of a local church must be the expression of Christ. Christ is not only the victorious and prevailing life, but also a practical, present, living Person. Whenever we testify in the meetings, others will be able to tell whether or not we have been taking Christ as our person. If we are faithful to take Christ as our person, we shall enjoy the presence of the Lord Jesus in the meetings. In fact, the meetings will even be His presence, for He will be expressed from within us.

We need to pray for ourselves and for others to have the reality of taking Christ as our person in our daily living. Everything we do should be done not by the self, but by Christ. His tastes and preferences need to become ours. Then Christ will be not only our life, but also our person. The Lord will thus expand in our heart, take possession of our heart, and make His home in our heart in a full way. Eventually, He will saturate our whole being with Himself, and we shall live no longer by the self, but by Christ. The more this becomes our experience, the more the meetings of the church will be the presence of the Lord Jesus. In such meetings there is little need for preaching, teaching, or the exercise of gifts, because Christ is expressed through the saints. Because Christ is so rich, available, present, and practical in the experience of the saints, they will be able to share Christ with one another. What a difference between such meetings and the "services" in today's Christianity!

CONSTITUTED INTO GIFTS

In Ephesians 4 we see that when the victorious Christ ascended, He led a train of vanquished foes and constituted them into gifts to His Body. We have pointed out that we become gifts through experiencing Christ's descending and ascending within us.

Paul is the most useful gift given by Christ to His Body. Before being constituted a gift to the church, Paul was an enemy of Christ and a persecutor of the church. Nevertheless, when the Lord Jesus appeared to him, Paul was defeated. He fell to the ground, and said, "Who art thou, Lord?" By calling on the name of the Lord Jesus, he was saved, and the Lord came into him. At that moment, Saul of Tarsus became a vanquished foe. In the years to follow, he went on to experience Christ's descending and ascending within him. Eventually, through this experience of the traveling Christ, Paul became an outstanding gift to the Body.

The principle is the same with us. Although we were once enemies of the Lord, one day He met us, perhaps as we were on our road to Damascus. The Lord vanquished us, captured us, and put us in His train of vanquished foes. Now, by descending and ascending within us, He is constituting us into gifts to His Body.

Many Christians think only the leading apostles, prophets, evangelists, and shepherds and teachers are gifts to the church. However, if we read 4:7 in context, we shall see that every member, including every one of us, is a gift to the Body. In 4:16 Paul speaks of every part, that is, every member. Every member of the Body may be a gift if he is constituted by the descending and ascending Christ.

PERFECTING THE SAINTS THROUGH THE MINISTRY OF CHRIST

Ephesians 4:12 speaks of the perfecting of the saints. To perfect the saints is not mainly to teach them; it is to minister Christ to them. What the saints need is not the knowledge of doctrine, but the ministering of Christ. Whenever someone ministers Christ to us, we spontaneously have the sense that we are fed and nourished, that we have received Christ as our food supply. Through this supply we are strengthened and enlightened.

However, it is altogether different when someone comes to us with enticing questions. When the serpent contacted Eve in the garden, he asked, "Has God said?" In like manner, negative ones often raise tempting questions. We need to realize immediately that such questions do not come from the Lord. Those who contact us in this way do not minister Christ. They do not supply us with food, they do not water us, and they do not strengthen, enlighten, or equip us. The effect of their questions is darkness and death. As soon as we are aware of this kind of speaking, we must close ourselves to it and refuse to take it in.

What the saints need is to have Christ ministered into them. This is necessary for the church life. In all our contact with the saints there should be the ministry of Christ as the life supply. The leading gifts are to perfect the saints through such a ministry of Christ. The more the saints are supplied with the living Christ, the more they are perfected.

GROWING IN PARTICULAR MATTERS

As the saints are perfected through the ministry of Christ, they will grow up into Christ. We have Christ within us, but in many matters we are still in the self. Hence, we need the growth that will bring us out of ourselves and into Christ. Teaching cannot do this. This can be done only through the ministry of Christ as food and nourishment.

The growth into Christ in 4:15 is equal to the putting on of the new man in verse 24. The only way to put on the new man is to grow up into Christ. The more we grow into Christ, the more we put on the new man. To put on the new man is to be in the proper church life. We cannot be in the church life if we do not grow into Christ. We need to grow up into Christ in all the details of our daily living, for example, in shopping and in talking. Often our talk is natural and devoid of Christ. The only way to be free from such a natural way of speaking is to grow out of it by growing up into Christ. If we grow in Christ in the matter of talking, our talk will eventually be in Christ. By growing up into Christ in this particular matter, we spontaneously put on more of the new man.

In some localities the saints love the Lord very much; however, they are quite natural. Nearly everything about them—their behavior, their virtues, their way of speaking—is natural. With them there is no sign of having grown up into Christ. This is disturbing to the indwelling Spirit, who longs for the church to be realized as the new man. In order to put on the church life as the expression of the one new man, we need to grow out of everything natural by growing up into Christ. If we have the perfection with the growth spoken of in 4:13 and 15, surely we shall put on the new man.

THE PROPER COMMUNITY LIFE

As we grow into Christ, we shall also put off the old man, especially regarding the former manner of life. The manner of life of the old man is the old social life, the old community life. By creation, every human being needs a community life. Before we were saved, we had a certain kind of social life. Now that we are saved our social life needs a change. This means that we need a change of community. The church life is the best "social life." We can testify that in the church life our former social life has been exchanged for the best community life. Praise the Lord for the "social life" in the church!

A STABLE CHURCH LIFE

However, if we proclaim that the church is our community life but we do not grow into Christ, we shall not be stable in the church life. Some say that they are for the church life. However, when they are disappointed with something in the church, they leave. This indicates that they have not truly put on the church life by growing up into Christ. The only way to put on the church life is to grow up into Christ in all things. Suppose a sister does not grow up into Christ in her shopping. As long as she lacks growth in this matter, her church life will not be altogether secure. The security of our church life depends upon our growing up into Christ in particular matters. If we do not grow up into Christ, we may be in the church life one day and gone the next. For a steady church life, we need to grow up into Christ in particular ways. Once again we see that to put on the new man is to grow.

What we need is not growth in a general way, but in particular ways. For example, a brother may need to grow up into Christ in the way he cuts his hair or in the way he deals with his wife. If we do not show any growth in such aspects of our daily life, others may rightfully question the security of our life in the church. Only by growing in particular things will our church life become steady, stable, and secure.

The more we grow in Christ, the more of the church life we put on.

The church life is not a matter of good character or good works. It is altogether a matter of growth into Christ in particular things. By growing day by day in Christ, we gradually put off the old social life and put on the church the new man as the new community life. As we grow, we take Christ both as our life and as our person. Growth depends upon Christ making His home in our hearts. If we do not give Christ the opportunity to make His home in us, we can neither take Him as our person nor have the genuine growth in Christ. We grow in Christ only by taking Him as our person. The more we take Christ as our person, the more we grow up into Christ in particular things. The result is that we put on more of the church life.

It is possible to be in the church life merely in an outward way. However, if we do not grow in Christ by taking Him as our person, we are not in the church life in reality. The reality and practicality of the church life consists in growing up into Christ, which in turn is based upon taking Christ as our person in particular matters. As we take Christ as our person and grow up into Him, the church life is constituted into our being, and we become part of the church. This is the proper church life.

LIFE-STUDY OF EPHESIANS

MESSAGE EIGHTY-ONE

THE CHURCH—THE EXPRESSION OF CHRIST

Scripture Reading: Eph. 1:23; 3:8b, 17a, 19b; 4:13; 5:18b

The church is the expression of Christ. It is not the expression of such things as doctrine, gifts, or power. Nevertheless, subconsciously or unconsciously, many think that the church should be characterized by the manifestation of spiritual gifts. Some believe that whenever Christians meet together there should be the exercise and demonstration of the so-called charismatic gifts of the Holy Spirit. However, the book of Ephesians, a book on the church, does not mention this kind of gift. There is not a word in this Epistle about speaking in tongues or healing. When Paul speaks of gifts in Ephesians 4, he is referring to persons who are made gifts to the Body. For example, the apostles, prophets, evangelists, and shepherds and teachers are gifts. As we have pointed out elsewhere, every member of the Body is a gift to the church. Hence, in Ephesians a gift is not what we have or what we do; it is what we are. To be such a gift is to be constituted with Christ as life. This causes our very being to become a gift to the Body.

INDIVIDUALISM AND DIVISIVENESS

We thank the Lord for the many Christians who have been helped through the experience of charismatic gifts. However, we cannot agree with the claim that all Christians will become one if they have certain charismatic experiences. According to my experience and observation, those who emphasize the Pentecostal or charismatic experiences are the most divisive. The more certain believers exercise their spiritual gifts, the more individualistic and divisive they become. This is the reason that there have been so many divisions among those who stress spiritual gifts. In Christian meetings they may not care much for the edification of others, but care primarily for the manifestation of their own gifts. Some excuse their individualism by saying that they take heed only to God, not to man, and claiming that everything they do is of the Spirit's inspiration.

FILLED IN SPIRIT UNTO ALL THE FULLNESS OF GOD

In 1:22 and 23 Paul indicates that the church is the Body, the fullness of the One who fills all in all. The church is the fullness of Christ. In 3:8 Paul says that he preached the unsearchable riches of Christ. (Paul does not say here that he preached doctrine or gifts.) We need to know the difference between the riches of Christ and the fullness of Christ. Most Christians confuse these terms, thinking that the riches of Christ are the same as the fullness of Christ.

In chapter three Paul goes on to speak of Christ making His home in our heart, with the result that we are filled unto all the fullness of God. Furthermore, in 4:13 he says that we need to arrive "at a full-grown man, at the measure of the stature of the fullness of Christ." In 5:18 he says that we should be filled in our spirit. Surely this is related to being filled unto all the fullness of God. Such a filling takes place in our spirit, not in the mind. In 5:18 Paul is not saying that we are filled with the Holy Spirit; he is emphasizing the fact that we need to be filled in our spirit, even filled unto all the fullness of God.

In 5:18 Paul presents a contrast between being drunk with wine and being filled in spirit. To be drunk with wine is to be filled in the body, whereas to be filled in our regenerated spirit is to be filled with Christ unto all the fullness of God. To be drunk with wine in the body causes us to be dissipated, but to be filled with Christ, the fullness of God, causes us to overflow with Him in speaking, singing, psalming, and giving thanks to God (vv. 19-20) and to subject ourselves one to another (v. 21). How important it is for us to be filled in spirit unto all the fullness of God!

THE RICHES OF CHRIST AND THE FULLNESS OF CHRIST

Let us now consider the difference between the riches of Christ and the fullness of Christ. The riches of Christ are what Christ is to us in all His divine attributes and human virtues. These riches are unsearchable. The fullness of Christ, the Body, issues from the enjoyment of the riches of Christ. Through the enjoyment of Christ's riches, we become His fullness to express Him. Christ, who is the infinite God without limitation of any kind, is so great that He fills all things in all things. Such a Christ needs the church to be His fullness for His complete expression.

We have pointed out that the riches of Christ are unsearchable. Included in these riches is Christ's divinity. He is the very God. Since Christ is the Son of God, another aspect of His riches is sonship. Furthermore, according to Isaiah 9:6, the Son is even called the eternal Father. This indicates that He has not only the sonship, but also the fatherhood. Second Corinthians 3:17 says that Christ the Lord is the Spirit. This is another item of Christ's unsearchable riches. Other items include Christ as light, life, love, righteousness, holiness, humility, patience, and submission. How long the list would be if anyone could enumerate all the aspects of the riches of Christ!

Christ's riches need an expression. When these riches come forth to be expressed, that expression is the fullness of Christ. When Christ was incarnated, God's riches were expressed. However, the incarnation by no means exhausted these riches. Rather, it was the overflow, the fullness, of the riches of God. Christ came forth from the bosom of the Father (John 1:18). But His coming forth did not at all exhaust the divine riches in the Father's bosom. On the contrary, the more that came forth, the more there was to come forth. Therefore, with Christ there were not only the riches, but also the fullness. For this reason, John 1:16 says, "For of His fullness we all received, and grace upon grace." Christ is the fullness of the Godhead. When He came to earth, He was the overflow of the riches of God. Hence, He became the fullness of God. Not only were the riches within Him, but the very fullness of the Godhead dwelt in Him bodily (Col. 2:9).

Christ is the fullness of God, and the church is the fullness of Christ. Christ's riches are so extensive that not only is Christ Himself filled with them, but these riches also fill up the members of His Body, the church. As we are filled with Christ's riches, we become His fullness. In this way the church becomes the fullness of Christ.

THE UNLIMITED EXPRESSION OF THE UNLIMITED CHRIST

The fullness of Christ comes out of the enjoyment of the riches of Christ. For the church to have the riches of Christ and not the fullness of Christ would be an indication that Christ is limited. But the fact that the church not only has Christ's riches but also is His fullness indicates that the Christ experienced and enjoyed by the church is unlimited. Limited riches cannot produce fullness. Only unlimited riches are capable of producing the fullness. As the expression of the unsearchably rich Christ, the church is the unlimited expression of the unlimited Christ. This means that the church is the fullness of Christ who is Himself the embodiment of the fullness of God. My burden in this message is simply to point out that the church must be such an expression of Christ.

BACK TO CHRIST

The church is not the expression of anything other than Christ. We have seen that many Christians are occupied with spiritual gifts. These gifts, however, are not Christ Himself. In like manner, doctrine and power are not Christ. Not even the Bible itself is Christ. Christ, a living and wonderful Person, is the embodiment of God. We should not allow anything to take the place of Christ. Spiritual gifts may be a means to partake of Christ, power may help us to realize Christ, and doctrines may be instruments used to impart Christ. However, many Christians allow gifts, power, teachings, and even the Bible to become substitutes for Christ. Instead of taking Christ and experiencing Christ directly, many devote their attention to gifts, power, and doctrine. This indicates that the means and the instruments that God intends to be used to gain Christ are actually used to replace Christ. The situation must be altogether different in the Lord's recovery. In the recovery, the Lord intends to bring us back to Himself, not to the various means or instruments. We thank the Lord for the gifts, the power, the teachings, and, in particular, for the holy Word. But most of all, we thank God for His Son, the Lord Jesus Christ. God's intention is to bring us back to Christ, back from everything that has become a substitute for Him or has distracted us from Him. Therefore, when we Christians meet together, we should pay our attention not to the manifestation of gifts or even to the teaching of the Word, but to the expression of the living Christ. In the meetings we should not be concerned about the way of meeting, but with the expression of the living Christ.

CALLING ON THE NAME OF THE LORD

In the Lord's recovery we are fighting a battle. Primarily we must fight against the use of good things as substitutes for Christ. In his subtlety, the enemy, Satan, uses many things to attract people away from Christ. Some are distracted from Christ by teachings or by their concept of what is correct Bible doctrine. For this reason, some condemn the practice of calling on the name of the Lord. They claim that this is not according to Scripture. Some have accused us of inventing new ways of worship. Others have asked us why we cannot go along with the methods of worship that have been practiced by Christians for centuries. What is wrong with calling on the name of the Lord? It is not my intention to cause other Christians trouble. But the Lord has charged me to tell His people of the need to call on Him. This is not a new teaching. Such a practice is first spoken of in Genesis 4:26. This verse says, "Then began men to call upon the name of the Lord." This verse and dozens of other verses as well indicate that to call on the name of the Lord is certainly a scriptural teaching and practice. Verse after verse in both the Old Testament and in the New Testament encourages us to call on the name of the Lord.

PRAY-READING

Others are offended by pray-reading and criticize us for this practice. According to them, this is our invention. It is not my desire to argue with anyone about things such as this. However, I wish to point out that Ephesians 6:17 and 18 speak of taking the word of God by means of all prayer. Hence, if we are truly scriptural, we will take the Word not only by reading, studying, and searching, but also by praying. With verses such as Ephesians 6:17 and 18 before us, who can say that to pray-read the Word is not according to the Bible? How much we need to turn from the traditional understanding and come back to Christ Himself and to the pure Word of God! This is the Lord's recovery.

EXPRESSING CHRIST IN THE MEETINGS

As Christians who live by Christ, whenever we come together we should follow the indwelling Spirit to express Christ. There is no need to have a set way in the meetings. The Spirit knows how to express Christ. In each meeting we should simply open to Him and follow Him. It is not always necessary to open the meeting with a hymn. Perhaps someone will stand and offer living praises to God. We should not come to the meeting according to our concept, for it is too much under the influence of religious tradition. However, if we would express Christ in the meeting, we need to experience Him in our daily life. Some have very little of Christ with which to function and to minister because they have little experience of Him. Hence, they are "pew members." In the meetings of the recovered church life, the saints who live by Christ need to express Christ in a living way. Only the Spirit knows the way to do this.

In some of the coming messages we shall consider the matter of speaking Christ to one another. Ephesians 5:18 and 19 exhort us to be filled in spirit, speaking to one another in psalms, hymns, and spiritual songs. We need to stand up to declare what Christ is to us and how we have experienced Him. In this way we shall speak Christ to one another, and Christ will be richly expressed in the meetings. Then in a very practical way the church will be filled unto all the fullness of God, with the overflow of all that God is. The church life will be not the expression of gifts, knowledge, or power, but the expression of the living Christ.

LIFE-STUDY OF EPHESIANS

MESSAGE EIGHTY-TWO

THE CHURCH—THE OVERFLOW OF CHRIST

Scripture Reading: Eph. 1:23; 3:19b; 4:13; John 1:16

We have seen that the church is the expression of Christ. In Ephesians 1 we are told that the church is the Body and that this Body is the fullness of the One who fills all in all. The church is the Body of Christ, and this Body is the fullness of the Person who fills all in all.

THE FULLNESS OF THE VAST CHRIST

The words "all in all" in 1:23 refer to the universe. Christ fills the entire universe. This is proved by 4:10 which says, "He Who descended is the same Who also ascended far above all the heavens that He might fill all things." For Christ to fill all things is for Him to fill the universe. Christ is so universally vast that He fills all things. This vast Christ needs a Body to be His fullness.

The fullness of Christ is the overflow of Christ. Christ is so unsearchably rich that He has an overflow, a fullness, a surplus. As His Body, the church is Christ's fullness, His surplus. This is a matter of great significance.

The Lord's recovery is not concerned mainly with the recovery of outward things. In God's economy outward things have relatively little value. God's economy is Christ with the church. The church comes into existence as we inwardly experience the riches of Christ and thus become His fullness.

THE DIFFERENCE BETWEEN THE CHURCH AND A SOCIAL ORGANIZATION

There is a big difference between the church and a social organization. The church may seem to be a social group composed of different kinds of people. Worldly people view the church in such a way, as just another social organization. We need to see the difference between the church and a social club. Social clubs may have high requirements for their members. They may insist on superior standards of dress, behavior, and character. Outwardly, the members of such clubs may be better than the saints in the churches. However, no matter how good a club may be, it is merely a human organization. In contrast to the church, it has nothing of Christ. But the church is the overflow, the surplus, of Christ.

The members of a club may be regulated outwardly according to certain requirements. Those who fulfill these requirements may have a very good appearance in the eyes of man. In certain respects, they may seem better than those in the churches. However, in the eyes of God the best of human standards and behavior is nothing but dung. In the church we do not need outward improvement or correction. On the contrary, we need Christ to swallow up all our shortcomings with Himself. If the members of the church are short in certain respects, this indicates that they need more of Christ. We must resist the temptation to change the church into a social club with standards and regulations. This has nothing to do with the Body of Christ. The Body of Christ is constituted solely of Christ wrought into the saints.

THE FOCAL POINT OF GOD'S ECONOMY

I am fully aware that in Ephesians, a book concerned with the church, Paul speaks about such things as wives submitting to their husbands, husbands loving their wives, children obeying their parents, and slaves obeying their masters. These things, however, are not the focal point of God's eternal economy. God's economy is not to have a good family life; it is to have a Body for Christ. If we are in the Body of Christ in a proper and practical way, we shall no doubt have a proper family life. However, we may have an outstanding family life and yet have nothing to do with the

Body of Christ. I have known unbelievers whose family life was better than that of many Christians. Although the family life of these unbelievers was good, it had nothing to do with Christ or with God's economy. It is crucial for us to see that the focal point of God's economy is not a standard of character or behavior; it is Christ with the church.

In his subtlety, Satan, the enemy of God, has used such things as Bible knowledge, spiritual gifts, and evangelism to keep believers from seeing God's economy. During the time of the Lord Jesus on the earth and of the Apostle Paul, Satan utilized the Old Testament to veil the Jewish people. When the Lord Jesus appeared to them as the very incarnation of God, they were not able to recognize Him. On the contrary, with the Scriptures in their hands, they sentenced the Lord Jesus to death. According to their concept, they were serving God in so doing.

Christians today should not regard themselves as superior to those Jewish religionists. It is entirely possible for Christians today to be deceived just as the Jews were. The enemy still uses the knowledge of the Bible to keep people from seeing Christ. Furthermore, he will use almost anything as a substitute for Christ and to keep people from seeing the revelation of God's economy concerning Christ and the church.

TRANSFORMED TO BECOME CHRIST'S OVERFLOW

We have pointed out that the church is the overflow of Christ. In order to be in reality the overflow of Christ, we need to be transformed. Second Corinthians 3:18 says that as we behold and reflect the glory of the Lord with an unveiled face, we are being transformed into the same image from glory to glory. Yes, the saints still have their shortcomings and failures, but they are nonetheless undergoing the process of transformation. The more we are transformed, the more we become the overflow of Christ.

It is easy to adjust people outwardly by asking them to conform to certain regulations. But it takes time for the divine life to grow within us. For example, in a very short period of time you can make an artificial flower. But to produce a real flower, a flower that has life and fragrance, may take several months. If we regulate others outwardly, we shall only delay the process of the growth in life. Therefore, we should be patient and allow the Lord to grow in the saints. Eventually, the growth in life will produce the desired change. This is the difference between the church and a social club.

As the Body of Christ, the church is a living organism constituted of the divine life. The divine life came into us at the time of regeneration, and now it is working within us to saturate every part of our being and to swallow up all our negative element. By this process the church becomes the Body in a practical way.

EXPERIENCING CHRIST FOR THE CHURCH LIFE

In the recovery the Lord is not working mainly to recover teachings, gifts, or practices. On the contrary, the recovery is a matter of experiencing Christ as life for the church life. If some feel that the goal of the Lord's recovery is the recovery of certain teachings and gifts, I would say that time will prove that this is a false expectation. More than ten years ago certain ones claimed that the Lord desires to recover the vast field of Pentecostal gifts. Those who made this claim were living in a dream, and they are no longer in the Lord's recovery. At the time I told them that they were dreaming and that if they would not wake up from their dream, they would suffer loss. They would be deceived by their dream. Those who did not give up that dream have in fact suffered loss spiritually. Today many of them are apart from the Lord's presence and grace.

The indwelling Christ can keep us safely in the way of the Lord. It is crucial that we all know the indwelling Christ and allow Him to make His home in our hearts. We should not desire to do a great work. Instead, we should be satisfied to allow Christ to live in us and for Him to use us to impart His element into others. If this is our situation, it is not we who work for the Lord, but Christ who does the work from within us. If we experience Christ in this way, then in reality and in practicality the church will be the Body of Christ. The church as the Body comes out of Christ Himself, for it is His overflow, His surplus.

Some years ago I spent ten hours talking to a certain brother. He did not believe that the Lord's work could be accomplished by the indwelling Christ. Rather, his full confidence was in the recovery of Pentecostal gifts. I told this brother that the Lord does not intend to have a great movement. On the contrary, His move will be on a relatively small scale, perhaps, as it often is, in a hidden way. The Lord will not do anything that is out of proportion to His Body.

NO FOREIGN ELEMENT IN THE BODY

Furthermore, anything that is of the Body of Christ must be of the life of Christ. For example, nothing artificial can truly be part of our physical bodies. Not even the best dentures are part of our bodies because they do not have the life of our bodies. Only what is produced by the life of our bodies can be part of our bodies. If you lose an arm, it may be replaced by an artificial limb, but that limb will not be a genuine part of your body. In the same principle, the Body of Christ must be of the life of Christ. There can be no foreign element in the Body. However, in today's Christianity there are many foreign elements or artificial things. None of these has anything to do with Christ as life. However, as we have pointed out, the church as the Body of Christ is the very fullness of Christ.

THE MEASURE OF THE STATURE OF THE FULLNESS OF CHRIST

In 4:13 Paul says, "Until we all arrive at the oneness of the faith and of the full knowledge of the Son of God, at a full-grown man, at the measure of the stature of the fullness of Christ." According to this verse, we need to arrive at three things: at the oneness of the faith and of the full knowledge of the Son of God, at a full-grown man, and at the measure of the stature of the fullness of Christ. The fullness of Christ, which is the Body, has a stature, for Paul speaks of the stature of the fullness of Christ. The stature of the fullness of Christ is equal to the stature of the Body of Christ. Chapter one reveals that the Body of Christ is the fullness of Christ, and chapter four, that the fullness of Christ has a stature. Therefore, the stature of the fullness of Christ is the stature of the Body of Christ.

In 4:13 Paul speaks not only of the stature of the fullness of Christ, but of the measure of that stature. As the Body of Christ, the church has stature. Because this stature grows, 4:13 speaks of its measure. This measure is the full-grown man.

In many believers the stature of the fullness of Christ has not grown very much. For this reason, with them there is very little measure. But as Christ grows within them, they will gradually increase unto the measure of the stature of the fullness of Christ. We need to press on until we all arrive at the measure of the stature of the fullness of Christ.

Presently we are on the way toward a full-grown man, toward the measure of the stature of the fullness of Christ. The day is coming when we shall all arrive at a full-grown man. Until then, we are still in the process. Because we are in the process, Paul speaks of the time when we shall "be no longer babes tossed by waves and carried about by every wind of teaching" (4:14).

As the Body of Christ, the church is the fullness that is daily growing within us. It is vital for us all to see that the church is an organism that comes out of Christ. Anything that is not of Christ cannot be part of the church. No matter how disciplined, regulated, or improved we may be, none of this is of the church if it does not issue out of Christ. Self-regulation, self-discipline, and self-improvement may produce an excellent society, but it cannot produce the church. As far as the Body of Christ is concerned, nothing that we have in ourselves has any significance. In relation to the Body, natural goodness is of no advantage. Whether we are good or evil, we still need Christ. Those who are evil surely need Christ. But those who are very good need Christ just as much. No matter what kind of disposition we may have, our natural being needs to be swallowed up and even consumed by the indwelling Christ. Then in reality we shall be the Body of Christ, His fullness.

RECEIVING OF HIS FULLNESS

John 1:16 says, "For of His fullness we all received, and grace upon grace." What is important is not that we merely learn about Christ or that we imitate Christ, but that we receive of His fullness. Christ is so rich that He has an overflow called the fullness. Of this fullness we may all receive grace upon grace. If we daily receive of His fullness, we shall eventually become His fullness, for we shall be constituted according to what we have received. This means that the more we receive of His fullness, the more we shall be constituted of His fullness and become His fullness. If we see this, we shall say, "Lord, save me from anything that is not Your fullness. Lord, I am willing to pay any price to enjoy You and to partake of Your fullness." May the Lord be merciful to us that we may daily experience Him and enjoy Him and thereby become the church that is His very fullness, His overflow.

LIFE-STUDY OF EPHESIANS

MESSAGE EIGHTY-THREE

EXPERIENCING THE RICHES OF CHRIST

Scripture Reading: Eph. 3:8b, 17a; 2 Cor. 2:10; 10:1; 11:10; 8:9; 12:9; 13:14

Ephesians 3:8 speaks of the unsearchable riches of Christ, and 3:17, of Christ making His home in our hearts. This indicates that the very Christ who is making His home in us is the Christ with the unsearchable riches. The unsearchable riches of Christ are for our enjoyment. Day by day and even hour by hour we need to enjoy these marvelous, wonderful, immeasurable, unlimited, and all-inclusive riches.

It is difficult to list all the items of the riches of Christ. If these items were few in number, it would be easy for us to point them out. But Christ's riches are beyond our ability to speak of them or to enumerate them. In order to get into the riches of Christ in Ephesians, it will be helpful to consider Paul's experience of these riches as revealed in the book of 2 Corinthians.

GIFTS, GRACE, AND TRANSFORMATION

The book of 2 Corinthians deals with grace, in contrast to 1 Corinthians, which deals with gifts. Paul concludes 2 Corinthians with the words, "The grace of the Lord Jesus Christ, and the love of God, and the fellowship of the Holy Spirit, be with you all" (13:14, Gk.). Because 2 Corinthians is a book of grace, in the concluding verse Paul mentions grace first. Grace is deeper and more subjective than gifts. Gifts are outward, but grace is inward. Furthermore, gifts are related to what we do, but grace is related to inward enjoyment.

It is significant that it is in 2 Corinthians, not in 1 Corinthians, that Paul says that we are transformed as we behold the glory of the Lord with an unveiled face (2 Cor. 3:18). To be gifted is one thing, but to be transformed is another. Although many Christians pay attention to gifts, not many concentrate on transformation.

Do you prefer to be gifted or to be transformed? Before you answer this question, consider the example of Balaam's donkey (Num. 22:23-33). Suddenly this donkey spoke to Balaam. How miraculous for a donkey to speak a human language! However, the donkey was not transformed into a human being. There was the gift of speaking, but there was not any transformation.

Transformation takes place slowly through the growth in life. It transpires so slowly that it may seem as if nothing is happening. For example, to a mother, her young child may look the same every day. Actually, the child is gradually growing.

In 2 Corinthians 4:7 Paul says, "But we have this treasure in earthen vessels, that the excellency of the power may be of God, and not of us." The treasure in the earthen vessels does not refer to gifts. Rather, it denotes something precious that is hidden. The vessel is outward, but the treasure is inward. Through the process of transformation over a period of time, the treasure takes over the vessel and swallows it up.

THE SUFFERINGS OF CHRIST

Another difference between 2 Corinthians and 1 Corinthians is that 2 Corinthians speaks a great deal about suffering, but there is no need for suffering in order to have spiritual gifts. It was not necessary for Balaam's donkey to suffer to have the ability to speak a human language. Transformation, on the contrary, requires a certain amount of suffering. For this reason, 2 Corinthians speaks not only of the grace of Christ, but also of the sufferings of Christ. In 2 Corinthians 1:5 Paul says that "the sufferings of Christ abound in us." The grace of Christ with the sufferings of

Christ produces transformation. Transformation is not a matter of our gifts or abilities; it is a matter of what we are in our inward being.

In 2 Corinthians 4:5 Paul declared, "For we preach not ourselves, but Christ Jesus the Lord." Although Paul did not preach himself or write an autobiography, occasionally he found it necessary to disclose certain aspects of his experience of Christ. In 2 Corinthians there are a number of such disclosures by which we can see how Paul enjoyed particular aspects of the riches of Christ. Later on in this message we shall consider these particular aspects.

Certain aspects of the riches of Christ are very great. Some of these are the fact that Christ is God, the Creator, the Son of God, the Redeemer, the Savior, the Father, and the life-giving Spirit. Other major aspects are related to incarnation, crucifixion, resurrection, ascension, descension, and indwelling. Furthermore, there are the aspects of Christ as life, love, power, holiness, and righteousness. All these are great items, and, to some degree at least, Christians do know them. However, Christians may have just a doctrinal knowledge of these riches of Christ without the experience of them. May the Lord have mercy on us so that we may not only know the various aspects of the riches of Christ, but also experience them and enjoy them.

CALLING ON THE NAME OF THE LORD

Romans 10:12 gives us a clue as to how we may enjoy the unsearchable riches of Christ. In this verse Paul says, "The same Lord of all is rich to all who call upon Him." The riches of Christ should not just be studied—they should be enjoyed. We do not enjoy them by meditating upon them. To meditate is to exercise the mind. In the New Testament we are not told to meditate. (The use of the word meditate by the King James Version in 1 Timothy 4:15 is not an accurate translation; the Greek word is better rendered "attend to.") If we desire to experience the riches of Christ, we should call on the name of the Lord Jesus. Many of us can testify that such calling is much sweeter and more enjoyable than meditating. The more we call on the name of the Lord Jesus, the more we taste His sweetness.

Some criticize our practice of calling on the name of the Lord Jesus. According to them, it is merely a psychological phenomenon with no spiritual value. If calling on the Lord's name simply produces a temporary psychological experience, then the same experience could be achieved by calling on the name of some other person. However, such is not the case. When we call on the dear name of the Lord Jesus, we enjoy His reality and taste His sweetness. Remember, the Lord's name is backed up by His Person. Thus, when we call on the name, we contact the Person, the reality of whom is the Spirit. For this reason, when we call on the name of the Lord Jesus, we receive the Spirit.

The name of the Lord Jesus is often associated with the Spirit in the Bible. For example, 1 Corinthians 6:11 says, "But ye are washed, but ye are sanctified, but ye are justified in the name of the Lord Jesus, and by the Spirit of our God." Jesus is the name, and the Spirit is the Person. Whenever we call on the name of Jesus, we experience the Person of the Spirit. Because this Person is real, living, near, and available, we experience Him and enjoy Him when we call on Him. The Lord Jesus is rich to all who call upon Him. What a wonderful way to enjoy the unsearchable riches of Christ!

LIVING IN THE PERSON OF CHRIST

The book of 2 Corinthians reveals the kind of life lived by the Apostle Paul. Paul lived by taking Christ as his life and person. He was constantly enjoying Christ and experiencing Him. In 2 Corinthians 2:10 he says that he forgave "in the person of Christ." Paul did not forgive in himself, that is, in his own person. When he forgave something, he forgave it in the person of Christ. This reveals that Paul lived in the person of Christ.

Everything we do should be done in the person of Christ. This means that when a brother loves his wife, he should love her in the person of Christ. Moreover, when a sister goes shopping, she should shop in the person of Christ. As long as we do a particular thing in the person of Christ, there is no problem.

It is rather difficult to render accurately the Greek word for person in 2 Corinthians 2:10. It may be rendered face or presence. The Greek signifies the area of the face around the eyes. This part of a person's face is the index of his feeling and inward being. By looking at this part of a person's face, we know how he feels about a certain thing. When Paul said that he forgave in the person of Christ, he was saying that he forgave in the index of the Lord's inward being.

We may experience something of this with our husband or wife. For example, someone may invite me to his home for dinner. By looking at my wife's eyes, I can tell by the expression through the index of her eyes whether or not she agrees with accepting this invitation. At other times, my wife may check the expression that I convey through my eyes. This is what the Apostle Paul was doing in 2 Corinthians 2:10 as he forgave in the index of the Lord's inner being. He did not care for himself or for his own feeling. He cared only for the Lord's thought and feeling as made known through the index of His eyes. What a living the Apostle Paul had! He was a person always living in the presence of the Lord, always looking at the index of His eyes. Hence, whatever he did was the Lord's doing, and whatever he said was the Lord's speaking. Paul was a person who lived by taking Christ as his person. Paul's old person had been nullified. It was no longer he who lived—Christ was the person living in him. This was the reason Paul said he forgave in the person of Christ.

Many Christians talk about spiritual gifts, but they know nothing about living in the person of Christ. How different are these Christians from the Apostle Paul! In 2 Corinthians 2:10 Paul seemed to be saying, "I do not forgive according to my personal feeling or preference. I forgive according to the index of Christ's inner being. I know that the Lord wants me to forgive. By looking at the index of

His eyes I know what is in His heart. Therefore, I forgive in the person of Christ."

This is the kind of life that builds up the Body of Christ. We may do some great work, but we may not accomplish anything as far as the building up of the Body is concerned. Only those who live in the person of Christ can build up the Body. Such a living is not a matter of power or behavior. It is altogether a matter of life, of living in the person of Christ. This is one way in which Paul experienced the riches of Christ.

THE MEEKNESS AND GENTLENESS OF CHRIST

In 2 Corinthians 10:1 Paul says, "Now I Paul myself beseech you by the meekness and gentleness of Christ." Paul did not say that he imitated the meekness and gentleness of Christ. To imitate Christ is one thing, but to live in Christ's meekness and gentleness is another. Paul enjoyed these aspects of Christ's unsearchable riches and they also should be our enjoyment today. As we contact others, we should not try to imitate Christ. Rather, we should contact them in the meekness and gentleness of Christ.

In order to enjoy the meekness and gentleness of Christ, we need to be in the Spirit, for all the riches of Christ are in the all-inclusive Spirit. When we turn to our spirit, contact Christ as the all-inclusive Spirit, and take Him as our person, His meekness and gentleness become our food, nourishment, strength, and satisfaction. There is no need for us to desperately attempt to restrain ourselves or to manufacture meekness or gentleness. The meekness and gentleness of Christ are our spontaneous enjoyment. We can actually feed on these aspects of Christ's riches. When we take Him as our person, we spontaneously enjoy His meekness and gentleness. Instead of self-effort, we simply enjoy whatever Christ is. This was the living of the Apostle Paul.

THE TRUTH OF CHRIST

In 2 Corinthians 11:10 Paul says, "The truth of Christ is

in me." Within Paul there was something true and real of Christ. Because he enjoyed the truth of Christ, His reality, he knew that what he was relating to the Corinthians was of the truth of Christ. This is a further indication that Paul lived not by the self, but by taking Christ as his person.

Paul did not boast that he had any truth of himself. On the contrary, he boasted of the truth of Christ. We should learn from this never to boast of ourselves. We need to forget what we are and not speak of ourselves. Instead, we need to live according to Christ and behave by the truth of Christ. As we contact others in the meekness and gentleness of Christ, we need to speak as the truth of Christ is in us.

THE GRACE OF CHRIST

In 2 Corinthians a number of verses speak of the grace of Christ. For example, 2 Corinthians 8:9 says, "For ye know the grace of our Lord Jesus Christ, that, though he was rich, yet for your sakes he became poor, that ye through his poverty might be rich." By grace, Christ lowered Himself and left His position for our sake. He gave up His riches so that we may become rich. We can do such a thing only through the grace of Christ. If we take His grace as our enjoyment, spontaneously we shall do the same thing Christ did. Actually, we shall not be the ones who do this, but it will be Christ living in us.

In chapter twelve Paul asked the Lord three times that the "thorn in the flesh" might depart from him (vv. 7-8). However, the Lord said, "My grace is sufficient for thee: for My strength is made perfect in weakness" (v. 9). Therefore, Paul could say, "Most gladly therefore will I rather boast in my weaknesses so that the power of Christ might overshadow me" (v. 9, Gk.). The Lord told Paul not to care about the thorn or about his sufferings, but to enjoy His sufficient grace. Paul realized in his experience that Christ's strength was made perfect in his weakness.

Today many complain of their weakness or lack of ability.

However, they need to see that in their weakness Christ's strength is made perfect. Their weakness gives them an opportunity to enjoy the strength of Christ.

In 2 Corinthians 12:10 Paul went on to say, "Therefore I take pleasure in weaknesses, in reproaches, in necessities, in persecutions, in distresses for Christ's sake: for when I am weak, then am I strong" (Gk.). Paul was strong because Christ's strength was made perfect in his weakness.

PAUL'S BLESSING

We have pointed out that the book of 2 Corinthians ends with a blessing: "The grace of the Lord Jesus Christ, and the love of God, and the fellowship of the Holy Spirit, be with you all" (13:14, Gk.). Today many pastors pronounce these words as a formal benediction. Paul here was not giving such a benediction. Rather, he was telling the saints that they could partake of the riches of Christ and enjoy them.

The grace of Christ issues out of the love of God. This means that the love of God is the source of the grace of Christ, and that the grace of Christ is the expression of the love of God. Furthermore, this grace is in the fellowship of the Holy Spirit. Through the fellowship of the Holy Spirit, the grace of Christ with the love of God becomes our enjoyment. This enjoyment is just what we need today.

If we all experience and enjoy the riches of Christ, we shall have much to speak concerning Christ whenever we come together. As we fellowship with others in the Lord, we shall speak of what Christ is to us. We shall not speak about doctrine or gifts, but about the genuine experience of Christ and the real enjoyment of the riches of Christ. The more the riches of Christ are dispensed into us, the more we shall be sanctified and metabolically transformed. As a new element discharges the old element, we shall be nourished, cherished, and, eventually, glorified. The goal of the Lord in His recovery is to bring His people into this experience. After the time of Paul, the enjoyment of the unsearchable riches of Christ was lost to a large extent. Praise the Lord that this experience is being recovered!

LIFE-STUDY OF EPHESIANS

MESSAGE EIGHTY-FOUR

OVERFLOWING TO SPEAK

Scripture Reading: Eph. 5:18b-19; 1 Cor. 14:1, 5, 23-24, 31-32

In 5:18 Paul charges us to "be filled in spirit." As members of the Body of Christ, we need to be filled in our spirit unto all the fullness of God. If we are filled in spirit, that with which we are filled will overflow from within us.

Verse 19 refers to this overflow: "Speaking to one another in psalms and hymns and spiritual songs, singing and psalming with your heart to the Lord." We do not overflow by meditating or by sitting silently in the meetings of the church. On the contrary, we overflow by speaking to one another. If we are filled in spirit unto all the fullness of God, we shall spontaneously speak to one another concerning Christ. Speaking, therefore, is the way to overflow.

A SPEAKING GOD AND A SPEAKING PEOPLE

Christians must be a speaking people. We should not be dumb, or silent, for the God we worship is the speaking God. Idols, on the contrary, do not speak; they are dumb. In 1 Corinthians 12:2 Paul mentions "dumb idols." Because idols cannot speak, those who worship idols are also dumb. A dumb god needs dumb worshippers. If you visit a country where there is the practice of idol worship, you can see that idol worshippers worship their gods in a dumb way. But our God is not dumb; He is the speaking God. Therefore, those who worship Him must also speak. However, many who attend the so-called services in Christianity do not speak. Instead, they worship the Lord in a dumb way. What is our situation in the meetings of the church? Are we silent, or are we bubbling over with words about the Christ we have experienced in our daily life? In the meetings we should praise the Lord and speak of what He is to us in our experience.

Many Christians realize that their religious services should not be altogether silent. Therefore, they arrange to have soloists, quartets, and choirs to provide music. They also may hire outstanding preachers to speak. Nevertheless, most of the people sit silently in the pews, and, for the most part, are dumb worshippers.

The very architecture of many places of Christian worship is conducive to silence. For example, many spontaneously become quiet when they enter Catholic cathedrals. The steep roof, the dimly-lighted atmosphere, and the stained glass windows all encourage dumbness. Some worshippers may burn candles before images or pray in front of statues. How devilish! In principle, this is the same as the idol worship practiced in pagan countries. Much of Christianity has been permeated by the concept of silent worship. In effect, many who attend the Christian services are dumb worshippers.

Since our God is a speaking God, we as His worshippers must also speak. At times, we should even make a joyful noise to the Lord, as we are charged to do in Psalm 100:1. In a number of other verses we are told to do the same thing (Psa. 66:1; 81:1; 95:2; 98:4, 6). Often when we come together we should make joyful noise to the Lord.

As we speak to one another of our experiences of Christ, we should not wait for some kind of formal beginning of the meetings. To do this is to remain under the influence of traditional Christianity. If we have been set free from tradition, we shall speak spontaneously as we come together in the meetings of the church. Some may even begin to speak on the way to the meeting. The meetings need to be filled with speaking concerning the riches of Christ.

Ephesians 5:19 also refers to "singing and psalming" to the Lord. Such singing and psalming are not only the overflow of being filled in spirit, but also the way to be filled in spirit. Whenever we are filled in our spirit unto all the fullness of God, the first thing we shall do is speak. Then we shall sing and psalm with our heart to the Lord.

Many pride themselves on being scriptural. I wonder, however, if they are scriptural according to 5:19. This verse, found in a book that deals with the church, tells us that after we have been filled in our spirit unto all the fullness of God, we need to speak. Many who regard themselves as scriptural are scriptural only in a traditional way. They are not scriptural according to Paul's word in verse 19.

THE BIBLICAL UNDERSTANDING OF PROPHECY

In 1 Corinthians 14:1 Paul says, "Pursue love, and desire spiritual gifts, but rather that ye may prophesy" (Gk.). Most people regard prophecy merely as a foretelling of future events. According to this understanding, someone predicts the future and concludes his speaking with the words, "Thus saith the Lord." For example, in 1963 some prophesied that a great earthquake would cause Los Angeles to fall into the ocean. Prediction, however, is not the primary meaning of prophecy in the Bible, especially in the New Testament.

In the Bible to prophesy has three meanings. First, it is to speak for someone, to speak on behalf of another person. When one prophesies in this way, he speaks not for himself, but for someone else. Hence, someone may be called upon to prophesy for the Lord, that is, to speak on the Lord's behalf. Second, to prophesy means to speak forth, to declare. In the Bible a person may not only speak for God, but he may also speak forth something of God. Third, to prophesy is to foretell, to predict. Therefore, the three meanings of prophesy are to speak for, to tell forth, and to foretell. However, the meaning of foretell is not the primary meaning.

Let us use the book of Isaiah as an example. Isaiah 1:3 says, "The ox knoweth his owner, and the ass his master's crib: but Israel doth not know, my people doth not consider." What kind of prophecy is this? Certainly it is not foretelling. Rather, it is a declaration, a speaking forth something that is of the Lord. The same is true of Isaiah 9:6: "For unto us a child is born, unto us a son is given: and the government shall be upon his shoulder: and his name shall be called Wonderful, Counselor, The mighty God, The everlasting Father, The Prince of Peace." This word is a declaration, a telling forth. It is not primarily a foretelling of a future event. Of course, in the book of Isaiah there are a number of instances of such foretellings or predictions. Nevertheless, most of the book of Isaiah is either a speaking for or a telling forth. Only a relatively small portion of the book consists of foretelling. Thus, the content of the book of Isaiah illustrates the fact that the primary meaning of prophecy is not prediction, but declaration and speaking on behalf of another, especially on behalf of the Lord.

As we preach the gospel, we may prophesy in this way. We may say to a group of unbelievers, "Friends, you must believe in the Lord Jesus. Otherwise, you will be eternally lost." To speak in this manner is to prophesy in the sense of uttering something of the Lord and on behalf of the Lord. To preach the gospel, therefore, is to declare something of the Lord and to speak on behalf of the Lord. Such preaching may contain an element of prediction—for example, the prediction of eternal loss for those who refuse to believe in Christ—but such prediction is not the main element. In a general way, we can say that whenever we speak regarding the Lord or for the Lord, we are prophesying. How different this is from the common and traditional understanding of prophecy!

If we intend to be scriptural in a comprehensive way, we need to accept the biblical understanding of prophecy. To prophesy is not to gossip or to speak for ourselves. Furthermore, it is not to speak forth something of ourselves. On the contrary, to prophesy is to speak for the Lord and to speak forth something of the Lord. As we have pointed out, such speaking may have the aspect of prediction. One who speaks for the Lord may say, "The Lord Jesus is faithful, available, near, and dear. Whenever we call on Him, He immediately comes, and we have the deep sense of His sweetness. But if we do not practice calling on the name of the Lord, our daily living will be pitiful." To speak in this way is to prophesy.

In 1 Corinthians 14:31 Paul says, "For ye can all prophesy one by one, that all may learn, and all may be comforted" (Gk.). If prophecy were mainly a matter of predicting the future, how would it be possible for all the saints to prophesy? But we all can speak for the Lord and utter something of the Lord. Even the new ones and the young ones can prophesy like this.

THE WAY TO BE SPIRITUAL

The way to be spiritual is to speak for the Lord and concerning the Lord. The more we speak, the more we shall be filled in our spirit. However, if we remain silent, we shall find that we cannot be filled in spirit. In our daily living we need to be those who speak. We can speak concerning the Lord even when we are alone. If you speak in this way day by day, you will see that it produces in you a genuine spirituality and that it causes you to be filled in your spirit. When we have no other person to whom to speak, we can speak to our pets or even to inanimate objects. For example, you may say to a flower, "Little flower, you are very pretty. But your beauty is vanity. The real beauty is the Lord Jesus Christ." How important it is that we all learn to speak!

We especially need to speak in the meetings of the church. In 1 Corinthians 14:23 and 24 Paul says that if we all prophesy when the whole church comes together into one place, the unlearned one will be convinced of all and judged of all. In verse 25 he goes on to say, "And thus are the secrets of his heart made manifest; and so falling down on his face he will worship God, and report that God is among you of a truth" (Gk.). Many believers regard 1 Corinthians 14 as a chapter that deals with speaking in tongues. However, in this chapter more attention is given to prophesying than to tongues-speaking. In verse 3 Paul says that prophesying is for the building up, exhortation, and comfort of the saints. Furthermore, the one who prophesies builds up the church (v. 4).

The more we speak for the Lord, the more our inward being is filled with Him. Often the reason we are offended by others is that our soul is empty. We are not occupied in a proper way. But when we are filled through speaking of the Lord, our being will be properly occupied, and there will be no room for anything negative to come in to usurp us.

OUR SPIRIT SUBJECT TO US

Concerning this matter of speaking for the Lord, some believe that they should wait until the Spirit comes upon them. This was the practice in the Old Testament. But it is not the way revealed in the New Testament. In the Old Testament the Spirit of God came upon people, but the Spirit was not dwelling in them. In the New Testament age, however, as believers in Christ, we have the Spirit within us. Hence, there is no need to wait for the Spirit to come upon us. In 1 Corinthians 14:32 Paul says, "And the spirits of the prophets are subject to the prophets." Since our spirit is subject to us, there is no need for us to wait for inspiration. Why should we wait for the Spirit to come upon us when we already have the Spirit in our spirit? We should take the initiative to exercise our spirit, giving our spirit the command to act. Then we should speak, not according to our thought, but according to the sense deep within. Every believer in Christ can speak in this way. This is the reason Paul tells us that we all can prophesy.

BUBBLING OVER WITH THE LORD

In the meetings of the church we all need to speak for the Lord and regarding the Lord. Everyone should be bubbling over with the Lord. If this is the experience of every one of us, there will be no need for so much singing or preaching in the meetings. In many Christian meetings singing and preaching are used to fill up time. Without singing and preaching, there would be large gaps in those meetings. The situation among us in the Lord's recovery must be altogether different. We must be those who experience Christ, who live by Him, and who are filled in our spirit with Him. If we are filled with Christ in our spirit, we shall overflow by speaking of Christ and for Christ. Whenever we come to the meetings, we shall speak to one another of our experience and enjoyment of Christ. Of course, we shall still sing, but not because we have nothing else to do. We shall not use songs and hymns to fill the gaps caused by the shortage of speaking regarding Christ.

We need to labor on Christ day by day just as the children of Israel labored on the good land. Through their labor, they gained produce to offer to the Lord at the time of the feasts. When they came into the Lord's presence, they had something in their hands to present to Him. The principle is the same with respect to experiencing Christ. Because many Christians do not labor on Christ, they do not experience Him in their daily living. Thus, when they come to meetings, they have nothing of Christ to present to God or to share with the saints. They have nothing to speak on behalf of the Lord.

May the Lord be merciful to us in the church life that we may contact Him day by day and live according to the index of His inner being. If we live by Christ, we shall be filled in our spirit unto all the fullness of God. Then spontaneously we shall overflow by speaking for the Lord. Through this kind of speaking we shall offer Christ to God and share Him with one another. Meetings that are filled with this speaking of Christ will be the expression of the living Christ. In principle, this is the proper way to have the church meetings.

I believe that the time is coming when the meetings of the local churches will be carried out in this way. However, we can do this only through experiencing Christ in our daily living. Only when we experience Christ do we have something to speak for Christ.

TESTIMONIES OF CHRIST

Many of the testimonies given by Christians concern miracles or material blessings. Some may testify about a good job or about a physical healing. But this is not the kind of testimony we need in the church meetings. We need testimonies of the experience of Christ. For example, we need to hear testimonies about how the saints have experienced

Christ in a particular way, perhaps as their tenderness, meekness, or gentleness. Furthermore, we need testimonies about living and acting according to the index of the Lord's inward being. We must confess that as far as such testimonies are concerned, there is still a great shortage among us. May the Lord be merciful to us that we in the local churches will be rich in the experience of Christ. Day by day we need to experience Christ as our life, our person, and our everything. Then we shall be filled with Him and spontaneously speak of Him. I encourage all the saints to practice speaking for Christ and of Christ. The way to take the Lord into us is to speak of Him. The more we speak, the more we shall be filled with Him; and the more we are filled with Him, the more we shall speak of Him. May we all be filled with Christ and be overflowing with the riches of Christ.

LIFE-STUDY OF EPHESIANS

MESSAGE EIGHTY-FIVE

ORDINANCES AND THE CHURCH LIFE

Scripture Reading: Eph. 2:11-18; Gal. 6:15

The book of Ephesians reveals that God's economy is to work Christ into His chosen people to produce the church. This book also exposes certain negative things that damage the church life. According to our natural concept, we may expect Ephesians to emphasize such negative things as sin and worldliness. Although these are dealt with, they are not the main factors revealed in Ephesians as causes of damage to the church life.

We all easily recognize that sin is damaging. Without even reading the Bible, we have the knowledge that sin is a cause of corruption. Therefore, when we read about sin in the Scriptures, we readily understand, for the concept of sin is already in our natural mentality. However, it is contrary to our natural concept to say that ordinances are more damaging to the church life than sin is. The verses which speak of ordinances may make little impression on us because they do not correspond to anything already in our natural concept.

FOUR CATEGORIES OF NEGATIVE THINGS

What are the basic factors that damage the church life according to the revelation in the book of Ephesians? We have indicated that sin and worldliness, although certainly causes of damage, are not the basic negative factors in this book. In Ephesians there are four categories of negative things that damage the church life. The first of these is the ordinances. In 2:14 and 15 Paul says that Christ "has broken down the middle wall of partition, the enmity, having abolished in His flesh the law of the commandments in ordinances." The law of commandments contained in ordinances is a cause of enmity. With the ordinances there are regulations, and these regulations are the law of commandments. This gives rise to enmity. Today there is enmity even among good, spiritual Christians, enmity caused by ordinances regarding certain practices. For instance, there may be enmity between those who practice baptism by immersion and those who practice baptism by sprinkling. Related to these practices there are ordinances with their law of commandments. These ordinances are the first basic category of negative things that damage the church life.

The second category is doctrine. In 4:14 Paul says that we should "be no longer babes tossed by waves and carried about by every wind of teaching." The word teaching here refers to doctrine. Although Christians may regard doctrine as a positive thing, this verse clearly indicates that it can be used to carry us away from Christ. Any doctrine, even a scriptural one, that distracts the believers from Christ is a wind of teaching that carries them away from God's economy. Doctrine, therefore, can be used to destroy the Body life. If we intend to have the proper church life, we must recognize the damage doctrine has caused to the Body of Christ.

In chapter four Paul goes on to speak of the old man (v. 22), the third category of negative things that damage the church. The old man is of Adam, created by God, but fallen through sin. Because the old man causes so much damage to the church life, we must put off the old man in order to have the proper practice of the Body life.

In 5:27 we see the fourth negative category: the spots and wrinkles. Spots are related to the natural life, and the wrinkles are related to oldness. Both spots and wrinkles are capable of causing serious damage to the church life in a very subjective way. The glorious church that Christ will present to Himself will not have spot or wrinkle or any such things, but will be holy and without blemish.

Perhaps you have read the book of Ephesians a number of times without realizing that these four categories of things can cause great damage to the church life. You may have read this book without paying attention to the matters of ordinances, doctrines, the old man, and spots and wrinkles. I myself read Ephesians for years before I began to see the seriousness of these four things with respect to the church life. In this message we shall deal in particular with the ordinances.

BABEL, ORDINANCES, AND DIVISION

The primary source of the divisions among Christians throughout the centuries has been ordinances. We may trace these ordinances all the way back to the time of Babel. God's intention in His creation of man was for mankind to be one. This was the reason that He created just one man, not a multitude of men. God's desire was to have one corporate man. However, as a result of Babel, mankind was divided into nations, into a number of different peoples. Between these nations, these peoples, there are many differences. Not only are there differences in a general way between the Jews and the Gentiles, but there are also differences among the various nationalities, for example, between the Chinese and the Japanese, and between the Germans and the French. These differences have created divisions, and divisions are related to ordinances.

From the time of Babel, mankind has been divided by ordinances concerning the ways of living and worship. The source of this dividing work is the subtlety of the enemy, Satan. Through ordinances Satan has spoiled the oneness of the humanity created by God for the fulfillment of His purpose. Humanly speaking, it is not possible for the oneness of divided mankind to be restored. Although there is such an international organization as the United Nations, it is a fact that the nations are far from united. On the contrary, they are divided by ordinances.

One of the main elements of ordinances is language. As we all know, the division of the peoples at Babel was related to differences of language. Hence, a primary element of ordinances is language. If we can overcome the difficulty presented by language, a great part of our problem with ordinances will be solved.

On the day of Pentecost God Himself did something very significant concerning language. Peoples of different languages were saved and brought into oneness. On that day the divisions caused by language were overcome, and the church as the one new man came into existence. For the church to be the new man means that the church is a new mankind, a new humanity, a new human race. The old humanity God had created for Himself had become divided by ordinances. But on the day of Pentecost the church came into being as the new man, the new humanity.

THE MAIN CAUSE OF DIVISION

However, throughout the centuries ordinances have crept in to divide Christians. Especially from the time of the Reformation Christians have been divided by ordinances concerning practices. Some Christians have made baptism by immersion an ordinance. With this ordinance as their basis, they have formed the Baptist denomination. Others have done the same thing with respect to their belief about presbytery or eldership. With an ordinance related to eldership as their basis, they have formed the Presbyterian denomination. This kind of thing has occurred again and again. The main reason Christians are divided is the ordinances concerning different religious practices.

It is possible to have an ordinance about any practice. For example, we may have an ordinance about pray-reading. Although we find pray-reading helpful, we should not make an ordinance concerning it or insist that others practice it. Either to impose pray-reading on others or to oppose the practice of pray-reading is wrong. No matter how much life supply you receive through pray-reading, do not make an ordinance about pray-reading. Furthermore, do not allow your local church to become a pray-reading church. In other words, do not insist that all who attend the meetings practice pray-reading. To insist on pray-reading in this way is to be divisive.

It is the tendency of Christians to create ordinances related to those practices which they personally find helpful. For this reason, there are ordinances about practices such as foot-washing and about speaking in tongues. Those who advocate speaking in tongues may have an ordinance imposing it, but those who oppose speaking in tongues may have an ordinance forbidding it. It is by ordinances like these that Christians have been divided. Therefore, it is of vital importance that we receive all genuine Christians and not become divided over ordinances.

Christian groups sometimes adopt rather unusual practices. One Christian group in Taiwan has the peculiar practice of chair-shaking. In their meetings they often kneel down, take hold of the legs of chairs, and then shake the chairs. They think that this is the best way to be freed from the natural mind and to be filled with the Spirit. Simply because we may not agree with this practice does not give us the ground to criticize those who do. Many of the Christians in this chair-shaking group are noted for their prevailing preaching of the gospel among the mountain people in Taiwan. Furthermore, a number of professional people have been attracted to this group and then have received spiritual help. I certainly do not oppose this chair-shaking, but I do oppose any ordinances that may be formed regarding it.

On the one hand, we may see the error of denominations. On the other hand, we may see the truth of the ground of oneness—the truth of one church in one city. We may also have come together to meet as the church on the proper ground. However, although we may have seen the truth of the church ground and may be for this truth in a definite and practical way, we may still have our ordinances. If we do not drop these ordinances, we shall eventually have a problem concerning the oneness.

We must exercise ourselves not to have any ordinances. We must admit, however, that it is not easy for us to drop them. Some believers have ordinances about musical instruments. I know of a certain Brethren assembly that was divided over the use of a piano. Eventually, two groups came into existence, one favoring the piano and the other opposing it. Both groups were formed because of ordinances.

In the early days of the church life in Los Angeles, some saints had a problem over the playing of tambourines in the meetings. Some had an ordinance in favor of tambourines, whereas others had an ordinance in opposition to it. I found myself having to fight against both kinds of ordinances in the attempt to preserve the proper oneness. To one brother who strongly opposed the use of tambourines I said, "Please tell me, what is the difference in the eyes of God between playing a tambourine and playing a piano?" This brother admitted that in the eyes of God there was no difference. But he was quick to point out that as far as he was concerned, there was a difference. When I said that this difference was due to his background, he agreed, but still went on to oppose the use of tambourines. Eventually, the ordinances concerning tambourines kept a number of saints from participating in the church life. This is only one of the many illustrations we could give to prove that ordinances can ruin the church life.

For the sake of the church life, we should not have any ordinances concerning the way to meet. Simply be one with the church in your locality, regardless of their way of meeting. Be one with the church simply because it is the church. Do not oppose any particular practice, and do not impose any practice. Either to impose or to oppose is to bring in ordinances.

A NEW CREATION IN CHRIST

The Apostle Paul was very clear about ordinances, and he knew the futility of debating whether certain practices are right or wrong. During his time, there was a heated debate about circumcision. No doubt many said that Paul was not scriptural because he discontinued this practice. In Galatians 6:15 Paul uttered a very significant word related to this controversy: "For in Christ Jesus neither circumcision availeth any thing, nor uncircumcision, but a new creation" (Gk.). Paul realized that neither circumcision nor uncircumcision had anything to do with God's economy. The only thing that avails as far as God's economy is concerned is a new creation in Christ. To be a new creation is to have Christ wrought into our being.

Applying this principle to our situation today, we see that the crucial question is not what we do about chair-shaking, tongues-speaking, or pray-reading. It is altogether a matter of Christ wrought into us and making His home in our hearts. As in the time of Paul, the only thing that avails is a new creation in Christ Jesus.

We need to recognize the fact that God uses many different ways to bring people to Himself. Some may criticize the practice of speaking in tongues, but many believers have been helped by this. In like manner, certain saints in Taiwan are helped by shaking chairs. Who are we to condemn them for this or insist that they discontinue this practice? If certain ones desire to speak in tongues, we should not stop them. The same holds true of pray-reading or of any other practice, as long as it is not sinful. The church must be all-inclusive, receiving all genuine believers in Christ. Only in this way can we preserve the oneness.

CHRIST OUR ONLY SOURCE

To see the matter of one city, one church, is good, but it is not adequate. If we do not deal with our ordinances, we shall eventually be divided by our opinions or practices. Christ should be our only source. We should not allow anything of our background or culture to be our source. Otherwise, we shall bring in different ordinances according to our various backgrounds and cultures. Christ, not our ordinances, is the source of the church life.

If we did not love the Lord, division would not present such a serious problem, for we would probably all be distracted by worldly endeavors. But because we love the Lord, we also love the Bible and care for the truth of the Bible. As a result, disputes may arise concerning doctrine. Such disputes may lead further to division. In that case, we would repeat the history of divisive Christianity.

RETURNING TO THE GENUINE ONENESS

In the Lord's recovery we need to be brought out of every kind of division and return to the genuine oneness. However, if we see only the ground of oneness but not this matter of the ordinances, our oneness will not be secure. Rather, we may be in danger of again becoming sectarian or divisive. We may attempt to impose a particular practice on others in the church. To do this is to have ordinances. The church meetings must be general; they must not specialize in certain practices. If someone desires to speak in tongues, he should be free to do so. However, he should not try to make speaking in tongues the focal point of the meeting. Our oneness does not consist in practices; it is in Christ as everything. Insistence on certain practices damages our oneness. We should give the saints liberty without insisting on any particular practice. Then the oneness will be preserved.

As long as the saints in a locality are for the Lord and are standing on the proper ground of the church, we should be one with them. Instead of imposing any practice on them, we should minister the riches of Christ. What we need is to be strengthened into our inner man and filled with the riches of Christ unto all the fullness of God. Then instead of trying to adjust others or to correct them, we shall minister Christ to them. The Holy Spirit will always honor what is of Christ. If we supply Christ to others, the Spirit will honor this, and they will be helped. In this way we shall practice the church life in a proper way, free from the damage caused by ordinances.

LIFE-STUDY OF EPHESIANS

MESSAGE EIGHTY-SIX

SLAYING THE ORDINANCES

Scripture Reading: Eph. 2:11-22

It is easy to understand those parts of the Bible that correspond to our natural concept. For example, we readily understand those verses that tell us we are sinful, that we are sinners under God's condemnation, and that we are in need of God's forgiveness. However, in 2:11-22 there are a number of matters which do not fit in with our natural concept. For this reason, they are not adequately understood by most Christians when they read Ephesians.

NEAR IN THE BLOOD OF CHRIST

One matter that differs from our natural concept is found in verse 13. Here we are told that in Christ Jesus we "who once were far off have become near in the blood of Christ." To whom have we become near? We have become near both to God and to one another. However, the emphasis in this verse is that the very blood of Christ through which we have been redeemed, brought back, brings us near to one another. According to verse 12, when we were apart from Christ, we were "alienated from the commonwealth of Israel, and strangers from the covenants of the promise, having no hope and without God in the world." If we consider verse 13 in the light of verse 12, we shall realize that here the emphasis is upon becoming near to one another. Because we were fallen, we were far off from Christ, from the commonwealth of Israel, and from the covenants of God's promise. But the redeeming blood of Christ has brought us back. Hence, in this blood we have become near both to God and to God's people.

THE GOSPEL OF PEACE

Another unusual expression is in verse 17: "And coming, He preached the gospel of peace to you who were far off, and peace to those who were near." The subject of this verse is Christ, the One who broke down the middle wall of partition, abolished the law of the commandments in ordinances, and reconciled the Jews and the Gentiles in one Body to God through the cross (vv. 15-16). This very One came to preach the gospel of peace to us who were far off. This is the coming of Christ as the Spirit to preach the good news of the peace which He has accomplished through His cross. When Paul went to Ephesus, Christ went with him. Paul's going was Christ's going. Having come as the Spirit in Paul, Christ preached the gospel of peace.

According to this verse, Christ did not mainly preach forgiveness or salvation. Rather, He preached the gospel concerning peace among the peoples. Have you ever realized that such a peace is related to the gospel? The gospel of peace involves not only the peace between man and God, but especially the peace between one man and another. For example, there is a need for peace between Germans and French, and between Chinese and Japanese. Just as there was enmity between the Jews and the Gentiles at the time of Paul, so there is enmity among peoples today. Among the different nations there is no real peace. Instead there is enmity. Hence, there is an urgent need not only for the preaching of the gospel concerning forgiveness, justification, salvation, grace, and regeneration, but also for the preaching of the gospel of peace.

Before the foundation of the world, God chose people from various nations to be part of the one Body and the one new man. Under the sovereignty of God, these different people have been brought together in the church life. According to the natural constitution, it is not possible for Chinese to be one with Japanese or French to be one with Germans. The only way for the different peoples to be one is through receiving the gospel of peace. One day the Lord came and preached peace as the gospel to us. We realized as a result that we are now one with saints of every nationality and race. Today all who believe in Christ have one source, and this source is Christ Himself. Our source should no longer be our culture or nationality; it must be Christ and Christ alone. Once we were divided by our different sources, but now we are one in Christ as the unique source.

It is easy to talk about this matter, but it is difficult to put it into practice. On the cross Christ abolished all the ordinances, and then He came to us preaching the gospel of peace. However, after we were saved and brought into Christ as the one source, the ordinances returned.

BROUGHT BACK

In verses 11 and 12 Paul tells us to remember our situation before we were saved. He reminds us that we were Gentiles in the flesh, the ones "called uncircumcision by those who are called circumcision in the flesh made by hand." He also reminds us that we were apart from Christ, alienated from the commonwealth of Israel and strangers from the covenants of promise. We were without hope and without God in the world. Verse 13 opens with the words, "But now in Christ Jesus." These words denote a change of source. Formerly we were outside of Christ; now we are in Christ and with Christ. In Christ Jesus we who once were far off have become near in the blood of Christ.

Why does Paul mention the blood of Christ with respect to our being made near to one another? This reminds us that before we became near, we were among the fallen people. We needed to be redeemed, to be brought back by the precious blood of Christ. It was because of the fall that the human race was divided and scattered. Because we were fallen, we needed to be redeemed, to be brought back to God. Redemption has been accomplished through the blood of Christ. In this verse the blood signifies redemption. As the redeemed ones, we are now the brought-back ones. When we were fallen, we were divided and scattered. But having been redeemed by the precious blood of Christ, we have spontaneously become near not only to God but also to one another.

OUR PEACE

In verse 14 Paul goes on to say, "For He Himself is our peace." The word our refers to the different peoples, to the Jewish and Gentile believers. The peace spoken of here is not that between God and man, but that between one man and another. Having accomplished full redemption for us, Christ Himself is our peace, our harmony. After God called a chosen race out of fallen mankind, there was a separation between Israel and the nations. Through Christ's redemption, this separation has been removed. Therefore, in the redeeming Christ we all are one. For this reason Paul says that Christ "has made both one." The word both denotes the Jewish and Gentile believers.

CREATING ONE NEW MAN

In the remainder of verse 14 and in verse 15 Paul declares that Christ has broken down the middle wall of partition, the enmity, "having abolished in His flesh the law of the commandments in ordinances, that He might create the two in Himself into one new man, making peace." When Christ was crucified, all the ordinances were nailed to the cross. He broke down the middle wall of partition by abolishing the law of the commandments in ordinances. His goal in doing so was to create the Jews and the Gentiles "in Himself into one new man." By Christ's abolishing the ordinances and creating the Jewish and Gentile believers into one new man, peace was made between all believers. Once again we see that the peace in this portion of the Word is the peace among those who believe in Christ.

In verse 16 Paul speaks of the Jews and the Gentiles reconciled to God in one Body through the cross. Then in verse 17 he tells us that Christ preached the gospel of peace to those who were far off, that is, to the Gentiles, and to those who were near, that is, to the Jews. The result is that "through Him we both have access in one Spirit unto the Father" (v. 18). All the concepts contained in these verses are not to be found in our natural understanding. For this reason, we need to be enlightened by the Lord to apprehend them.

FELLOW-CITIZENS AND MEMBERS

In verse 19 Paul continues, "So then you are no longer strangers and sojourners, but you are fellow-citizens of the saints and members of the household of God." The phrase "fellow-citizens of the saints" indicates the kingdom of God, and the phrase "members of the household of God" indicates the house, the family, of God. On the one hand, we are citizens of the kingdom; on the other hand, we are members of the household. The household is a matter of life and enjoyment, whereas the kingdom is a matter of right and responsibility.

ALL DIFFERENCES REMOVED BY THE CROSS

The point we are burdened to emphasize in this message is that on the cross Christ has slain all the ordinances. These ordinances were related to the differences between the peoples. Many Christians know that on the cross Christ dealt with sin, the flesh, the self, the old man, the world, and the Devil. But not many also realize that on the cross Christ dealt with the ordinances. Hallelujah, all the ordinances have been slain! How we thank Him for revealing this to the churches in His recovery! The cross has dealt with sin so that we may be saved; with the world, the old man, the flesh, and the self, so that we may be sanctified; and with the Devil, Satan, that we may be victorious. Now we see that the cross has also slain the ordinances so that we may be one new man.

Although we are different as far as physical characteristics are concerned, actually there should no longer be any difference among those in the one new man. According to Colossians 3:11, in the new man "there cannot be Greek and Jew, circumcision and uncircumcision, barbarian, Scythian, slave, freeman, but Christ is all and in all." Not only is there no natural person in the new man, but there is no possibility for there to be any natural person. In the new man there is only one person—Christ who is all and in all. The differences between the peoples have been removed by the cross. What a wonderful gospel this is! The ordinances that once divided the peoples have been abolished, and now we have true peace. We are no longer strangers—we are fellow-citizens of the saints. We are no longer sojourners—we are members of the household of God. We all are citizens of God's kingdom and "folks" in God's family.

This revelation is made real to us in the mingled spirit. In the spirit we are one new man in Christ. But if we consider our situation by analyzing in the mind, the natural differences will become apparent once again. Those from a certain country or region may regard themselves as superior to others. This will give all the others a sense that they are strangers. The same thing is true whenever those from a particular local church regard their church as superior. If we would be faithful to the vision in this portion of the Word, we need to remain in the spirit where we shall experience the genuine building up with others. Paul's concluding point in this chapter is that both universally and locally the church must be built up as God's dwelling place in spirit.

MINISTERING LIFE IN ALL KINDS OF MEETINGS

Concerning the meetings, we should not hold on to any ordinances. We may enjoy releasing our spirit in a particular way, but we should not insist that others follow that way. Even if the meetings in certain localities are very different from those to which we are accustomed, we should still be able to minister life and supply the riches of Christ to others. Furthermore, we should also be willing to receive help from others. In this way we shall have true fellowship and experience a mutual supply.

We should not even allow the terminology with which we are familiar to be a hindrance to fellowship. Other Christians may not be familiar with the word economy. In such a case, it may be better for us to speak of God's will than about

God's economy. We may share with others that God's will is to work Christ into us. We may prove our point by quoting Ephesians 3:17, a verse which speaks about Christ making His home in our hearts.

We should always focus our attention on Christ and not become involved in disputes over doctrines or practices. Admittedly, it takes a great deal of learning and experience to know how to minister Christ to others in this way. Nevertheless, it is important for us to learn how to adapt to meetings that differ from our own and how to function in those meetings properly. For example, if those in a certain locality have the practice of offering long prayers or giving long testimonies, we should simply follow their way, not insist on short and quick prayers and testimonies. If, however, we insist on our way of praying or testifying, we may offend others and cause them to think unnecessarily that we are strange or peculiar.

It is important for all of us to learn to minister life in all kinds of Christian meetings. We should never despise the ways of meeting that are different from ours. On the contrary, in any meeting we should be able to dispense into the saints the riches of Christ. If in our experience we have truly slain all the ordinances, we shall be able to do this. For the sake of oneness and for the ministry of life, we shall be able to adapt to the way practiced by others in their meetings.

Do not think that simply because those in a particular locality emphasize the Pentecostal gifts, they are not a proper local church. As long as they have the standing of the church, they are the church in that locality, even if the meetings are filled with the activities often associated with Pentecostalism. If they are genuine Christians who have seen the way of the church and have begun to practice the church life, we must recognize them as the church. Their meetings may differ from ours, but that does not mean that they are not the church in that locality. If you insist that they are not a genuine local church, they may say the same thing about the church in your locality. If you are involved in arguments about the way to meet, you may claim that your way is right, but they may insist that their practice is correct. To be entangled in such arguments is to be involved in ordinances once again. If we hold on to certain ordinances and insist on certain practices, we immediately become sectarian. Therefore, for the proper church life, we must set aside all the ordinances and concentrate on ministering Christ to the saints.

THE CHURCH LIFE WITHOUT ORDINANCES

We in the Lord's recovery have no intention to form another denomination. Rather, we need to be rescued from all divisiveness and receive all genuine Christians. In the meetings we may practice pray-reading and calling on the name of the Lord, but we should not allow either of these practices to become ordinances. Perhaps in the years to come the Lord will give us something new related to the release of the spirit. Regarding our faith in Christ and our belief in the Bible, we cannot change. But as far as the way to meet, we should always be open to receive something new and better from the Lord. In this way we shall practice the church life without ordinances.

LIFE-STUDY OF EPHESIANS

MESSAGE EIGHTY-SEVEN

THE ORDINANCES VERSUS CHRIST

Scripture Reading: Eph. 2:11-22

THE CROSS DEALING WITH THE ORDINANCES

Ephesians 2 is an important chapter because it reveals that Christ died on the cross in order to create in Himself one new man. For the new man to come into being, the law of the commandments in ordinances had to be abolished. Christians realize that on the cross Christ dealt with sin, the old man, the flesh, the world, and the Devil, Satan. But very few Christians have seen that on the cross Christ also dealt with the ordinances.

It is rather easy to understand that the cross of Christ deals with sin. It is also easy to realize that the old man and the flesh are problems that are dealt with by the cross. In like manner, when we read in the New Testament that the death of Christ has also dealt with the world and with Satan, we have no problem with understanding these truths. However, we may not realize that ordinances also present a serious problem.

Ordinances are related to different ways of living and worship. They do not appear to be negative. On the contrary, they seem quite good. For example, some ordinances are related to table manners. Who can say it is not good to be properly regulated when we eat? However, different peoples have different kinds of table manners. Therefore, regulations concerning table manners can be a source of division and enmity between peoples.

Ordinances are involved in the matter of worship. The Jews worship God according to their ordinances, and the

Moslems worship according to their ordinances. This is also true with the various denominations today. Because ordinances seem helpful, it is difficult to recognize that they also need to be dealt with by the cross.

REDEMPTION IN RELATION TO GOD'S PURPOSE

The fall of mankind was the source of all ordinances. If man had not fallen, there would be no ordinances today. After God created man, He did not give him a list of ordinances. But as soon as man fell, the ordinances began to come in. Then, at Babel, the man created by God for His purpose became divided and scattered into a number of races and nations which began to fight against one another. This made it impossible for God's eternal plan to be fulfilled.

If we view the redemption of Christ from the angle of God's purpose, our concept of redemption will be broadened. Most Christians view Christ's redemption only from the perspective of their personal salvation. They are not concerned with the fulfillment of God's purpose, but are concerned only with being saved from hell and assured of spending eternity in heaven. Their concept of Christ's death on the cross is extremely narrow. It is crucial for us to see that God's eternal purpose is to dispense Himself into man and to become one with man in order to express Himself through man. But Satan has sought to frustrate the fulfillment of God's purpose by damaging humanity through dividing it into different peoples who war against one another. Christ came to redeem fallen mankind in order that God's purpose may be fulfilled, not merely that we may be saved from hell and assured of heaven. In order to redeem divided mankind, Christ died on the cross to deal with all the negative things, including ordinances. On the cross Christ abolished all the regulations regarding living and worship, regulations that have divided the nations. God does not care for any ordinances. He cares only that we are one and that Christ is wrought into us. Christ abolished all the ordinances not that we may go to heaven or that we may be spiritual or victorious. He abolished the ordinances in order to create in

Himself one new corporate man. He created the new man not only within Himself as the sphere, but also with Himself as the very element. By abolishing the ordinances and creating the Jewish and Gentile believers into one new man, Christ has made peace. Now those of different nationalities have peace in Christ.

IN CHRIST

In 2:11 and 12 Paul reminds us of our situation when we were apart from Christ. We were alienated from the commonwealth of Israel, we were strangers from the covenants of the promise, we had no hope, and we were without God in the world. We had no goal and no God. But one day we were called by God, and we answered His call by calling on the name of the Lord Jesus. When we did this, the Triune God came into us. No matter where we may go, even if we try to run from the Lord or to stop believing in Him, He will always be with us. How wonderful that we have become involved with Christ! However, even when it does not seem so wonderful in our experience, we cannot get away from Him. We may try to leave Him, but He will never leave us.

As saved ones, we are in Christ. He is our sphere and our source. Now in Christ Jesus we who once were far off from God and from one another have become near in the blood of Christ. As verse 14 says, the very Christ who is our peace has made us one and has broken down the middle wall of partition. He has reconciled us to God in one Body, and He has come to preach to us the gospel of peace (vv. 16-17). The result is that we are no longer strangers and sojourners, but fellow-citizens of the saints and members of the household of God (v. 19).

Although Christ is our sphere, our source, and our peace and although He has abolished the ordinances, many Christians still hold to certain ordinances. In their practice, they care more for ordinances than for Christ. Many Christians neglect Christ and pay attention to the very ordinances He abolished on the cross. What a pitiful situation!

BUILT ON CHRIST AS THE FOUNDATION

Now we are in Christ. He should be the unique foundation upon which we are built. In 2:20 Paul speaks of the foundation of the apostles and prophets. This refers to the Christ in whom the apostles believed and whom they ministered to others. The foundation of Moses was the law, and the foundation of the prophets was prophecy. But the only foundation of the apostles and prophets is Christ. In 1 Corinthians 3:11 Paul said, "For other foundation can no man lay than that is laid, which is Jesus Christ." The foundation in Ephesians 2 is not related to any kind of ordinances; it is Christ Himself. The foundation of Judaism is composed of the Sabbath, circumcision, and the dietary regulations. But when the apostles came forth to minister, the unique foundation laid by them was the living Christ.

The church is built on Christ, not on ordinances or regulations. Today, however, all the denominations have another foundation besides Christ. For example, the Baptist denomination has immersion as a foundation along with Christ. It seems that underneath Christ as the foundation the denominations have something other than Christ as their basic foundation. The church has been divided by the different ordinances used as foundations.

May the Lord open our eyes to see how dreadful it is to cling to ordinances. We may claim to see the church, and we may declare that we are meeting as the local church. But if we still insist on particular practices, those practices will become ordinances. Spontaneously, the ground of oneness will be damaged or even lost. Instead of meeting on the ground of oneness, we shall meet on the ground of our ordinances. If a certain ordinance becomes our ground, we cease to be the church and become a sect. Whenever we insist on a particular practice, we lose the unique ground of oneness. This is why we should not insist on things such as pray-reading or calling on the name of the Lord, even though we may receive great benefit from them.

THINGS WE MUST OPPOSE

There are only a few things we must oppose. These include idolatry, immorality, divisiveness, and the denial of Christ's deity. In the church absolutely no ground can be given to idols. Idolatry is an insult to God. Likewise, the church cannot tolerate immorality, which damages the humanity created by God for His purpose. Furthermore, a factious, sectarian person must be rejected if he does not cease from his divisiveness after being warned. Fourthly, we cannot receive into the church anyone who refuses to recognize the deity of Christ, who denies that Christ is God incarnate. These things are leaven which must be purged out of the church life. But apart from these four things, we are not told in the New Testament to reject believers for any other reason. According to Romans 14:1, as long as a person has the faith, we must receive him, even if he is weak. Nowhere in the New Testament are we instructed to reject someone if he does not believe in immersion. Neither are we told not to receive those sisters who do not wear head coverings. Believers should not be rejected over things such as the size of cup used at the Lord's table or over the practice of foot-washing. Apart from the four things we have mentioned, there is no legality in the church life. We must receive all the saints and have nothing to do with ordinances.

The Christ who is our peace, our source, and our sphere must be our unique foundation. There must not be any other kind of foundation in addition to Christ. We need to check with ourselves concerning this. Do we have any foundation in addition to Christ? If we do not have any ordinances, then Christ will truly be our only foundation.

THE CORNERSTONE

Christ should also be our cornerstone. As the cornerstone, He joins the two walls, the one of the Jewish believers and the other of the Gentile believers. In Ephesians 2 Christ is referred to specifically as the cornerstone (v. 20). When the Jewish builders rejected Christ, they rejected Him as the cornerstone (Acts 4:11; 1 Pet. 2:7), which would join the Gentiles to them for the building of God's house.

If we hold only to the all-inclusive Christ, not to any ordinances, He will be the cornerstone to join us together for the building of God's dwelling place.

THE UNIVERSAL CHURCH AND THE LOCAL CHURCH

In verse 21 Paul goes on to say, "In Whom all the building, being fitted together, is growing into a holy temple in the Lord." In Christ who is the cornerstone, all the building, including both Jewish and Gentile believers, is fitted together and is growing into a holy temple. This temple is the universal church. As we shall see, verse 22 refers to the local church.

The local churches should not have an independent attitude, and they should not be isolated from one another. If we have an independent attitude, we may become a local sect instead of a local church. Christ has just one Body in the universe. If each local church were an independent body for Christ, this would mean that Christ has a great many bodies. No matter how many local churches there may be, Christ still has just one Body. For this reason, the local churches need to be fitted together and to grow into the one universal temple. In Christ as the foundation and the cornerstone, all the building, the universal church, is fitted together and is growing in the Lord.

Some of those who have an attitude of independence concerning the church in their locality may point to the differences between the seven churches in Revelation 2 and 3 as a justification for their attitude. However, the seven churches as the seven golden lampstands are the same in nature, substance, and pattern. Furthermore, the New Jerusalem in eternity will have the same appearance and the same material on each of its four sides. The local churches should not be organized. But if all the churches hold only Christ, they will be fitted together as God's universal building.

Suppose the churches in a certain place hold the attitude

that, as independent local churches, they want to go on by themselves and have nothing to do with other churches. In the eyes of the Lord, they may become local sects. All the churches should hold to Christ, be fitted together, and grow together into a holy temple in the Lord. When the churches are fitted together, whatever riches are experienced by one church will be spontaneously transfused into all the other churches. For example, a doctor may inject something into a person's arm, but the injected element is soon transfused throughout the person's body. In this way the whole body receives the benefit of the injection. How foolish it would be for certain members of the body to regard the injection as only for themselves! Whatever one church receives is for the whole Body. Therefore, we should not try to confine any experience of Christ to our locality. We should realize that whatever we receive of Christ is to be transfused into the rest of the Body.

In verse 22 Paul says, "In Whom you also are being built together into a dwelling place of God in spirit." The word "also" here indicates that the building in verse 21 is universal and that the building in this verse is local. According to the context, the holy temple in verse 21 is universal, whereas the dwelling place of God in verse 22 is local.

PUTTING OUR TRUST IN CHRIST

After all we have said about not holding to the ordinances but holding to Christ, some may still have questions about things such as the method of baptism. These questions may indicate that those who ask them still have ordinances. Nevertheless, some may persist with their questions by saying that we need to be practical and must know how to baptize new converts. Whenever we face practical problems such as this, we should remember Paul's word in verse 18: "For through Him we both have access in one Spirit unto the Father." Instead of arguing, we should turn to our spirit, pray, and have fellowship. The Lord is near, present, and available. If we seriously seek His leading, He will certainly guide us, and we shall know how to take care of the various practical matters. I can testify that throughout the years the Lord Jesus has been very real, precious, present, and available to us. We simply need to open ourselves to Him regarding everything that concerns us. As we do so, we should be willing to set aside any concept that occupies us. Then the Lord will lead us in a living way.

In our concern for the church, we should remember that Christ nourishes and cherishes the church. He is much more concerned about the church than we are. Therefore, we should place our trust in Him. As long as we do not have anything related to idolatry, immorality, divisiveness, or the denial of the deity of Christ, none of the mistakes that may be made will be serious. Do not try to avoid mistakes by holding to ordinances. Our confidence should be in the all-inclusive Christ and in Him alone. If our trust is in anything other than Christ, that thing will become an ordinance which will damage the church life. But if we take Christ as our everything, all the local churches throughout the world will grow and go on in a healthy way.

LIFE-STUDY OF EPHESIANS

MESSAGE EIGHTY-EIGHT

UNIVERSAL BUILDING AND LOCAL BUILDING

Scripture Reading: Eph. 2:21-22

Chapter two of Ephesians concludes with the matter of the building. In verse 21 we see the universal building, and in verse 22, the local building. Verse 21 says, "In Whom all the building, being fitted together, is growing into a holy temple in the Lord." The phrase "all the building" denotes the universal building, the church throughout the universe. The words "in Whom you also" in verse 22 denote the local building, the building among those in the city to which this Epistle was sent. The building, therefore, has a universal aspect and a local aspect. It is significant that this chapter of Ephesians concludes with the building of the church in these two aspects.

For centuries, this matter of the building has been neglected. Very few servants of the Lord have given it adequate attention. Beginning in 1938, among us the Lord began to emphasize the importance of the building. Message after message has been given on this crucial subject. Among them are the messages printed in *The Vision of God's Building*. The messages in that book cover God's building as revealed from the beginning of the Bible to the end.

FORSAKING ALL ORDINANCES

If we would be built up universally and locally, we must forsake all ordinances. To hold to certain ordinances is to build without a proper foundation, that is, without Christ as the unique foundation. Many Christians are not clear about Christ as the unique foundation, and they do not know God's building. Therefore, they have spent years wandering from one denomination or Christian group to another. Such believers may be stones for God's building, but they have not yet been built in. Some church-traveling Christians may claim that the reason for their wandering from group to group is a sense of dissatisfaction. However, the underlying reason is ordinances.

Ordinances may be related to our natural disposition. Some have a quiet disposition and prefer Christian meetings where the believers worship in silence. They wander from group to group in quest of a meeting to match their disposition. They may think that a particular group suits their taste, only to learn that certain practices there do not match their disposition. Such Christians are not satisfied with any group. They cannot find a group that is fully in accord with their disposition.

If we have seen a clear vision of God's economy and know what the recovery is, we shall be willing to forget our disposition, to deny our taste, and to care only for the Lord's recovery. The recovery is not based on any practice; it is based on Christ who is our peace, our foundation, our cornerstone, and our everything. The vision of God's economy must control us, direct us, and restrict us. Such a vision will surely cause us to stand on Christ as the unique foundation. Then instead of being wandering stars (Jude 13), we shall be those who can be built up with others. We shall be eternally settled in God's economy. Those who have seen this vision and are governed by it can be built up with others on the unique foundation of the all-inclusive Christ. They will not allow any ordinances to become their foundation.

Once again I wish to use pray-reading as an example. We thank the Lord for pray-reading. Although we have not made pray-reading an ordinance, some have left the church life simply because they did not care for this practice. Do you think that someone who leaves the church for such a reason has truly seen what the church is? I do not think so. One who has seen the vision of the church will never leave.

Some Christians have criticized us not only for the practice of pray-reading, but also for praising the Lord loudly, for calling on the name of the Lord Jesus, and for allowing believers to be baptized again, that is, to be "buried." Others have criticized us for emphasizing the fact that Christ is versus religion. If we in the local churches have something related to idols, immorality, division, or the denial of the deity of Christ, we should be criticized. However, it is wrong to criticize us for such things as pray-reading the Word or calling on the name of the Lord Jesus. If believers are helped spiritually by these practices, what right have others to criticize them? Those who do not follow these practices should nevertheless be one with those who receive benefit by following them. Suppose a certain brother is convicted of his oldness and deadness and is led of the Lord to bury himself in the waters of baptism. After his burial, he is refreshed, renewed, and living. He may even praise the Lord in a loud, excited way. Should he be condemned because he was baptized a second time or because he praises the Lord with a loud voice? Certainly not! Nevertheless, some believers may criticize such a one because they still have ordinances related to baptism or to loud praises.

Many years ago there was a certain Presbyterian pastor who was the top theologian in China. As a Presbyterian, in his teaching he should have opposed the practice of immersion and favored sprinkling. However, as he was praying one day on a mountain, he experienced the outpouring of the Holy Spirit. As he was running down the mountainside, he saw a pool of water and threw himself into it. After that experience, he became a different person, very living in the Lord. Those who hold to ordinances may criticize him. But the Lord does not honor ordinances. In Christ neither circumcision nor uncircumcision avails anything, only a new creation (Gal. 6:15).

CARING ONLY FOR CHRIST

Although there are millions of Christians on earth today, very few have been built up with others. The reason for this lack of building is that so many believers still hold on to ordinances. Perhaps you were a member of a certain denomination. However, because of your ordinances, you were not one with others, and you were not able to be built up with them. Rather, you were waiting for the situation to change to fit your ordinances. When there was no change or improvement, you moved to another group, hoping to find there a situation to suit your preference. This has caused many to travel from one denomination to another. Some have testified that they were not satisfied until they came into the church life. Although it is true that we are satisfied spiritually in the church, we must be careful not to hold to any ordinances. In our experience Christ must be everything to us: our peace, our foundation, our cornerstone. We should not care for anything other than Christ. Whether the meetings are noisy or quiet makes no difference. We are not for noise or for silence—we are for Christ. By caring only for Christ, we can easily be one with others and be built up with them locally and universally on Christ as the unique foundation.

Recently I have been burdened of the Lord to give a number of messages dealing with ordinances. I believe that the Spirit of the Lord within us realizes how important it is for us to be clear about this matter. As more saints turn to the way of the Lord's recovery, it is possible for ordinances to be brought in or for dissenting opinions to be expressed. Therefore, it is crucial that we learn to care only for Christ, particularly as we visit localities where the way of meeting differs from that to which we are accustomed. We should not evaluate a meeting according to whether or not the saints practice pray-reading, exercise tongues-speaking, or pray long prayers or short ones. We should care for Christ and for Christ alone. If we care only for Christ, we shall not have any problems with oneness. The more we care for Christ and drop all manner of ordinances, the more we shall be built up in Christ locally and also universally.

NO ORGANIZATION

In speaking of the universal building, we must be careful to distinguish such building from organization. Although we are absolutely for the proper building, we are opposed to organization. The churches will be built together universally, but this does not mean that they will be universally organized.

NO ISOLATION

According to the truth of the Body, the Body is universally one. For this reason, the local churches should not be isolated from one another. Isolation is contrary to the truth concerning the oneness of the Body. Because each local church is part of the Body universally, no local church should be isolated from the others. This is especially true today with modern means of communication and transportation that permit the rapid spread of news and information around the world. Something of life may be released in Los Angeles today and be known in dozens of other places within hours. How wrong it is for a church to try to be independent! The Body is receiving a continual transfusion. If we isolate ourselves from the other churches, we cut ourselves off both from the transfusion and from the circulation of life in the Body. Such a thing violates the law of the Body. Although we must shun organization, we need to be built up universally as the one Body.

BUILT UP IN CHRIST

In 2:22 Paul speaks of the local building: "In Whom you also are being built together into a dwelling place of God in spirit." The word "you" refers to the local saints. Furthermore, the word "also" indicates that the building in verse 22 is local. According to the context, the dwelling place of God in this verse is local, whereas the holy temple in the preceding verse is universal.

Paul is careful to point out that it is in Christ that the local saints are built together into a dwelling place of God in spirit. They are not built in ordinances, in practices, or in opinions. We can be built up only in the all-inclusive Christ who is our peace, foundation, and cornerstone.

UNIVERSAL BUILDING ACCOMPLISHED ONLY THROUGH LOCAL BUILDING

It is important to see that the universal building can be accomplished only through the local building. If we are not built up with others in our own locality, we should not expect to be able to be built up in any other locality. All those who are burdened to migrate for the spread of the church life must firstly be built up in their own locality. If you have not yet been built up in your local church, I encourage you not to migrate. Before we can be built up universally, we must be built up in a practical way locally.

If you have been in a locality for a period of time without being built up with others, there must be a reason for this lack of building. The reason may be your natural cleverness or your reservations concerning the church life. Yes, you have stopped wandering from group to group, and you have come into the church life to stay. However, in order for you to be built up locally, your disposition, your being, must be dealt with. Nothing tests your spiritual maturity as much as this matter of building. Furthermore, the local building is a great help in your spiritual growth. If you are willing to be built into the church in your locality, you will have the abundance of the growth in life. The building must begin with the local aspect and then spread to the universal aspect. Some saints have not grown very much because they have not been built into the church locally. The reason for the lack of building is that they have too many reservations. Although they are in the local church, they have the tendency to withdraw or to hold back when certain situations arise in the church. It is this holding back that keeps them from being built up. Instead of withdrawing or holding back, we should be willing to be broken and even "wrecked" in order to be built up with others. What a difference this makes to our growth in life! If we grow in this way, the church life will spread both through us and with us, and we shall be useful in any coming migration. However, if we are not built up locally, we shall not be a help to any future migration. Only those who have been built up locally can support the spread of the church life through migration. Any who have reservations about the church, yet who desire to participate in a migration, will be a cause of frustration.

THE SPREAD OF THE LORD'S RECOVERY

The spread of the Lord's recovery is the move of the living Christ in our spirit in a corporate way. The Lord's move is with the saints not individualistically, but corporately. As those who seek the Lord, we should not hold anything back from Him. On the contrary, we should always give in to Him and be willing to be broken so that we may be built into the church in our locality. Then wherever we may be, the recovery of the Lord will spread through us. This is altogether different from a movement of man or an organization. For the genuine move of Christ as the life-giving Spirit in His Body, we need the local building.

We thank the Lord for the many churches raised up through migration. We also thank Him for the many who have been useful in migration because they had experienced some amount of local building before they migrated. At the same time, we must admit that there has been some frustration in certain places. The reason for this frustration is that certain ones still have reservations. They still have the tendency to hold back from the church life. This underscores the fact that the success of migration depends on the degree of building. If we are built up in an absolute way, migration will proceed also in an absolute way. But if we compromise with the local building, we shall also compromise in any future migration.

In conclusion, I wish to emphasize again that how much building we have universally as well as locally depends on how much we give up the ordinances and realize in a practical way that Christ is everything in God's economy. Since He is the all-inclusive One, we should not hold on to anything in place of Him. If we hold to Christ as everything to us, we shall experience the genuine building, first locally and then universally. This will make us useful in migration for the expansion of the church life.

LIFE-STUDY OF EPHESIANS

MESSAGE EIGHTY-NINE

GROWTH BY FEEDING FOR THE BUILDING

Scripture Reading: Eph. 4:11-16; Rom. 14:1-3, 5-6; 16:17; 1 Cor. 5:9-11; Titus 3:10; 2 John 7, 9-11

God created mankind for the fulfillment of His eternal purpose. However, through the fall, mankind was divided and scattered. When Christ died on the cross to accomplish redemption, He slew all the ordinances in order to bring His chosen people back into oneness and to create in Himself one new man. However, the enemy, Satan, has used ordinances to divide the new man Christ has created. The divisions, denominations, and sects in Christianity have their source in these ordinances.

THE CAUSE OF DIVISION

Today the Lord is seeking to recover His church by bringing His people out of the divisions. To be brought out of division is to be brought out of ordinances as the source of division. Therefore, in order to recover the church, the Lord must cause His people to set aside the ordinances that have been the cause of division. If we are not clear about this matter of ordinances, we may bring ordinances into the church life and cause a repetition of the divisiveness that has occurred in the history of Christianity. We do not want the history of Christianity to be repeated among us in the Lord's recovery.

Certain dear ones who love the Lord's recovery may not be clear about ordinances. If they insist on practices that correspond to their ordinances, they will cause problems in the churches. Although we may see the ground of the church, we cannot be in the church life in a secure way until we have a thorough understanding of ordinances. It is not sufficient simply to forsake divisions. We also need to recognize that ordinances are the source of division.

As the Lord's recovery spreads throughout the world, people with different backgrounds will be brought in. Since there is no organization nor human control in the recovery, it is possible in certain places for saints to insist on various practices. If this should happen, the church life would be seriously damaged through division. Therefore, I encourage you all to bring this matter of ordinances to the Lord. Ask Him to make you crystal clear about the seriousness of having ordinances in the church life. No ground whatever can be given to the insistence upon any practice. For the building up of the church we must be willing to drop all ordinances.

ORDINANCES AND DOCTRINE

We have pointed out that in Ephesians, a book concerned not with personal salvation but with the church in a corporate way, there are at least four categories of things that damage the church life: ordinances, doctrine, the old man, and the spots and wrinkles. After a number of messages concerning ordinances, we come now to the subject of doctrine. Most doctrines are based on ordinances, and ordinances are produced from doctrines. It is difficult to say which comes first, doctrines or ordinances. On the one hand, doctrines produce ordinances, but, on the other hand, ordinances provide the basis for doctrine. Nevertheless, we can be clear that these two matters are intimately related and cannot be separated.

THE NEED FOR HUMAN COOPERATION

Chapter one of Ephesians speaks of the Body, the fullness of the One who fills all in all. Chapter two speaks of the one new man and concludes with a word about God's building. For the sake of the new man, God is dispensing Himself into His chosen people, as revealed in chapter three. All Three of the Godhead are involved in this dispensation. We are strengthened by the Spirit into the inner man, so that

Christ may make His home in our hearts, with the result that we are filled unto all the fullness of God. In 3:8 Paul speaks of the riches of Christ. If the new man is to be built up as the habitation of God in spirit, surely the riches of Christ need to be dispensed into every part of this new man. In order for such a dispensation to take place, the inner man of all those who make up the one new man must be strengthened by the Spirit. Then Christ with all His riches will be able to make His home in our hearts. Eventually, the new man will be filled unto all the fullness of God. This indicates that the new man will be a God-filled man, a corporate entity mingled with the Triune God.

Chapter three of Ephesians ends with the new man filled unto all the fullness of God. This, however, is not the end of the book. There is still the need for human cooperation. Although Christ has abolished all the ordinances in order to create the new man, the church as the new man still needs to be built up. Christ does not build the church directly. Rather, He uses the apostles, prophets, evangelists, and shepherds and teachers to perfect the saints to carry out the direct building up of the church. As the Head, Christ presents certain gifts to His Body for the perfecting of the saints. Having been perfected through the ministry of these gifts, the saints build the church directly. Hence, the church is not directly built by Christ or by the apostles, prophets, evangelists, shepherds and teachers; it is built directly by the perfected saints. This indicates that the building of the church requires the cooperation of God's people.

Some readers of Ephesians may think that Paul should have stopped at the end of chapter three. According to their opinion, the end of this chapter is the high point and completion of the book. They see only the fact that Christ has accomplished everything. Yes, Christ has been incarnated, has passed through human life, and has died on the cross to accomplish redemption and to deal with all negative things, including ordinances. After His all-inclusive death, He rested in the tomb. This rest was a true Sabbath. Then on the first day of the week He was resurrected from among the dead, and a new age with a new humanity came into being. On God's side, everything has been accomplished. But in His economy God requires human cooperation. His economy is based on the principle of incarnation, that is, of God and man mingled and working together to accomplish God's goal. In John 15 the Lord Jesus said, "Apart from Me you can do nothing" (v. 5). However, it is also true that apart from us Christ can do nothing. We can tell the Lord, "Lord Jesus, just as I need You, You also need me. We can do nothing without You, and You can do nothing without us." If we would speak to the Lord in this way, He would agree. The very fact that Christ was incarnated indicates that God's economy has both the divine aspect and the human aspect.

This principle applies to the book of Ephesians. The first three chapters emphasize the divine aspect. These chapters reveal that Christ has accomplished everything and that the new man has been filled with the riches of Christ unto all the fullness of God. Then in chapters four through six we see the human aspect, the aspect of our cooperation with the Lord. Hallelujah, we need God, and God needs us! If we fail to cooperate with Him, we cause a serious problem. Therefore, it is crucial that we fulfill our responsibility to cooperate with God in the carrying out of His economy.

NOT MERE TEACHING, BUT GROWTH

Many Christians think that what is mainly needed on the human side is teaching. Yes, in chapter four Paul does mention shepherds and teachers. However, the concept here is altogether different from the religious concept in today's Christianity. Christianity has become a religion of doctrine. No other religion in the world has as many doctrines as Christianity has. Consider how many books are put out by Christian writers every year. Surely no other religion can equal it in the number of books published annually. Most of these books merely feed the desire for doctrinal talk. Furthermore, most of these books are related to ordinances. Because someone favors a particular practice, he writes a book in order to advocate it.

Paul's concept in Ephesians 4 is absolutely different from the concept in today's Christianity. The basic concept in this chapter is that of growth until we all arrive at a full-grown man. As all mothers know, growth of children comes by feeding, not mainly by teaching. When we all arrive at a full-grown man, we shall no longer be children spiritually. On the human side the main need is not doctrine; it is growth. We need to grow until we arrive at a full-grown man.

We need to become a full-grown man so that "we may be no longer babes tossed by waves and carried about by every wind of teaching in the sleight of men, in craftiness with a view to a system of error" (4:14). Notice that here Paul does not speak of every wind of heresy or false doctrine, but of every wind of teaching. Such teaching may include sound, fundamental, scriptural doctrine. However, even this kind of doctrine may be used by the sleight of men in craftiness with a view to a system of error. Any teaching, even a scriptural one, that distracts believers from Christ and the church is a wind that carries them away from God's central purpose. Teachings that distract us from God's economy are instigated by Satan in his subtlety with the sleight of men, in order to frustrate the building up of the Body of Christ. The teachings systematized by Satan cause serious error and thus damage the practical oneness of the Body life. If this matter were not serious, Paul would not use so many strong terms to describe it.

Doctrine may be likened to a baited hook used to catch fish. Ignorant of the hook, the fish go for the bait and are caught. In like manner, many Christians have been lured by the "bait" of doctrine, only to be caught on the "hook" concealed within it. Because many of the Lord's people are ignorant of the "hook" inside an enticing doctrine, they have been systematized by the enemy in a very subtle way.

In verse 15 Paul goes on to say, "But holding to truth in love, we may grow up into Him in all things, Who is the Head, Christ." Paul does not say that we shall grow up into the knowledge of Bible doctrine. On the contrary, he says that we shall grow up into Christ as the Head. This indicates that what is needed on the human side for the fulfillment of God's economy is growth. Only by growth shall we be no longer children who are carried about by every wind of teaching.

FEEDING, EATING, AND DRINKING

Growth comes through feeding and through eating and drinking. Apart from this process, it is impossible for anyone to grow. Therefore, what we need today is not the mere teaching of doctrine; it is the feeding with processed spiritual food. We need to feed others with the riches of Christ that we have "cooked" and processed in our experience. In this way others will receive nourishment and be able to grow. According to the religious concept, the members of the church need to be regulated through teaching. But the concept in God's economy is that God's people mainly need to be fed by having the riches of Christ ministered to them.

Daily my wife serves me nourishing food. For this reason, I am strong, healthy, and full of energy. I do not need my wife to teach me; I need her to feed me. It is the same in the church life. What we need is not more teaching, but more of the riches of Christ dispensed into us. I can testify that throughout the years the saints have grown through being fed.

Growth takes time. Change produced through regulation, on the contrary, comes very quickly. For example, a new believer may be taught how he should dress or cut his hair. This, however, would produce mere outward change, change without any growth in life. The change produced by genuine growth needs time. For example, you can make an artificial flower in an hour, but it takes months to grow a real flower. What the church needs is the feeding that produces the genuine growth in life. Such feeding does not come from mere doctrine.

We have pointed out that Christianity is a religion of doctrine. The so-called Sunday morning services in Christianity are filled with the teaching of doctrine. The meetings in the Lord's recovery must be completely different. Instead of teaching doctrine, we need to minister nourishment to the saints. We need to feed them with the riches of Christ. In this way the saints will gradually grow in life.

I thank the Lord for all the feeding that has taken place in the church in Los Angeles. Only in a few instances have certain ones become preoccupied with doctrine. This preoccupation has caused great loss both to them and to others. Most of the saints have not been interested in acquiring mere doctrinal knowledge. Instead, they have appreciated the feeding which has nourished them and made them strong. In all the churches in the Lord's recovery we need more feeding with the riches of Christ and less teaching of doctrine.

I can testify that I have no interest in doctrinal discussion and no appetite for it. When some ask me questions about things such as absolute grace, eternal security, the mode of baptism, speaking in tongues, or various views of the rapture, I simply have no desire to talk about these things in a doctrinal way. My only desire is to minister the riches of Christ to the saints so that they may grow in Him.

A BOOK OF LIFE

Have you ever noticed that in the book of Revelation there is no emphasis on doctrine? By contrast, this book speaks of the sevenfold, intensified Spirit, that is, of the seven Spirits burning before the throne of God. Revelation also speaks of the seven stars, the seven lampstands, the tree of life, and the river of water of life. There is nothing about absolute grace or eternal security. Actually, the Bible as a whole is not primarily a book of doctrine; it is a book of life. We should come to the Scriptures not primarily to learn doctrine, but mainly to be nourished by the living bread. We need to be like the prophet Jeremiah who said, "Thy words were found, and I did eat them" (Jer. 15:16). Let us drop the doctrines and the ordinances and concentrate on nourishment. If we do this, we shall eventually arrive at a full-grown man and no longer be those carried about by winds of teaching. If someone comes to you with doctrinal questions, perhaps you should read him Ephesians 4:14. Those who want to discuss doctrine under the guise of having fellowship may be influenced by the cunning craftiness of Satan. Remember to beware of the "hook" concealed within the "bait."

PROPER NOURISHMENT AND GENUINE GROWTH

We should try our best not to become involved in discussions over doctrine, especially as we contact new ones or visit Christian meetings in other places. Furthermore, we should certainly not criticize others according to a doctrinal standard. Instead of talking about doctrine, we should enjoy Christ and minister Christ to others. This is the Lord's way in His recovery. In the recovery what we need is not doctrine, but the proper nourishment that leads to genuine growth. Let us beware of Satan's subtle use of doctrine to distract us from God's economy, and let us pay attention to feeding, nourishment, and growth. This is the need in the Lord's recovery today.

LIFE-STUDY OF EPHESIANS

MESSAGE NINETY

DROPPING DOCTRINES BY THE GROWTH OF LIFE

Scripture Reading: Eph. 4:11-14; 1 Tim. 1:19; 3:9; 6:12a; 2 Tim. 4:7; Titus 1:13b; Jude 3

We have pointed out that doctrine is included among the four categories of negative things that damage the church life. The other three categories are ordinances, the old man, and the spots and wrinkles. Because in our natural, religious concept, doctrine is positive and is viewed positively by most Christians, it is difficult to speak about doctrine in a negative way. Doctrine, however, can frustrate the building up of the Body of Christ. In 4:14 Paul speaks of the negative effect of doctrine: "That we may be no longer babes tossed by waves and carried about by every wind of teaching in the sleight of men, in craftiness with a view to a system of error." Not many Christians have paid adequate attention to this verse, a verse which indicates that doctrine can damage the Body of Christ.

According to the four Gospels, the Lord Jesus had a difficult time with those religious people who were steeped in doctrine. The scribes, Pharisees, elders, and chief priests argued with Him over doctrine. Little did they realize that they were actually arguing with God, the One who inspired the Old Testament on which their doctrines were based. In their blindness they used the Scriptures to argue with the One who inspired the Scriptures and whose coming the Scriptures foretold. Those who were occupied with doctrine missed the opportunity to gain Christ. They did not realize that when the Lord Jesus was on earth, God was not concerned for doctrine, but for Christ.

DAMAGED BY DOCTRINE AND PHILOSOPHY

After the church had been established and had begun to spread, problems in the churches were caused by doctrine. Romans 14 indicates this. The doctrines concerning eating and observing days were derived from Judaism, not from heathen philosophy. Although the Roman Empire did persecute the church, this persecution did not damage the church life. However, damage was caused by religious doctrine. The situation that made it necessary to call the conference described in Acts 15 was caused by doctrine. Just as doctrine caused damage to the church life in the first century, it can damage the church life in the Lord's recovery today.

The church life has also been damaged by philosophy, especially by Gnosticism with all its concepts. If we bring in concepts derived from our cultural background, we shall cause problems in the church life. The church life in the Lord's recovery can still be damaged by doctrine and philosophy.

Most Christians appreciate those who are knowledgeable in the Scriptures. But, in a sense, it may be a dreadful thing to acquire a vast knowledge of the Bible, if our Bible knowledge causes us to miss Christ. Remember that it was those who knew the Scriptures—the Pharisees and the scribes—who persecuted the Lord Jesus and the apostles. The principle is the same today. The ones who are most opposed to the Lord's recovery are those with a certain amount of Bible knowledge.

GOD'S CONCERN

God's concern is with Christ and the church, not with doctrine or Bible knowledge. However, many Christians care more for doctrine than for Christ and the church. God's economy is not to have a group of people who know the Bible. It is to work Christ into His chosen people for the building up of the Body. We must condemn any doctrine that distracts us from Christ or that hinders us from being built up in the Body. Even doctrines that are scriptural or fundamental may be used by the enemy to distract us from Christ and the church. Satan hates to see God's people built up in the Body. Although God's goal is to produce the Body by working Christ into us, most of His people have been distracted from God's economy and from His eternal purpose. Doctrines are among the good things utilized by Satan in his subtlety to distract God's people from God's will. The reason God has put His seal upon the recovery of the church is that in the recovery we are pursuing God's goal, not mere doctrinal knowledge.

THE SUBJECTIVE HOLD OF DOCTRINE

Deep within, even unconsciously, some of us may still be holding on to certain doctrines. These doctrines hidden within us may cause us one day to become dissenting. This can happen to sisters as well as to brothers. Actually, doctrines often have a stronger hold on sisters than on brothers. According to my experience, it is much harder for a sister to let go of a doctrine than it is for a brother. The reason is that, as far as doctrine is concerned, sisters are subjective, whereas the brothers are objective. Hence, it is difficult for sisters to change their doctrine. The trouble in the church life caused by doctrine is often backed, supported, and strengthened by sisters. This tendency for sisters to hold on to doctrine can frustrate, damage, and even destroy the church life.

We have pointed out that although Christ has done everything necessary to produce the church, there is still the need for the church to be built up in a practical way. This involves our cooperation. The last three chapters of Ephesians emphasize human cooperation for the building up of the Body.

PERFECTED THROUGH GROWTH

Ephesians 2:22 speaks of the building up of the church, but it gives only the principles; it does not give the details. However, the details are found in 4:16. "Out from Whom all the Body, fitted and knit together through every joint of the supply, according to the operation in measure of each one part, causes the growth of the Body unto the building up of itself in love." By growing up into the Head, the members of the Body have something to share with one another. Furthermore, there will be the operation in the measure of each part, and the result will be the growth of the Body unto the building up of itself in love. In order to have the reality of this verse, we must be perfected by the gifts given to the Body by the Head. The saints are not perfected merely by learning doctrine. On the contrary, they are perfected through being fed. This feeding causes them to grow. For example, an infant does not need anything to be added on to his body to perfect him. As he grows, the members of his body develop and begin to function normally. A mother does not perfect her baby by teaching him to use the various parts of his body; she perfects him by feeding him. The more a child grows through receiving proper nourishment, the more the members of his body will come into their function. In the same principle, the members of the Body are perfected not by teaching, but through the feeding that causes them to grow.

THE ONENESS OF THE FAITH AND OF THE FULL KNOWLEDGE OF THE SON OF GOD

According to 4:13, the saints need to be perfected until they arrive at three things: at the oneness of the faith and of the full knowledge of the Son of God, at a full-grown man, and at the measure of the stature of the fullness of Christ. Then we shall be no longer babes tossed by waves and carried about by every wind of teaching (v. 14). Instead, we shall hold to truth in love so that we may "grow up into Him in all things, Who is the Head, Christ" (v. 15). The more we grow, the more we shall drop our doctrines. After someone is saved, he needs to have Christ ministered to him as his spiritual food and drink. This will cause him to grow. As he grows, he will gradually lay aside his doctrinal concepts. Eventually he will realize that nothing is more important than having Christ wrought into him.

As we grow in life, we arrive at the oneness of the faith. However, if we hold to our different doctrinal concepts, we shall not have this oneness. The emphasis on doctrine has destroyed the oneness among Christians. If we are nourished with the element of Christ and gradually lay aside our doctrinal concepts, we shall arrive at the oneness of the faith and of the full knowledge of the Son of God. The more we grow, the more we arrive at such a oneness.

This aspect of oneness is of two things: the faith and the full knowledge of the Son of God. The faith here does not refer to the act of believing; it refers to those things in which we believe, such as the divine Person of Christ and His redemptive work for our salvation. This is the faith spoken of in Jude 3; 2 Timothy 4:7; and 1 Timothy 6:21. The full knowledge of the Son of God is the realization of the revelation concerning the Son of God for our experience. The more we grow in life, the more we shall cleave to the faith and to the realization of Christ, and the more we shall drop all the minor doctrinal concepts which cause division.

In the New Testament faith has both an objective meaning and a subjective meaning. When used in a subjective sense, faith denotes our action of believing. Used in an objective sense, it denotes the object of our belief. In 1 Timothy 1:19 the word faith is used in both a subjective and an objective sense. Here Paul says, "Holding faith, and a good conscience; which some having put away, concerning the faith have made shipwreck" (Gk.). The first reference to faith in this verse is subjective; it denotes our capacity to believe. The second use of faith is objective; it denotes the object of our belief.

Faith in Ephesians 4:13 refers to those things which all Christians believe. We all believe in the Triune God—the Father, the Son, and the Spirit. We believe that Christ, the Son of God, was incarnated, was crucified for our redemption, was resurrected from among the dead both physically and spiritually, that He has ascended to the right hand of God, and that He is coming again. Furthermore, we believe that the Bible is God's Word, inspired by the Holy

Spirit word by word. This is our faith, the "common faith" (Titus 1:4), the "faith which was once delivered unto the saints" (Jude 3).

FAITH AND DOCTRINE

We must be careful to distinguish the faith from doctrines related to such things as the keeping of days, dietary regulations, the method of baptism, speaking in tongues, and foot-washing. Remember that our faith consists of those things which a person must believe in order to be saved. To be a genuine Christian it is necessary to believe in the Triune God and in Christ, the Son of God, our living Savior, who died on the cross for our sins and was raised bodily from among the dead. However, it is possible to be saved and not believe in foot-washing or in tongues-speaking.

Although Paul in Ephesians 4 makes a clear distinction between the faith and doctrine, many Christians confuse these two things. Instead of contending for the faith, they contend for their particular doctrine. Nowhere in the Scriptures are we told to fight for doctrine. However, we must contend for the faith that is related to our "common salvation" (Jude 3). Our common salvation comes from the common faith. Although all genuine Christians have the faith and salvation in common, we may not have all doctrines in common. The different denominations emphasize different doctrines and hold on to them. Although we are not to fight for doctrine, we must be willing to fight for the faith. In 1 Timothy 6:12 Paul charges Timothy, "Fight the good fight of the faith" (Gk.). Therefore, we should contend for our faith, but we should not fight for our doctrine.

In Romans 14 Paul shows us that as long as someone has the faith, we should receive him, even though he may differ from us with respect to doctrine. We should not dispute over matters such as eating and the observing of days. If someone regards a particular day as special, he is free to do so. But if someone else views every day as the same, he is also free. As far as doctrines are concerned, we must be liberal toward others, because doctrines have nothing to do with our common salvation.

If someone comes to you denying that Jesus is the Son of God, you must earnestly contend for the faith. You must be ready to fight for the truth that Jesus Christ is the Son of God incarnated. However, you should not argue over things such as foot-washing. If someone comes advocating this practice, you may tell him that you care only for Christ and do not want to be involved in discussion about doctrine. How pitiful it is that so many Christians are under the dominion of doctrine and are preoccupied with it!

LAYING ASIDE DOCTRINAL TOYS

Many Christians play with doctrines just as children play with toys. From my experience with my grandchildren, I have learned that the best way to get a child to drop his toys is to offer him something good to eat. The same is true with helping Christians to drop the doctrines that preoccupy them. The more we enjoy Christ and are nourished by the ministry of Christ, the more willing we shall become to lay aside our doctrines. Years ago, the saints in a certain place were preoccupied with their doctrinal toys. But as the years have gone by and they have enjoyed the ministry of Christ, they have gradually dropped these toys. The more they have grown in Christ, the less they care for toys.

The only way we can drop our doctrines is by the growth in life. We need to grow until we arrive at the oneness of the faith and of the full knowledge of the Son of God. Although we all are saved, we have come into the church life from different backgrounds. Because of these different backgrounds, we have different doctrines and philosophies. We may say that we care only for Christ and the church, but we may still be occupied with doctrine. Do not try to teach others to set aside their doctrines. Just as children will play with their toys until they grow up, so the believers will be occupied with doctrine until they grow more in Christ. If the saints grow in the Lord, eventually they will lay aside the doctrines which preoccupy them.

As we grow, we shall arrive not at the oneness of doctrine, but at the oneness of the faith and of the full knowledge of the Son of God. This is the kind of oneness we desire in the local churches. Our oneness is not a oneness of Bible knowledge; it is a oneness in the knowledge of the living Christ, a oneness constituted of the common faith and of the knowledge of Christ. Our main concern is not that the saints acquire the knowledge of the Bible. It is that they know the Lord Jesus in a living way. In the meetings of the church our emphasis is not on Bible teaching; it is on helping the saints to know the living Christ and to grow in Him. Only by growing in this way shall we be no longer children tossed by waves and carried about by winds of doctrine.

THE PROCESS OF GROWTH

Through the growth of life, we shall also arrive at a full-grown man and at the measure of the stature of the fullness of Christ. The fullness of Christ is the Body of Christ, Christ's expression. With this Body there is a stature with a measure. When the Lord's work in His recovery began in this country a number of years ago, we could see very little of the measure of this stature. Praise the Lord that over the years the measure of the stature has increased! This increase is the result of the perfecting of the saints through the ministry of Christ. However, as we all admit, we are still in the process of growth. The more we grow, the more we shall be able to function and to have the growth of the Body unto the building up of itself in love. This is our need today.

LIFE-STUDY OF EPHESIANS

MESSAGE NINETY-ONE

FAITH BUT NOT DOCTRINE

Scripture Reading: Eph. 4:13-14; Jude 3; 1 Tim. 1:19; 3:9; 6:12a; 2 Tim. 4:7; Titus 1:4, 13b

In 4:13 Paul speaks of the oneness of the faith, and in 4:14 he refers to the winds of teaching, of doctrine. This indicates that we need to distinguish between the faith and doctrine. Regarding the faith—what we must believe in order to be saved—the New Testament is strong, strict, and consistent. In Jude 3 we are even told that we "should earnestly contend for the faith which was once delivered unto the saints." Concerning the faith, we must be ready to fight. We should not merely insist on the faith and stand for it, but fight for it at any cost, even at the cost of our life. The faith for which we must fight is the common faith, the Christian faith, the faith that saves us.

LIBERAL WITH OTHERS REGARDING DOCTRINE

In contrast, in the New Testament we are never charged to fight for doctrine. As far as doctrine is concerned, the New Testament is liberal. Take the example of eating what has been sacrificed to idols. If you read what Paul says about this in Romans and in 1 Corinthians, you may be puzzled. In some places Paul indicates that it is permissible to eat what has been offered to idols. However, in other places he strongly advises against this practice. Years ago, I spent a great deal of time trying to understand this. Troubled by what seemed to be an inconsistency in Paul's writings, I wondered why he did not tell us in a straightforward way whether or not we should eat things that have been sacrificed to idols. Only after I had been delivered from preoccupation with doctrine did I come to understand that Paul wrote different things on different occasions about eating because he was liberal with respect to doctrine. He knew that under certain circumstances it was permissible to eat, whereas in other circumstances it was not. Only when you have been delivered from preoccupation with doctrine will you be able to understand that certain matters pertaining to doctrine are relative to the situation. This is why Paul could say one thing on one occasion and something else on a different occasion.

FOUR NEGATIVE THINGS

Concerning the eating of meat or the observing of certain days, Paul did not take a definite stand. On the contrary, in these matters he was liberal. But in Romans 16:17 he said strongly, "Now I beg you, brothers, keep a watchful eye on those who make divisions and causes of falling contrary to the teaching which you have learned, and turn away from them." As far as doctrines go, Paul was liberal, but as far as divisiveness was concerned, he was definite. He told us to mark out those who cause division and to avoid them.

In 1 Corinthians 5:7-11 Paul deals with fornication and idolatry. In verse 9 he charges the saints "not to company with fornicators." Fornication damages humanity, and idolatry is an insult to God. Although Paul was liberal with respect to doctrine, he would not tolerate anything related to fornication or idolatry. His word about these things is strong and definite.

In Titus 3:10 Paul says, "A man that is factious, after the first and second admonition, reject" (Gk.). A factious person is divisive and sectarian. After such a one has been admonished once or twice, he should be rejected if he continues in his divisiveness. There can be no compromise or neutrality. Therefore, regarding idolatry, fornication, and divisiveness Paul was very strict, and we must be strict also.

According to the Second Epistle of John, we see that we must also reject those who deny the incarnation of Christ. Verse 7 says, "For many deceivers are entered into the world, who confess not that Jesus Christ is come in the flesh. This is a deceiver and an antichrist." This verse indicates that even in the first century there were certain ones who called themselves Christians, but who did not confess that Christ was God come in the flesh. In other words they denied the fact that Christ was God incarnated. In verse 9 the writer goes on to say, "Whosoever transgresseth, and abideth not in the doctrine of Christ, hath not God. He that abideth in the doctrine of Christ, he hath both the Father and the Son." The word transgress here means to go a little farther. The Bible reveals that Christ is God incarnated. Those who denied this went too far; they had given up the teaching that Christ is God incarnate. Hence, the Apostle John warned the believers concerning this kind of person: "If there come any unto you, and bring not this doctrine, receive him not into your house, neither bid him God-speed: for he that biddeth him God-speed is partaker of his evil deeds" (vv. 10-11). We cannot receive those who do deny the incarnation of Christ.

According to the New Testament, there are four things which we cannot tolerate: idolatry, fornication, division, and the denial of the deity of Christ. Concerning the faith, we must be bold, strong, and definite, ready to contend for the faith once delivered to the saints. However, as far as doctrines are concerned, we must be liberal with others. Nevertheless, we cannot tolerate idolatry, fornication, division, and the denial of the incarnation of Christ.

PRACTICING ROMANS 14

Apart from the four negative things mentioned above, we cannot find a fifth item in the New Testament concerning which we should be strict in accepting others. Yes, the New Testament commands us to love one another. However, it does not say that we should reject a person if he does not follow the teaching about loving others. The same is true regarding the doctrine of foot-washing. In John 13 the Lord Jesus speaks of washing one another's feet. However, this chapter does not say that we should refuse to have fellowship with another believer because he does not practice foot-washing. In the same principle, although the New

Testament speaks emphatically about baptism, we are never told to reject a believer because he has not been baptized. We should not separate ourselves from those believers who differ from us in doctrine.

We need to remember Romans 14 and practice it. Today many Christian teachers are talking about the Body in Romans 12 without paying adequate attention to Romans 14. Apart from Romans 14 we cannot practice the Body life revealed in Romans 12. Only through being liberal toward others with respect to doctrine can we have the Body life.

Among many Christians today there is no practice of the Body life. Instead, there is division after division. In fact, there is more division among earnest Christians than among those who are worldly or indifferent to the Lord and His Word. When Christians are revived and renewed in reading the Bible, they are more easily divided over doctrine. Because of the divisiveness in today's Christianity, most Christians do not have the Body life. This is especially true in the charismatic movement. Although many in this movement are fond of talking about the Body, there is more divisiveness in the charismatic movement than in any other aspect of Christianity. The reason for this is that Christians talk about Romans 12, but neglect Romans 14. I repeat, only by practicing Romans 14 do we have the reality of the Body described in Romans 12.

According to Romans 14, there is room in the church life for those with different doctrines. Some believe that they can eat everything, whereas others eat only herbs. In like manner, some observe certain days, whereas others regard every day the same. Do you realize that in the church life there can be different doctrines, and there should be? Take the example of head covering. Some sisters wear a head covering in the meetings, but many sisters do not. This indicates that among the sisters there are different doctrines concerning head covering. It is a very positive sign that the church can include both those sisters who wear a head covering and those who do not. I have been in Christian meetings where sisters without a head covering were not welcome. Furthermore, the sisters who wear a head covering have different kinds of coverings and coverings of different colors. But I have been in meetings where the sisters were required to wear head coverings of the same size, style, and color. Praise the Lord that in the church life we are not divided over different matters such as these! How wonderful that in the church we receive those with different doctrines concerning head covering!

Although we may differ in doctrine, we are truly one. But those who are preoccupied with doctrine often argue about whether or not certain doctrines or practices are scriptural. However, we can declare that the most scriptural meeting is the meeting in which believers with different doctrines are received. As we contend for the faith and reject the four categories of negative things we have mentioned, we are liberal toward others with respect to doctrine. This is the only way to preserve the oneness. If we dispute over doctrine, we shall repeat Christianity's history of division.

ESCAPING FROM THE SNARE OF DOCTRINE

About a century and a half ago, the Brethren were raised up by the Lord and came to see many truths in the Bible. Certainly this was of the Lord. However, the Brethren eventually were snared by doctrinal knowledge and were divided again and again. In some cases they cared more for their interpretation of the Bible than for Christ. For this reason, there are hundreds of divisions among the Brethren today. If you visit certain Brethren assemblies, they may argue with you about doctrine, yet have little care for the Spirit or for the living Christ. How pitiful to care for our interpretation of the Bible but to neglect the Lord Jesus!

In the Lord's recovery we have escaped from the trap of doctrine and are being brought back to the Lord Himself. How I praise the Lord for rescuing me from doctrinal knowledge! We in the Lord's recovery have no appetite for doctrine. At the same time, we reject idolatry, fornication, division, and the denial of Christ's deity. Although we are strict about these negative things, we are liberal toward others about doctrine. We are not for doctrines, practices, or ordinances. We care only for Christ as the Head and the church as the Body. Therefore, we are truly one.

GOD'S INTENTION

God's intention is not to gain a people who are merely moral and godly in a religious sense. His intention is to have a people who have been regenerated, sanctified, purified, transformed, and built up as the one new man. He desires to have the church as the new man with Christ as his person. Our concern is to become this new man filled and saturated with Christ. God's concern is that we be filled with Christ, nourished by Christ, and built up in Christ as a proper church.

THE LORD'S RECOVERY AND THE LORD'S COMING

Everyone in the Lord's recovery needs to be clear about the Lord's move on earth today. Do not think of the recovery as an ordinary Christian work or movement. The recovery of the church life is not merely another kind of typical Christian work. No, the recovery is unique and of tremendous significance.

The Lord's recovery is related to the Lord's coming back. According to the prophecies in the Bible, two signs of the Lord's coming back are the re-formation of the nation of Israel and the return of Jerusalem to Israel. As we all know, these two things have taken place, the re-formation of Israel in 1948 and the return of Jerusalem in 1967. According to the Lord's word in Luke 21:24, the return of Jerusalem indicates the fullness of the age of the Gentiles. Since these two signs have taken place, we believe that it will not be too long before the Lord comes back. Furthermore, the world situation is focused on the Middle East, particularly on problems related to oil. The world situation is coming more and more into line with biblical prophecy.

The Bible also tells us that the Bride must be prepared. Consider the situation of today's Christianity, and ask yourself where the Bride is being prepared. Is the Bride being prepared in Catholicism? in the denominations? in the charismatic movement? in the independent groups? I sincerely believe that the Bride is being prepared in the Lord's recovery. We admit that we are imperfect and rather weak, but it is nevertheless a fact that no other Christians love the Lord Jesus more than those in the local churches. Recently we received a report that certain missionaries in Taiwan, although critical of the local churches, admitted that the Christians in the churches were the most mature to be found on that island. We simply cannot deny the fact that so many of the saints in the Lord's recovery love the Lord Jesus in an absolute way.

May the Lord impress us that it is not an insignificant matter to be in His recovery. The time is short, and the Lord's coming is close. Surely before He comes back the Bride must be ready for Him. There may not be time for the Lord to begin another work apart from the recovery as a preparation of the Bride. If the Bride is not being prepared in the recovery, please show me where this preparation is taking place. We in the churches must not boast, and we must not be proud. To be either boastful or proud is foolish. Nevertheless, we must admit the fact that no Christians love the Lord more than those in the churches in the Lord's recovery. We praise the Lord that however weak and imperfect we may be, He is going on among us. We believe that the church life will spread in Europe and eventually reach Jerusalem. We believe that when the Lord sets His feet on the Mount of Olives at the time of His coming back, there will be a church in Jerusalem to meet Him. What a shame it would be to Him if there were no church in Jerusalem at His coming! Oh, may we all be clear that we are not involved in an ordinary Christian work. We are in the Lord's recovery, in His move on earth today. Praise Him, He is marching on! Let us go forth with Him to meet Him in His coming. May the Bride be made ready!

LIFE-STUDY OF EPHESIANS

MESSAGE NINETY-TWO

THE PERFECTING OF THE NEW MAN

Scripture Reading: Eph. 4:7-16

In 2:15 Paul speaks of the creation of the one new man: "Having abolished in His flesh the law of the commandments in ordinances, that He might create the two in Himself into one new man, making peace." Then in 4:13 he speaks of arriving at a full-grown man, and in 4:24, of putting on the new man. The full-grown man in verse 13 is the new man in verse 24. Hence, in Ephesians the new man is referred to three times.

Some versions make a serious error in rendering 4:24. For example, the Revised Standard Version says "put on the new nature." What a poor translation! The Greek word here is *anthropos,* the same word used for man in 2:15. The New American Standard Version also makes a serious mistake by rendering this verse, "put on the new self." Very few Christian writers have recognized that the new man in 4:24 is the church. In his *Expository Dictionary of New Testament Words,* W. E. Vine points out that the new man in 4:24 is the church which is Christ's Body. He clearly connects 4:24 to 2:15. No doubt the one new man in 4:24 is the new man in 2:15, for the same term is used in each case.

In 2:15 we have the creation of the new man. We may regard this creation as the birth of the new man. Just as a child is perfected through growth, so the new man created in Christ is also perfected through growth. This is the reason Paul refers to the new man in chapter four as well as in chapter two.

PERFECT ORGANICALLY AND FUNCTIONALLY

We may distinguish between something that is perfect, or

complete organically and something that is perfect according to its function. At birth, an infant is perfect organically; that is, the infant has all the necessary organs. However, a child is not functionally perfect at birth. Organically, a mother cannot help her child, for she cannot add any organs to the child. But she can help him functionally by feeding him so that he will grow normally. Although only God the Creator can produce an organism that is perfect organically, we as parents must help our children become perfect functionally. We fulfill this responsibility by nourishing our children and cherishing them. In order to develop properly and to function normally, every child needs to be nourished and cherished. This principle also applies to the church as the new man. In 2:15 we see the creation of the new man organically, but in 4:13-16 we see the perfecting of the new man in relation to his function.

In this respect, 4:16 is an extremely important verse. Here Paul says, "Out from Whom all the Body, fitted and knit together through every joint of the supply, according to the operation in measure of each one part, causes the growth of the Body unto the building up of itself in love." Our growth in life is to grow into the Head, Christ, but our function in the Body is to function out from Him. The phrase "each one part" refers to every member of the Body. Every member of the Body of Christ has its own measure which works for the growth of the Body. The Body causes the growth of itself through the supplying joints and working parts. The growth of the Body is the increase of Christ in the church, which results in the building up of the Body itself.

There is no verse such as 4:16 in Ephesians 2. In chapter two we have the birth of the new man, but not the function of the new man. At birth, the new man is organically perfect; however, he is not yet able to function. Just as a child needs to be perfected through nourishing and cherishing, so the organically perfect new man needs to be perfected through the growth of life in order to function in a proper way.

Our physical life portrays this. Only God can create a being that is organically perfect. However, after a child is born, God does not come in to feed him or cherish him. This is the responsibility of the parents, especially of the mother. The more the child is nourished and grows, the more he will function normally.

In the same principle, the new man created by Christ must be perfected in order to function. Through the growth spoken of in chapter four, the new man comes into function. Through the operation in the measure of each part, the Body grows unto the building up of itself in love. The creation of the new man was the responsibility of the Lord alone. We have nothing whatever to do with this. But we must fulfill our responsibility to perfect the new man through nourishing and cherishing. As the new man is perfected in this way, he grows and becomes perfect functionally.

GROWTH THROUGH FEEDING

We have pointed out that the new man can become perfect in relation to his functions only through receiving the proper nourishment. This, however, is not a superficial matter. On the contrary, it is one of the deepest concepts in the whole book of Ephesians. In Christianity today the ministers, pastors, and preachers mainly teach the people and thereby build up a religion instead of the Body. Many of those among us who formerly were ministers or missionaries can testify of this. Because those in Christianity rely on doctrine, they mainly build up something else in place of the Body. The Body does not become functionally perfect through the teaching of doctrine. Actually, in Ephesians 4, a chapter that speaks of the perfecting of the new man through the growth of life, doctrine is depreciated. Paul says that when we are no longer children, we shall no longer be carried about by winds of doctrine. What is needed for the building up of the Body and for perfecting the new man functionally is the growth of life. This comes only through feeding.

GIFTS FOR THE PERFECTING OF THE SAINTS

In 4:8 we are told that the ascended Christ gave gifts

to men. The gifts here do not refer to abilities for service, but to the gifted persons mentioned in verse 11—apostles, prophets, evangelists, and shepherds and teachers. After conquering them and rescuing them from Satan and death through His death and resurrection, Christ in His ascension makes rescued sinners such gifts with His resurrection life and gives them to His Body for its building up. Hence, the four kinds of gifted persons mentioned in verse 11 are those who have been endued with a special gift. These gifted ones are given "for the perfecting of the saints unto the work of the ministry, unto the building up of the Body of Christ" (v. 12). The more the saints are perfected, the more they grow. Through growth their function comes forth, and they function according to the effectual working in their measure.

THE ASCENDED CHRIST PRODUCING GIFTS

Let us consider in more detail how Christ gave the gifts to His Body. How are the believers constituted as gifts and presented to the Body? The case of the Apostle Paul is an excellent example. Paul was not perfected by attending a theological seminary. As we all know, when he was Saul of Tarsus, he was an extremely religious person. Having been born into Judaism and raised in it, he opposed Christ and persecuted the church. He had even been authorized by the high priest to go to Damascus for the purpose of arresting and imprisoning those who called on the name of the Lord Jesus. But when he was on the way, the Lord Jesus appeared to him. In Galatians 1:13 Paul said, "For ye have heard of my conversation in time past in the Jews' religion, how that beyond measure I persecuted the church of God, and wasted it." Then Paul went on to say that "it pleased God...to reveal his Son in me, that I might preach him among the heathen" (Gal. 1:15a, 16a). God caused Christ to be wrought into Paul so that he could minister Him to others. In this way, Christ presented Paul as a gift to the Body. By this process Christ constitutes us into gifts that are given to the Body. Firstly, Christ is wrought into us to become our life, our person, and our everything. Then we minister to others the very Christ who has been wrought into us.

Only the ascended Christ can produce gifts for the Body. Notice that in 4:8-11 the gifts are spoken of in relation to Christ's ascension. Verse 8 says, "Having ascended to the height, He led captive those taken captive and gave gifts to men." The height refers to the third heaven to which Christ has ascended. "Those taken captive" refers to the redeemed saints who had been taken captive by Satan before they were saved by Christ's death and resurrection. In His ascension Christ led them captive; that is, He rescued them from Satan's captivity and took them to Himself. Having rescued us from Satan, He constitutes us into gifts for the Body.

The ascension was the peak and the climax of Christ's work. The other basic steps of Christ's work are incarnation, crucifixion, and resurrection. Ascension is related to the coming of the Spirit. After Christ had accomplished redemption through His crucifixion and after He had resurrected and ascended to the heavens, He came down as the life-giving Spirit. Through the crucifixion of Christ all the enemies were conquered. Hence, the cross is the center of Christ's victory. Furthermore, by His death on the cross, Christ solved all the problems in the universe. This was the reason that after His crucifixion He could rest in the tomb and thereby enjoy a real Sabbath. Then in His resurrection He released all the divine riches. Following this, He ascended to the third heaven, and all the divine fullness was committed to Him along with all of God's chosen people. Saul of Tarsus was among these chosen ones given to the ascended Christ.

It is important to be clear concerning Christ's descension as the Spirit after His ascension. As we have pointed out, according to Ephesians 2, Christ even came to preach the gospel of peace. This indicates the coming of the ascended Christ. When Saul of Tarsus was persecuting the churches, he did not realize that what he was persecuting was related to the heavens, that the church on earth was related to the ascended Christ. The Lord Jesus appeared to Saul of

Tarsus, and spontaneously, even in his ignorance, Saul called upon His name, saying, "Who art thou, Lord?" Because Saul opened himself to the Lord and called on Him, the Lord with the divine fullness could enter into him and then proceed to constitute him into a gift to the Body. In this way the one who persecuted the churches became one who could perfect the saints. Paul became such a gift not through education, but by being saturated with the divine fullness. Therefore, Saul of Tarsus eventually became the Apostle Paul who could feed the saints, preach the unsearchable riches of Christ, and minister Christ to his fellow believers so that they would be nourished, grow, be perfected, and come into their function.

HOW CHRIST CONSTITUTES US INTO GIFTS

In today's Christianity there is not the proper function of the members of the Body. Hundreds, even thousands, of believers may meet together, but they sit in their pews without functioning. The reason for this is that in Christianity there is not the feeding that leads to genuine growth. Only those who have been properly nourished will be able to function.

In the Lord's recovery we need to return to what was in the beginning. In the beginning, especially with Paul, the saints were richly fed and nourished. If we would be perfected, what we need is not doctrine. Rather, we need to be constituted with Christ. Like Saul of Tarsus, we all were once enemies of Christ and persecutors of the churches. But one day the Lord Jesus came to us and captured us. I can testify that as I was on the way to my Damascus, the Lord appeared to me and interfered with my plans. Although I was ambitious to become successful in the world, I had no choice except to follow the Lord. Many of us have had the same kind of experience. The Lord Jesus came to us, and we were caught by Him. Now we need to take Him into us more and more until we are saturated with Him. In this way we shall become functioning members of the Body, gifts constituted by the Christ who has been crucified and resurrected and who has ascended and descended.

EVERY MEMBER FUNCTIONING

We have seen that by His death Christ conquered all the enemies and solved all the problems. We have also seen that through His resurrection He released all the divine riches, and that through His ascension He received God's chosen people with the divine fullness. From the time of His ascension, Christ has been working to constitute the vanquished foes into gifts for His Body. Firstly, He comes to these vanquished foes and gets into them. Then He gradually fills them and saturates them with Himself. Eventually, those who once were His enemies are transformed and constituted into useful gifts that can be presented to the Body. These gifts will not merely teach others, but will transfuse Christ into them. In this way the members of the Body receive nourishment and are cherished. Then they will be sanctified, purified, and transformed to become functioning members. As a result, the whole Body will be fitly framed together and compacted by every joint of supply, according to the effectual working in the measure of every part. This will make growth of the Body unto the building up of itself in love.

I believe that the day is coming when everyone in the local churches will be a functioning member. Consider how children grow by receiving nourishment. The more they grow, the more they function. The principle is the same with our spiritual growth as members of the Body. The more we grow by being nourished and cherished, the more we shall function properly in the church life. If the saints are absolute with the Lord, in a relatively short time many will come into function. I have the full assurance in the Lord that soon this will be the situation in the Lord's recovery.

LIFE-STUDY OF EPHESIANS

MESSAGE NINETY-THREE

THE CORPORATE LIFE OF THE NEW MAN

Scripture Reading: Eph. 4:17-32

We have seen that in chapter two we have the creation of the new man and in chapter four, the growth of the new man. In order for the new man to grow, we need to experience the crucified, resurrected, ascended, and descending Christ. This means that the all-inclusive Christ must be wrought into us to be our everything. Then the organically perfect new man will also become perfect functionally.

GROWING AND FUNCTIONING THROUGH THE EXPERIENCE OF CHRIST

The new man is not perfected mainly by teaching. Teaching may actually be a frustration to our growth in life. Before the new man could be created, all the ordinances had to be abolished. Now for the new man to grow, we must be careful about doctrine. Ordinances are obstacles to the formation of the new man, and doctrines are frustrations to the growth of the new man. I hope that all those who take the lead in the local churches will realize that we should not place our trust in doctrine to produce growth in the saints. Growth only comes through the experience of Christ. The degree to which we can minister Christ is in direct proportion to our experience of Christ. The more we experience Him, the more we can minister Him to others. As we minister Christ, others will be nourished.

The very Christ who was crucified and resurrected and who has ascended to the third heaven is now working within us to constitute us into functioning members of the Body. He carries out this work by making His home in our hearts and by saturating us with Himself. As He saturates us, we are sanctified, purified, nourished, cherished, and transformed. The result is that we become perfected functionally. In this way the Body grows and builds itself up. The Body is not built directly by the Head or by the gifts mentioned in 4:11; it is built up directly by those members who have been perfected by the gifted ones.

Concerning this crucial matter, I pray that we all shall have a clear sky. I can testify that the sky above me is crystal clear regarding the growth of the new man. In these days may the Lord make all His faithful seeking ones transparently clear about the one new man. How blessed we are to be living at a time when the Lord is recovering these things! Ephesians 4 has never been as clear to us as it is in these days.

All those who desire to migrate for the spread of the church life must realize that migration is not a movement. It is the move of the one new man, that is, the move of the all-inclusive Christ in His Body. It is the move of Christ, the heavenly Solomon, in His palanquin. If the Lord is to move among us in such a way, we should not function in an individualistic way. Rather, we should function in the Body in the way of coordination. In order to function in this way, we need to experience Christ and to grow in Him. The measure of our growth will be the sphere, the realm, of our function. If we fail to function, there will be a gap in the Body. But if we function excessively, we shall cause a cancer in the Body. As the Head of the Body, Christ thoroughly knows the situation of the Body. According to His mercy, may the Body be preserved both from any shortage and from cancer caused by overfunction.

We praise the Lord for opening His Word to us. We thank Him for showing us that the vital need is for Christ to be wrought into our being. The more we are saturated with Christ, the more we become in reality parts of the Body with a particular measure of function. Then wherever we may be we shall function properly, and the Body will grow. This will cause Satan, the enemy of God, to tremble. It will also hasten the coming back of the Lord Jesus.

PUTTING ON THE COMMUNITY LIFE OF THE NEW MAN

Because the book of Ephesians is a book on the church, we should view everything in it from the perspective of the church. If we fail to do this, we shall wrongly apply many things in this book. As we read 4:17-32, we should apply these verses corporately, not individualistically. These verses are not written in relation to the lives of individuals, but in relation to the corporate life of the one new man. The new man must become our daily living. In verse 24 Paul speaks of putting on the new man. To put on the new man means to have the church life, which is the new life of the new mankind created by Christ in Himself. The church is a new humanity. Corporately we need to put on another humanity. It is crucial for us to have this view as we consider the second half of Ephesians 4.

To put off the old man is not merely to put off the old nature; it is to put off the old way of life, the former way of living. Our old way of living was not entirely an individualistic way of life, for it involved our social life, our community life. No human being can be altogether individualistic. Human nature is inherently social. To be a human being is to live in society and to have some kind of community life.

In the church we have the best community life. If there were no church meetings, we would feel aimless, and our existence would be meaningless. We enjoy coming together in the meetings. The fact that the saints often linger after the meetings are dismissed indicates that in the church we have a genuine community life. If we would be the one new man, we must put off the community life of the old man and put on the community life of the new man.

Visiting Chinatown is part of Chinese social life in America. It is part of the living of the old man that must be put off if we are to practice the church life as the one new man. Many of those who go to Chinatown may discover that they have a difficult time praying after they come home. The reason for this is that, while they were in Chinatown, they were walking according to the vanity of the mind instead of being renewed in the spirit of the mind.

For the sisters to put off the old man in a practical way, they need to put off their old way of shopping. I believe that most sisters find it difficult to pray when they are in a department store because their way of shopping is according to the living of the old man. It seems that the old man who was buried in baptism is resuscitated in the department store. We need to keep the old man in the tomb in a practical way.

Sometimes in the church life those of a certain nationality may cluster together and converse in their native language instead of English. This practice shows that it is not easy to put off the old man. We automatically prefer our old community life. The reason today's Christianity is so weak is that it is permeated with the old man and his community life. In the denominations it is very difficult to see anything of the one new man. In the church life in the Lord's recovery, we should no longer live according to the former conduct of the old man. We need to be renewed in the spirit of our mind and put on the one new man.

The Lord's intention today is not simply to gather us together, but to cause us to put off the life of the old man. We must put off not only our old nature, but also our former manner of life. Our way of life must become absolutely new in nature, manner, and practice. The church life is the daily living of the new man in the new nature and manner. May we all look to the Lord and pray, "Lord, deliver my mind from vanity and fill it with the reality of the Spirit. Cause my mind to be occupied, possessed, and saturated by the reality of Jesus." If we pray in this way, the Chinese brothers and sisters will find it hard to go to Chinatown, and the sisters will find it hard to shop in the old way. Then we shall have not only the creation of the new man, but the new man growing and functioning with a proper daily living. This is strategic to God's economy. If the Lord can have this among us, He will gain a great victory. To have personal victories over things such as our temper cannot compare to the corporate victory of putting on the living of the new man in a practical way. The church life is the life of the corporate new man with a new nature and a new manner. Everything related to the living of the one new man is new.

In 4:24 Paul says that the new man is according to God. This means that the new man is according to God Himself, with God's life and nature. Since the new man is according to God, it must have a life that is divine. Such a life will not be individualistic; it will be corporate. I believe that before long the living of the new man will be realized in the Lord's recovery. In various localities the Lord will have a people whose daily living is the corporate life of the new man. This is the church life according to God's plan.

We do not have the church life simply by coming together in the meetings to sing, pray-read, praise the Lord, and give testimonies. The church life is the daily walk of a corporate man, a walk that is absolutely new in nature and in manner. If we walk according to the spirit of our mind, we shall be those who live such a corporate life. We shall have the proper community life in which everything is new. May the Lord hasten the day when concerning this matter our sky is clear and we are fully in the light!

THE VANITY OF THE MIND

In verse 17 Paul charges us to "no longer walk as the nations also walk in the vanity of their mind." Those who walk in this way are "darkened in their understanding, estranged from the life of God because of the ignorance which is in them, because of the hardness of their heart" (v. 18). It is possible to be a saved person, one who has the life of God, yet walk in the vanity of the mind. For example, some may do their shopping in the vanity of the mind and thereby become alienated from the life of God. Others may go to Chinatown and be estranged from the life of God. As they sit in the restaurant enjoying a Chinese meal, they may sense that, because they are living according to the former manner of life, they are cut off from the life of God. Because of the insulation within them, they do not sense the flow of the heavenly electricity. Whenever we return to the old manner of life, we shall spontaneously sense that we are darkened within and estranged from God's life. If we persist in living according to the former manner of life, we shall eventually become calloused and insensitive. We may even cease from feeling because we do not care for our conscience.

The church life is definitely a community life. But it is a community life altogether different from that of the old man. The community life of the one new man is new in every way.

Consider how many terms Paul uses to describe the life of fallen man in verses 17 through 19. He refers to vanity, darkness, estrangement, ignorance, and hardness. Whenever we live according to our old community life, we do not sense any shining or brightness within. We may reason that it is permissible to do a certain thing, but we realize that it causes us to be alienated from the life of God and to be in darkness.

A MATTER OF THE LIVING CHRIST

The church life is not a matter of right and wrong; it is a matter of the living Christ. You may argue that it is not wrong for you to go shopping at a certain department store. You may insist that such a thing is not sinful. There may in fact be nothing wrong with it, but it causes you to be darkened and estranged from the life of God. You may be right in every way, but you do not experience Christ as your life and as your person. This is the reason that after you go shopping you may not be able to pray for a period of time. The church life is higher than the standard of right and wrong; it is a living that is according to Christ. If Christ is the One living in us, He will not allow us to do certain things. For example, He will not be pleased for us to go shopping according to our former manner of life. Such a way of living is not according to the living of Christ.

THE TRUTH IN JESUS

In 4:20 Paul speaks of learning Christ and in verse 21, of having been "taught in Him as the truth is in Jesus." In a note on 4:21 J. N. Darby points out that in Greek there is an emphatic article before Jesus. He then goes on to say that this indicates that "'Jesus' is personally brought into relief." The truth in Jesus is the real situation of the life of Jesus as recorded in the four Gospels, a life filled with truth, reality. Jesus lived a life of always doing things in God, with God, and for God. God was in His life, and He was one with God. This is the truth in Jesus. Jesus lived in a way that always corresponded to God's righteousness and holiness.

In verse 24 Paul says that the new man is created according to God in righteousness and holiness of the truth. This truth no doubt is the very truth in Jesus. Our standard of living should not be according to the law or according to the standards of society; it must be according to the truth in Jesus, the reality lived out by Jesus when He was on earth. Hence, the life of Jesus should be our life today in the church. In other words, the living of the new man should be exactly the same as the living of Jesus. The way Jesus lived on earth is the way the new man should live today.

If we would live in such a way, we should not reason according to right or wrong. Instead, we should consider the various aspects of our daily life according to the truth as it is in Jesus. For example, if we are about to go shopping, we should ask whether the Lord Jesus is going shopping. The life of the one new man must be that of the reality of Jesus. If we all live in a way that is heavenly, divine, righteous, holy, and glorious, we shall have a wonderful community life in the church. This is the corporate life of the new man.

NOT GRIEVING THE HOLY SPIRIT

Toward the end of chapter four Paul says, "And do not grieve the Holy Spirit of God, in Whom you were sealed unto the day of redemption" (v. 30). I am concerned that day by day and even hour by hour many of us are grieving the indwelling Holy Spirit. We grieve Him because we do not live according to the new manner of life. Instead, we walk according to the vanity of the mind. Because we do not stay in the spirit of the mind, we grieve the Holy Spirit. This is a further indication that the new man needs not only creation and growth for function, but also the practical daily living with a new manner of life. This is the church life.

LIFE-STUDY OF EPHESIANS

MESSAGE NINETY-FOUR

THE SPIRIT AND THE CHURCH

Scripture Reading: Eph. 1:17; 2:22; 3:5, 16; 4:23; 5:18; 6:18

In 4:17 Paul says, "This therefore I say and testify in the Lord, that you no longer walk as the nations also walk in the vanity of their mind." The nations are the fallen people, who have become vain in their reasonings (Rom. 1:21). They walk without God in the vanity of their mind, controlled and directed by their vain thoughts. Whatever they do according to their fallen mind is vanity. Hence, the basic element in the daily life of fallen mankind is the vanity of the mind.

If you study the Bible from Genesis 6 through Revelation 20, you will see that all of fallen mankind lives in the vanity of the mind. Mankind has fallen from the spirit into the mind. God purposely created man with a spirit with the intention that man would live and walk in the spirit. But through the fall man's spirit was deadened, and man began to live according to the vanity of the mind. Those who are fallen have all their living directed by their thoughts. Every fallen person without exception is under the dominion of his thoughts. Before we were saved, our words and deeds were according to the thoughts of the fallen mentality.

WALKING ACCORDING TO THE SPIRIT OF THE MIND

In the church as the new man, we should live not according to the vanity of the mind, but according to the spirit of the mind (4:23). This is the key to the daily living of the corporate one new man. Formerly, our mind was filled with vanity; now it must be permeated with the spirit. We need to walk according to the spirit that is spreading into our mind and filling it. In this way the daily walk of the new man will be in the spirit of the mind. This is the secret of the church life.

A SPIRIT OF WISDOM AND REVELATION

The human spirit is mentioned in every chapter of Ephesians. Ephesians 1:17 says, "That the God of our Lord Jesus Christ, the Father of glory, may give to you a spirit of wisdom and revelation in the full knowledge of Him." The spirit here is the regenerated human spirit indwelt by the Spirit of God. Such a spirit is given to us by God so that we may have wisdom and revelation to know Him and to know His economy.

In relation to the church, we need a spirit of wisdom and revelation. As far as the church is concerned, a naturally keen mind is of no avail. Rather, the spirit is of primary importance. Just as we must use the proper organs to see, hear, and taste, so we must use the proper organ—the spirit—in dealing with the church.

Furthermore, our spirit must be a spirit of wisdom and revelation. Wisdom is in our spirit so that we may know the mystery of God, whereas revelation is of God's Spirit to show us the vision by opening the veil. We firstly have wisdom, the ability to understand, that we may know spiritual things. Then the Spirit of God reveals the spiritual things to our spiritual understanding. Knowing that the spirit is of crucial importance in relation to the church, Paul prayed that the Father of glory would grant us such a spirit of wisdom and revelation.

OUR SPIRIT BEING GOD'S DWELLING PLACE

In 2:22 Paul says, "In Whom you also are being built together into a dwelling place of God in spirit." This refers to our human spirit indwelt by the Holy Spirit. God's Spirit is the dweller, whereas our spirit is His dwelling place. Therefore, the dwelling place of God is in our spirit.

If we want to practice the church life, we need to be in the spirit. The natural mind is of no use in the church life as the one new man. In school or in business we need to rely on our mind, but in the church we must depend on the spirit, realizing that in the natural mind there is nothing but vanity. According to 2:22, God's dwelling place among His people today is in their spirit, not in their mind.

REVELATION IN SPIRIT

Speaking of the mystery of Christ, Paul says in 3:5, "Which in other generations was not made known to the sons of men, as it has now been revealed to His holy apostles and prophets in spirit." Once again the spirit here refers to the human spirit regenerated and indwelt by the Holy Spirit of God. Thus it can be regarded as the mingled spirit, the human spirit mingled with God's Spirit. Such a mingled spirit was the means by which the New Testament revelation concerning Christ and the church was made known to the apostles and prophets. We need the same spirit to see such a revelation today.

The "sons of men" in this verse are represented by the "holy apostles and prophets." When God revealed the mystery of Christ to these representatives of mankind, He revealed it to their spirit. By this we see that the spirit, not the mind, is the crucial organ with respect to God's economy.

THE INNER MAN

In 3:16 Paul goes on to speak of the inner man: "That He would grant you, according to the riches of His glory, to be strengthened with power through His Spirit into the inner man." The inner man is our regenerated spirit with God's life as its life. In order to experience Christ as the embodiment of God, we need to be strengthened into our inner man. However, by nature the brothers are strong in the mind and in the will, whereas the sisters are strong in the emotion. May the Lord cause us to become strong in the spirit, in our inner man!

We all need to be strengthened into our inner man so that Christ will be able to make His home in our hearts. Our heart is composed of all the parts of the soul—the mind, emotion, and will—plus the conscience, the main part of our spirit. These are the inward parts of our being. Through regeneration, Christ came into our spirit (2 Tim. 4:22). Subsequently, we should allow Him to spread Himself into every part of our heart. Since our heart is the totality of all our inward parts and the center of our inward being, when Christ makes His home in our heart, He is able to control our entire inner being and supplies and strengthens every inward part with Himself. The secret of Christ making His home in our heart is the strengthening of our inner man. Because Paul knew this secret, he prayed that the Father would grant us, according to the riches of His glory, to be strengthened with power into the inner man.

THE RENEWING SPIRIT

As we go on to chapter four, we see that the strengthened spirit must become the renewing spirit in our mind. In 4:23 Paul says, "And are renewed in the spirit of your mind." Once again, the spirit here is the regenerated spirit of the believers mingled with the indwelling Spirit of God. Such a mingled spirit spreads into our mind and thereby becomes the spirit of our mind. It is in such a spirit that we are renewed for our transformation (Rom. 12:2; 2 Cor. 3:18).

Our strengthened spirit is the means for our entire being to be renewed. When our spirit has become strong, it will spread into our mind and cause it to be renewed. When our spirit renews our mind, it proceeds to renew our emotion and our will. By such a renewing spirit the church has the proper living as the one new man.

FILLED IN SPIRIT

In 5:18 Paul goes on to speak about being filled in spirit. This verse says, "And do not be drunk with wine, in which is dissipation, but be filled in spirit." To be drunk with wine is to be filled in the body, whereas to be filled in our regenerated spirit is to be filled with Christ (1:23) unto all the fullness of God (3:19). To be drunk with wine in the body causes us to be dissipated, but to be filled with Christ causes us to overflow with Him in speaking, singing, psalming, and giving thanks to God (5:19-20). It also causes us to subject ourselves one to another (v. 21). What we need for the church life is not to be filled in our minds with objective knowledge, but to be filled in our spirit with the riches of Christ unto all the fullness of God.

PRAYING IN SPIRIT

The last reference in Ephesians to the regenerated human spirit indwelt by the Spirit of God is in 6:18. Here Paul charges us to pray "at every time in spirit," that is, to pray in our spirit mingled with God's Spirit. This reference to the spirit is in the context of spiritual warfare. When the church has become the new man with the normal functions and the proper daily living, and when the spots and wrinkles have been removed by the nourishing and cherishing of Christ, the church becomes a mighty warrior, a soldier to fight the battle for God's interests. In order to engage in spiritual warfare, we need to pray in the mingled spirit.

I hope that we all are impressed with the place of the human spirit in the book of Ephesians. In chapter one we have the spirit of wisdom and revelation; in chapter two, the spirit as the place of God's dwelling; in chapter three, the spirit as the means of receiving revelation and as the organ that needs to be strengthened; in chapter four, the renewing spirit that spreads into our mind to renew all our inward parts; in chapter five, the spirit being filled with Christ unto all the fullness of God; and in chapter six, the mingled spirit as the organ in which we pray to fight the battle for the Lord. As we consider all these references to the spirit in this short book, we see that the church life is altogether a matter in the spirit. In order to practice the church life, we need to turn to our spirit and remain there. The daily living of the corporate new man is absolutely in the spirit of the mind.

A CLEAR SKY

A number of times we have spoken about the importance of having a clear sky. Actually, to have a clear sky is simply to have a clear spirit. Spiritually speaking, our spirit is our sky. Therefore, when our spirit is clear, our sky is clear as well. However, if our spirit is cloudy, our sky also will be cloudy.

In 4:17-19 Paul says that those who walk in the vanity of the mind are darkened in their understanding and estranged from the life of God because of the ignorance which is in them. He points out that their hearts are hard, that they have ceased from feeling, and that they have given themselves over to lewdness. Therefore, to be in the vanity of the mind is to be in thick darkness. By contrast, the believers, who were once darkness, are "now light in the Lord" (5:8). Therefore, we should "walk as children of light." In 5:14 Paul says, "Awake, sleeper, and arise from among the dead, and Christ shall shine on you." Whenever we are in the spirit, we are in the light, under the Lord's shining. As a result, we have a clear sky. The more clear our spirit is, the more clear our sky becomes.

If we exercise the mind instead of the spirit, the sky within us will be cloudy. The same is true if we are strong in our emotion or will instead of in our spirit. However, if we deny our natural mind, emotion, and will and take a definite stand with the Lord in our spirit, our sky will immediately and spontaneously become clear. When we hesitate in following the Lord, our sky is cloudy. But when we are definite and absolute in following Him, it is clear.

The reason we hesitate to follow the Lord is that we consider too much in the mind or care for our emotional concerns. Possibly you are afraid of offending someone. A brother may be concerned about his wife's reaction to his decision to take the way of the church. Such considerations and concerns cloud our spirit. But if we set aside our considerations and concerns and make a firm decision to follow the Lord absolutely, our sky will be clear. There will be no clouds in our spirit. In our spirit we have no worries and no concerns, only the indwelling Holy Spirit.

If we walk according to the vanity of the mind, we shall be in darkness and estranged from the life of God. But if we turn to the spirit of the mind, Christ will shine upon us, and we shall have a clear sky. The reason certain ones who have been with us for a number of years have not improved much is that they live in the vanity of the mind. Rarely do they turn to the spirit of the mind. If such brothers and sisters turn from the vanity of the mind to the spirit of the mind, they will undergo a great change. Listening to messages is of little help unless we are in the spirit of the mind instead of in the vanity of the mind. We cannot receive spiritual help from messages if we exercise the mind rather than the spirit. We need to leap out of the vanity of the mind and walk according to the spirit of the mind.

A NEW ELEMENT WROUGHT INTO US

As we walk according to the spirit of our mind, we are renewed. To be renewed is not to be adjusted, corrected, or improved in a mere outward way. It is to have a new element, the divine element, wrought into us. This means that in the church life we should not care for outward correction or adjustment; we should care for inward renewing.

If we would be renewed, we need to put off the old man and put on the new man. Notice that Paul does not say that we should try to improve the old man. Many saints do not have the intention of putting off the old man and of putting on the new man. Instead, their intention is to improve themselves, even to perfect themselves. They may try to adjust themselves in order to adapt to the church life. This is a mistake. In the genuine church life there is no adjustment or correction; there is simply the putting off of the old man and the putting on of the new man. Actually, this putting off and putting on is the renewing.

For something to be renewed means that the old element is replaced by a new element. Our spirit is a renewing spirit because it is indwelt by the living Christ as the renewing element. Because we have the element of newness in our spirit, we can be renewed in the spirit of the mind as the renewing spirit spreads into our mind. The more we turn to the spirit of the mind and walk in the spirit of the mind, the more our mind will be renewed. Then in a practical way the old element is replaced by the new element. In this way we put off the old man and put on the new man.

THE EXPRESSION OF GOD

The result of such a daily living is that we have the image of God. This means that our life becomes the expression of God. In 4:24 Paul says that the new man is according to God. This means that the church life is according to God Himself and is God's expression. God's goal is to gain a people through whom He can express Himself. In the church as the new man according to God, this divine goal is fulfilled. This is altogether different from religion, which teaches people to behave themselves outwardly. God's intention is not simply to get a people who are outwardly kind, gentle, and humble. His intention is to have a Body, the new man, for His expression. In order for this goal to be attained, the new man must firstly be created in Christ. Paul speaks of this in chapter two. Then, according to Paul's word in chapter four, the new man must grow and live by walking in the spirit of the mind and must be renewed daily. The result is that the corporate new man will become the image of God, His expression. In this way God's intention is fulfilled.

THE DIVINE CHARACTER EXPRESSED THROUGH HUMAN VIRTUE

In 4:24 Paul says that the new man was created according to God in righteousness and holiness of the truth. Righteousness is a matter of being right with God and man according to God's righteous way; holiness is a matter of being separated unto God from anything common and of being saturated with God's holy nature.

In this verse the Greek word rendered holiness is *hosiotees*. It denotes a genuine piety. Hence, some versions adopt the rendering "piety." If we consider this verse in context, we shall see that the church life is a life of genuine piety. Unfortunately, this word has been damaged by traditional use and given a religious meaning. In the New Testament, this word sometimes translated piety is virtue according to the divine character expressed through humanity. On the one hand, it involves human virtue; on the other hand, it expresses the divine nature and character. We need to have a daily walk in which the divine character is expressed through our virtue.

This kind of living is very different from mere human virtue. As human beings, we have certain virtues. But these virtues need to become the expression of the divine character. For example, the New Testament teaches wives to submit to their husbands. Confucius also taught this. Actually Confucius taught a threefold submission: to the father, to the husband, and, if the husband should die, to the son. What is the difference between submission according to the teaching of Confucius and submission according to the teaching of the Bible? The submission that is according to the teaching of Confucius is nothing more than a human virtue. In this kind of submission there is nothing of the flavor of Christ and nothing of the divine character. But if a sister in the Lord is filled in spirit and submits to her husband out of this filling, there will be in her submission some amount of the flavor of Christ. This means that in her submission there will be the expression of the divine character.

Let us take another example, the matter of honoring our parents. The Bible surely teaches us to honor our parents. Confucius taught the same thing. But the difference between the honoring of parents that is in accord with the teaching of Confucius and that which is in accord with the Bible is that in the former there is no flavor of Christ, whereas in the latter there is both the flavor of Christ and the expression of the divine character. When we are filled in spirit unto all the fullness of God and honor our parents out of such an infilling, there will be the expression of God in our relationship to our parents. Our behavior will not be a mere human virtue; it will be a virtue with the divine character and with the flavor of Christ. As we honor our parents, there should be the sweet savor of Christ. This is the expression of God through human virtue. Suppose a young man honors his parents from a spirit filled unto all the fullness of God. In this virtue there will be the divine character. This is the expression of God in humanity.

This expression of God is absolutely different from mere ethical behavior. Although the followers of Confucius may attain a high ethical standard, there is no flavor of Christ in their virtue. I repeat, in our virtue there needs to be the character of God and the flavor and taste of Christ. Such a divine expression through human virtue is conveyed by the Greek word for holiness in 4:24. The church life must be filled with such an expression of divine character through human virtue.

In our honesty and generosity there needs to be the expression of the divine character. There are two kinds of honesty and two kinds of generosity: an honesty and a generosity that are mere human virtues, and an honesty and a generosity that express the character of God. In the church life our honesty and generosity must have the flavor of Christ. As others contact us, they should not only have the sense that we are virtuous; they should be able to sense in our virtue the flavor of Christ and see the expression of the divine character.

The key to the church life is the spirit of the mind. If we live according to the spirit of the mind, there will be in the church life the expression of the divine character. Then we shall be a corporate people with the flavor of Christ and the expression of God. If we simply give others the impression that we are good, righteous, and kind, our church life is a failure. There must be in our goodness, righteousness, and kindness the expression of the Triune God. The church life must be filled with the aroma and flavor of Christ and with the character of God. Such a living is the living of the Triune God through our humanity. For centuries, God has been longing for such a church life. We pray that before long this kind of church life will be fully practiced among us in the Lord's recovery. May the Lord be satisfied by seeing such an expression of Himself through the corporate new man on earth!

LIFE-STUDY OF EPHESIANS

MESSAGE NINETY-FIVE

THE BEAUTY OF THE BRIDE

Scripture Reading: Eph. 1:9-11, 13b-14, 17-23; 3:16-17a, 19b; 5:25-27, 29-30, 32

SPOTS AND WRINKLES

In previous messages we have considered three categories of negative things that damage the church life: ordinances, doctrine, and the old man. Now we come to the fourth category of these negative things—the spots and wrinkles. Paul refers to this in 5:27, where he says that Christ will "present the church to Himself glorious, not having spot or wrinkle or any such things."

In Ephesians Paul deals with the four categories of negative things in a very good sequence. Related to the creation of the new man, we have the ordinances. Related to the growth of the new man for function, we have doctrine. Furthermore, related to the daily living of the new man, we have the old man with his old way of life. For the creation of the new man, the ordinances must be abolished and slain. For the growth of the new man, doctrine must be depreciated. For the proper daily living of the new man, the old man must be put off. However, after these three categories of negative things have been dealt with, we must still face the problem of the spots and wrinkles.

Because they are so subjective, the spots and wrinkles are more difficult to deal with than the ordinances, the doctrines, and the old man. We cannot simply abolish the spots and wrinkles or put them off, for they are in our organic tissue and natural makeup. Spots are of the natural life, and wrinkles are a matter of oldness. Humanly speaking, there is no way for us to remove such things. However, God has a way.

The water of life in the Word can metabolically wash away these defects by the transformation of life. The more Christ sanctifies the church and cleanses her through the washing of the water in the Word, the fewer spots and wrinkles there will be. Furthermore, as Christ nourishes and cherishes the church, the spots and wrinkles will be removed metabolically. Every flaw, defect, and imperfection will be removed by Christ's transforming life.

IMPARTING THE RICH ELEMENT OF CHRIST

Instead of trying to correct others or to adjust them outwardly, we need to minister to them the sanctifying, purifying, nourishing, and cherishing element of Christ. This element will produce an inward change that will take away the oldness and the defects. We should not rely on any method or way. If a particular way is prevailing, it is not because of the way itself, but because of the life contained in that way and released by it. What we should impart to others is not a method or way of doing things; we should impart the rich element of Christ that will sanctify, purify, nourish, and cherish them. If you contact Christians whose way of meeting is different from yours, do not try to change them. Instead, take the opportunity to minister the riches of Christ to them. We should not care for a way, a method, or a form. We should care only to release the riches of Christ and to impart them to others. It is Christ who sanctifies and cleanses. Through His transforming work, all the spots and wrinkles are removed and replaced by His living element.

EXPERIENCING THE SANCTIFYING ELEMENT OF CHRIST

We have pointed out that spots and wrinkles are more difficult to deal with than ordinances, doctrine, and the old man because these defects and imperfections are subjectively part of our natural being. They have been interwoven into our organic tissue. Therefore, only the inner supply of life can deal with them. If we want the spots and wrinkles to be removed, then we must rely only on the sanctifying, purifying, nourishing, and cherishing element of Christ. It is not as difficult to deal with ordinances as it is with doctrines; doctrine is not as difficult to deal with as the old man; and the old man is not as difficult to deal with as the spots and wrinkles. Even though we may have no problems with ordinances, doctrine, or the old man, we must still inquire whether or not we are troubled by spots and wrinkles.

The spots and wrinkles must be removed in order for the Bride to be prepared for Christ. To be sure, the Bride presented to Christ will not have any spots or wrinkles. Revelation 19:7 says, "Let us rejoice and exult, and let us give the glory to Him, for the marriage of the Lamb is come, and His wife has made herself ready." Certainly the wife by this time will have been purified from all the spots and wrinkles.

We should not place our trust in mere outward change. Such change can take place suddenly without having any effect on the spots and wrinkles in our being. God's concern is not that we simply change with respect to our outward appearance; His concern is that the spots and wrinkles be washed away by the sanctifying element of Christ. Only through such a process of sanctification can we become a beautiful and glorious Bride for Christ, a Bride without blemish or imperfection. We should forget about trying to improve ourselves and concentrate instead on experiencing the sanctifying riches of Christ. We all need more experience of the purifying element of Christ. The more we experience this element, the more our defects and shortcomings will be metabolically removed. As the result of this process, we shall become a beautiful Bride ready to be presented to Christ. Only by the supply of life from Christ can our natural defects and organic blemishes be removed.

If we are clear about this, we shall realize that mere teachings can do nothing to eliminate spots and wrinkles. To repeat, only the sanctifying element which comes through the nourishing and cherishing of Christ can deal with such things. Praise the Lord that the element of Christ is gradually eliminating our defects!

THE PREPARATION OF THE BRIDE

I believe that we are living in a day in which the Lord is preparing His Bride. Furthermore, I have the full assurance that we are presently undergoing this process of preparation. Otherwise, when, where, and with whom will Revelation 19 have its fulfillment? This chapter is in the process of being fulfilled among us in the Lord's recovery.

We need to connect Revelation 19 with Ephesians 5. Apart from Ephesians 5, there is no way for the Bride to be prepared, and hence no way for Revelation 19 to be fulfilled. It is very significant that the Lord has spoken to us about ordinances, doctrines, the old man, and the spots and wrinkles. It is crucial that we experience the nourishing, cherishing, sanctifying, and purifying riches of Christ to remove our oldness and defects. When all such things have been removed, we shall become a church that is holy, glorious, and without blemish. Then we shall be the Bride in Revelation 19. When the Bride has been prepared, Christ will come as the Bridegroom. Praise the Lord that we are in the process of becoming a holy and glorious Bride for Christ! How we praise the Lord for showing us the way to be prepared as the Bride, made ready for His coming back! Christ will have a church without ordinances, doctrines, the old man, and the spots and wrinkles. Such a church will be the beautiful Bride to satisfy the desire of His heart.

BEAUTY FOR PRESENTATION

In chapter one we have a general sketch of the church, and in chapter two, the creation, birth, and formation of the one new man. Then in chapter four we have the growth of this new man for functioning. Also in chapter four we see the daily life of the new man. Then in chapter five we come to the presentation of the church to Christ. At the time of this presentation, the church will be the Bride, not the new man. As the new man, the church needs the functions. But as the Bride, the church needs beauty. The growth in chapter four is for the function of the new man, whereas the beauty in chapter five is for the presentation of the Bride.

The spots and wrinkles do not affect the function of the church. However, they very much detract from the beauty of the church. What a man looks for in a bride is not firstly ability; it is beauty. The church as Christ's Bride must also be beautiful. For this reason, Paul goes on from the function and daily living of the new man in chapter four to the presentation of the Bride without spot or wrinkle in chapter five. If we grow in the Lord, eventually our functions as members of the Body will come forth. However, we may function properly and have an excellent daily living according to the spirit of the mind, but still not be beautiful in the eyes of the Lord because of our spots and wrinkles. After saying so much about the church in chapters one through four, Paul goes on in chapter five to speak about the church as the Bride. In this chapter he says nothing concerning the creation of the church, the growth of the church, or the daily living of the church. Instead, he speaks of the beauty of the church. When Christ presents the church to Himself, the church will not be a strong man; she will be a beautiful Bride. Christ is the universal Man. As this universal Man, He needs the church to be His Bride to match Him. In order to be the Bride of Christ, the church must become beautiful and have all the spots and wrinkles removed.

THE WAY TO BE PREPARED

We have seen that with respect to the creation of the new man, the function of the new man, and the daily living of the new man, we face problems with ordinances, doctrine, and the old way of life. But with respect to the presentation of the church as the Bride, we have the problem of the spots and wrinkles. The crucial question is how these blemishes can be removed. Any bride would want to have a healthy, radiant complexion on her wedding day. If she is concerned about blemishes, she should begin long beforehand to prepare herself for her wedding by eating nutritious foods that will give her a healthy complexion. In the same principle, today we must prepare ourselves to be the Bride by taking in the element of Christ's riches as our nourishment. Christ is the food for the church. Therefore, as she prepares herself to be presented to Christ, the church must eat Christ. There is no other way to be prepared. Eating Jesus is the way. By eating Him we become a beautiful and even glorious Bride.

THE REFLECTION OF CHRIST

Christ is now preparing us to be His Bride. The time is coming when He will present the Bride to Himself. Surely at the time of her presentation to Christ, the Bride will not have any wrinkles or spots. In His Bride Christ will behold nothing but beauty. This beauty will be the reflection of what He is. Do you know where the beauty of the Bride comes from? It comes from the very Christ who is wrought into the church and who is then expressed through the church. Our beauty is not our behavior. Our only beauty is the reflection of Christ, the shining out of Christ from within us. What Christ appreciates in us is the expression of Himself in us. Nothing less than this will meet His standard or win His appreciation.

Firstly, Christ must come into us and then be assimilated by us. Then He will be able to shine out of us. This shining is the glory of the Bride, the manifestation of divinity through humanity. Real beauty is the expression of the divine attributes through humanity. Nothing in the universe is as beautiful as this expression. Therefore, the beauty of the Bride is Christ shining out of us. It is a matter of divinity expressed through humanity. Through our humanity there is an expression of the divine color, the divine appearance, the divine flavor, the divine nature, and the divine character. Hallelujah for such a beauty!

On the day of his wedding, a bridegroom cares much more for the beauty of his bride than for her ability. In like manner, in the church life our beauty will eventually be much more important to the Lord than our function. At the beginning of the church life, we may emphasize ability and function. But eventually we shall place more emphasis on beauty. The Lord Jesus cares much more for our beauty than for our function. Do not pay that much attention to becoming capable, qualified, and gifted in function. At first, this may count for something in the church life. But eventually the Lord will show us that what He cares for is not our ability; He cares for the beauty of Himself expressed through our humanity. Christ does not intend to present a capable church to Himself. The church that will be presented to Him will be glorious and beautiful, a church without spot, wrinkle, or any such thing. If our blemishes and imperfections are to be removed, we need to take in more and more of Christ. He should not simply energize us for our function, but also beautify us that we may be His Bride.

BEAUTIFIED BY THE INDWELLING CHRIST

We need to go on from the function in Ephesians 4 to the beauty in Ephesians 5. In caring for their children, mothers may value strength in a boy, but they appreciate beauty in a girl. Likewise, in the church as the one new man there is strength and ability, but with the church as the Bride there is beauty and glory. We should learn somewhat to depreciate our ability and strength, for as part of the Bride, we shall be not male, but female. At the time of the wedding, what the church will need is beauty, not strength. Oh, the church is being beautified by partaking of Christ, by digesting Christ, and by assimilating Christ! The more we experience the indwelling Christ in this way, the more He will replace our spots and wrinkles with His element, and the more His riches with the divine attributes will become our beauty. Then we shall be prepared to be presented to Christ as His lovely Bride.

CLOTHED IN FINE LINEN

We have pointed out that the experience of Ephesians 5 is necessary for the fulfillment of Revelation 19. Ephesians shows how Christ prepares the Bride by sanctifying, cleansing, nourishing, and cherishing us with Himself. In this way we are metabolically transformed and we become beautiful and glorious, ready to be presented to Christ according to Revelation 19.

Speaking of the wife, the Bride of Christ, Revelation 19:8 says, "And it was given to her that she should be clothed in fine linen, bright and pure; for the fine linen is the righteousness of the saints." Because the Bride is clothed in this way, the declaration can be made that she "has made herself ready" (v. 7). This indicates that by the time of Revelation 19 the Bride will have been prepared. For the Bride to be prepared means that she has the "fine linen, bright and pure." Pure refers to nature, whereas bright refers to expression. This fine linen is "the righteousness of the saints." No doubt, these righteousnesses are related to the righteousness in Ephesians 4:24, where we are told that the new man was created in righteousness. The fact that the clothing of the Bride is pure means not only that it is without dirt, but also that it is without mixture. The fine linen which is the righteousness of the saints does not refer to the righteousness (which is Christ) for our salvation (Phil. 3:9; 1 Cor. 1:30). The righteousness we received for our salvation is objective, that we might meet the requirement of the righteous God. However, the righteousnesses of the Bride here denote the subjective righteousness, Christ as the righteousness which has been constituted into our being. The more this subjective righteousness is wrought into the church, the more she is prepared to become the Bride. Those who compose the Bride have been redeemed and regenerated. But they need to have the subjective righteousness interwoven into their very being in order to have the fine linen, bright and pure. Actually, it is this linen that is the beauty of the Bride.

THE LORD'S WORK IN HIS RECOVERY

There is no doubt that Revelation 19 will be completely fulfilled. Furthermore, we believe that the process of fulfillment is taking place today. Since Jerusalem has been restored to the nation of Israel, the coming back of the Lord Jesus should not be far off. The Bride, however, cannot be prepared quickly. This preparation is a gradual work that takes place over a period of time. Certainly the Lord must be doing a work on earth to prepare His Bride. Where is this work being carried out? With whom is it taking place? Some may say that the work of preparing the Bride is among the spiritual ones in Catholicism, the denominations, and the independent groups. According to this view, Christ will gather together all these spiritual ones and form them into His Bride at the time of His coming. However, this is not the Lord's way. He is not coming to collect those who will constitute the Bride; He is coming to present to Himself the Bride who has already been prepared. This preparation, I believe, involves the work of building corporately. Those who make up the Bride must not only be mature in life; they must also be built together as the one Bride. Therefore, I firmly believe that the Lord is preparing His Bride among those in His recovery.

I am burdened that we would all realize that the Lord's recovery is not another Christian movement or an ordinary Christian work. The work in the recovery is the Lord's genuine work to prepare His Bride. I believe that in the years to come, more of those who seek the Lord faithfully will turn to the way of His recovery. They will realize that nowhere else do they have the inward confirmation. When we turned to the way of the Lord's recovery, we had the sense deep within that the Lord had put His seal on the way we are taking. The primary work of the Lord in His recovery is not to preach the gospel throughout the earth; it is to prepare His Bride.

The Lord's intention is not to revive Christianity as a whole. In His recovery, He is calling out a remnant of those who love Him and who are faithful to Him. He is sending out the call to overcome the degradation of Christianity so that a number of those who seek Him may be prepared as His Bride. In this matter, the Lord is moving on, and we are going on with Him. What a privilege to be alive in this age!

LIFE-STUDY OF EPHESIANS

MESSAGE NINETY-SIX

HEAD OVER ALL TO THE CHURCH

Scripture Reading: Eph. 1:9-11, 22-23; 3:17a

The deepest chapters in Ephesians are chapters one and three. The positive things unfolded in these chapters are far beyond our ability to grasp or apprehend. For example, in 1:10, Paul says, "Unto a dispensation of the fullness of the times, to head up all things in Christ, the things in the heavens and the things on the earth, in Him." I do not think that very many Christians have an adequate understanding of this verse. This word does not refer to the preeminence of Christ, to the authority of Christ, or to the expression of Christ. This verse is unique, and no other verse in the Scriptures can be compared to it. When we read about husbands loving their wives or about wives submitting to their husbands, we readily understand, for such things as love and submission fit into our natural concept. But in order to grasp the meaning of verses such as 1:10, we need a spirit of wisdom and revelation.

GOD'S ETERNAL ADMINISTRATION

As we consider 1:9 and 10, we see that the economy or dispensation which God purposed in Himself is to head up all things in Christ at the fullness of the times. The times refer to the ages. The fullness of the times will be when the new heaven and new earth come, after all the dispensations of God in all the ages have been completed. When God's economy has been completed, Christ will head up all things universally. God has made Christ the Head over all things (1:22). Through all the dispensations of God in all the ages, all things will be headed up in Christ in the new heaven and the new earth. This will be God's eternal administration and economy.

Because our physical body has a head, it is possible for our body to stand upright. Although we stand on our feet, it is actually the head which enables us to stand erect. This indicates that our head causes our entire body to be headed up. If a person has his head cut off, his body will collapse. Because the head causes every part of the body to be headed up, all the things that are on the body—clothing, shoes, eyeglasses—are headed up also.

The entire universe is under Christ's heading up. However, some things are still in a state of collapse because the process of the heading up of all things in Christ has not yet been completed. At the economy of the fullness of times, everything will be headed up in Christ. Nothing will continue to be in a state of collapse, and nothing will fall. In Christ God will head up all things. At present many things in the universe are still falling or collapsing. But at the dispensation of the fullness of the times, nothing will fall. Not even a leaf will fall from a tree.

CHRIST'S NEED FOR THE BODY

We have pointed out that our head functions to head up every part of our physical body. In the same principle, God is using Christ to head up all things in the universe. As the universal Head of all things, Christ needs a Body. This Body is the church. Just as clothing and other items rest on a person's body, so one day everything in the universe will rest on Christ's Body, the church. We have seen that if a person has his head cut off, his body and everything on it will collapse. The principle is the same with Christ as the Head over all things to the church. If all the things in the universe are not headed up in Christ through His Body, they will remain in a state of collapse.

Scientists have their explanations for such phenomena as the falling of leaves from trees. They put forth their reasons for the various physical changes that take place in the universe. These scientific explanations and reasons may be correct temporarily, but they will not be correct eternally. I do not know physics or biology, but I do know the process of the divine heading up of all things. Furthermore, I believe 1:10 when it says that in the dispensation of the fullness of times this process will reach its completion. From that time onward, nothing in the universe will collapse. Everything will rest on the church as the Body of Christ. Christ is the Head, and the church is the Body. Christ is heading up the Body, and all the billions of items in the universe will rest on this headed-up Body. Although we do not see a full picture of this today, we do see it in miniature. We also can enjoy a foretaste of the heading up of all things in Christ.

We should not think that a person can stand upright mainly because his legs, ankles, and feet are strong. We have pointed out that it is actually the head that enables us to stand erect. Apart from the heading up of the body by the head, the body and everything on it will fall down. This is a picture of the heading up of all things in Christ. Firstly, Christ heads up His Body. Then in the dispensation of the fullness of the times, God will head up all things in Christ through the Body.

THE INHERITANCE, THE SEAL, AND THE PLEDGE

In 1:11 Paul goes on to say, "In Whom also we were made an inheritance, having been predestinated according to the purpose of the One Who operates all things according to the counsel of His will." It is possible to render the Greek translated "were made an inheritance" as "have obtained an inheritance." Unless we have some understanding of verse 10, we shall not be able to understand verse 11. The words, "in Whom" in verse 11 refer to Christ as the Head. In Him, the universal Head, we were made God's inheritance. The Greek verb translated "were made an inheritance" means to choose or assign by lot. Hence, this clause literally means we were designated as a heritage. We were made an inheritance to inherit God's inheritance. On the one hand, we were made God's inheritance (v. 18) for God's enjoyment;

on the other hand, we were made to inherit God as our inheritance (v. 14) for our enjoyment.

In verse 13 Paul says, "In Whom you also, hearing the word of the truth, the gospel of your salvation, in Whom also believing, you were sealed with the Holy Spirit of the promise." As verse 14 explains, the Holy Spirit of the promise is "the pledge of our inheritance, unto the redemption of the acquired possession to the praise of His glory." To be sealed with the Holy Spirit is to be marked with the Holy Spirit as a living seal.

We have been made God's inheritance. At the time we were saved, God put His Holy Spirit into us as a seal to mark us out, to indicate that we belong to God. This Spirit is the pledge, foretaste, guarantee, token payment, a part payment in advance. Since we are God's inheritance, the Holy Spirit is a seal upon us. Since God is our inheritance, the Holy Spirit is the pledge of this inheritance to us. God gives His Holy Spirit to us, not only as a guarantee of our inheritance, securing our heritage, but also as a foretaste of what we shall inherit of God, affording us a taste beforehand of the full inheritance.

We need to understand verses 13 and 14 in the light of verses 10 and 11. We have seen that in Christ God is in the process of heading up all things in heaven and on earth. However, without the church as the Body to match Christ as the Head, it will not be possible for God to head up all things in Christ. The heading up of all things is accomplished by the Head, but it cannot be accomplished without a Body for the Head. This Body is God's inheritance, God's possession. Because we were lost, we had to be redeemed, purchased back, by God. Through redemption we have become God's acquired possession. We, God's redeemed ones, the church, are God's possession, acquired by His purchase with the precious blood of Christ (Acts 20:28). In God's economy, God becomes our inheritance, and we become God's possession. As God's inheritance and possession, we are the Body of Christ, through which all things in the universe are being headed up in Christ.

SATURATED WITH THE SPIRIT FOR THE HEADING UP OF ALL THINGS

It is important to see how God acquires His inheritance and His possession. Firstly, He purchased us by the blood of Christ. Secondly, He sealed us with His Spirit. The Spirit as the seal upon the Body is actually God Himself. This means that God put Himself as the seal upon the church purchased by the blood of Christ. The Spirit as the seal is upon the Body not simply in an objective way. On the contrary, through the process of sealing, the seal will permeate and saturate our whole being in a very subjective way. The more we, God's inheritance, are saturated with the Spirit as the living seal, the more heading up there will be in the universe. As God's inheritance and possession, we have been predestinated and purchased. Now we are in the process of being thoroughly saturated with the Spirit. When God's possession has been wholly saturated with the Spirit as the living seal, the heading up of all things in Christ will be completed.

When everything in the universe has been headed up in Christ, everything will be in order. Nothing will be out of place, and nothing will collapse or fall. During autumn, leaves fall from the trees. This indicates that something is out of order. Surely in the new heaven and the new earth leaves will no longer fall from trees, for by then everything will be in perfect order, having been headed up in Christ. As we have seen, this heading up of all things in Christ depends on God's possession, the church, being saturated with Himself.

In the church life in the Lord's recovery, we can experience a foretaste of the heading up of all things. When the church life in a particular city is strong, that city will be brought more into order. For example, policemen who work in the area of Elden Hall in Los Angeles have told us that the presence of the church has produced many positive changes in that area. There has been an improvement of the neighborhood, especially with respect to the crime rate. This illustrates that it is through the church that God is heading up all things in Christ. The more the church as God's possession is saturated with the Triune God, the more heading up there will be. Firstly the church is headed up, and then the things related to the church and that rest on the church will be headed up also. If we allow Christ to saturate us thoroughly, eventually we shall see the completion of the heading up of all things in Christ.

THE TRANSMISSION FROM THE HEAD TO THE BODY

Humanity is the center of God's creation. The heading up of all things in Christ takes place as the Triune God works Himself into man as the center of His creation. According to 1:22, God has subjected all things under the feet of the resurrected and ascended Christ and "gave Him to be Head over all things to the church." The little word "to" is very important because it implies a kind of transmission. Whatever Christ, the Head, has attained and obtained is now being transmitted to His Body, the church. By means of this transmission, the church shares with Christ all His attainments. The church shares in His resurrection from among the dead, His being seated in His transcendency, the subjection of all things under His feet, and His headship over all things. As the element of Christ is transmitted into the church, all that He has accomplished, attained, and obtained is transfused into the church as well. Through this marvelous transmission we become the Body of Christ, the fullness of the One who fills all in all. Then, as His Body, we shall become the means by which God will head up all things in Christ. The crucial factor here is the divine transmission, the transfusion of Christ into our being.

CHRIST MAKING HIS HOME IN OUR HEARTS

In Ephesians 3 we see experientially that the very Christ who is Head over all things is actually transmitted into us. According to verse 17, Christ is making His home in our hearts. For Christ to make His home in our hearts means that He is transmitted into us in a full way. We may say that our heart is the battery and that Christ is the heavenly electricity that is being transmitted into the heart of the battery. In this way, the battery is charged with all that Christ is and with all that He has obtained and attained. By means of such an inward transmission or transfusion, Christ makes His home in our hearts. Hence it is the heavenly transmission that brings Christ into our hearts. Then, just as blood circulates from the heart throughout our physical body, so the Christ who has been transmitted into our heart spiritually will spread into every part of our inner being. Through this transmission and the spread of Christ within us God is heading up all things in Christ through the church.

ONENESS IN THE HEAVENLY TRANSMISSION

Many Christians are amazed when they behold the oneness of the saints in the church life. They are surprised that those with different racial, cultural, and national backgrounds can be truly one. In their amazement at such a oneness, some have thought that we must have set up an organization to maintain this oneness. However, we do not have such an organization, and there is no possibility that any organization could produce such a oneness. We are not one by means of organization; we are one in the divine transmission. If the heavenly transmission of Christ into our inner being should cease, our oneness will be terminated. We can be one simply because we are being headed up in Christ through the transmission of Christ into our being. This is what enables us to live together in oneness in the church life.

We believe that in the years to come God will head us up even more. As a result, the condition of the church will become much better than it is today. Eventually, in the dispensation of the fullness of times, the whole universe will be headed up in Christ through the church. We have often spoken of the building up of the church. But the emphasis in this message is on being headed up in Christ through the divine transmission. The more Christ is transmitted into us, the more the process of heading up will advance. I have the full assurance that if the Lord delays His coming back, many more Christians will be headed up in Christ through His Body. The worldly people will be surprised at such a heading up, for the more they try to unite through such organizations as the United Nations, the more divided they are. The day is coming when the earth will see not only the uniting, nor even just the building up, but the heading up of all things in Christ. Christ is Head over all things to the church, and now He is in the process of heading up all things through the church. This is what the Lord is doing among us today.

LIFE-STUDY OF EPHESIANS

MESSAGE NINETY-SEVEN

THE CHURCH AS GOD'S WARRIOR

Scripture Reading: Eph. 6:10-18

VARIOUS ASPECTS OF THE CHURCH

In Ephesians 1 we have a general view of what the church is and how the church comes into being. Then in chapter two we see that the church is the new man created by Christ in Himself. In chapter three we have a clear vision of Christ making His home in the hearts of those in the church. For Christ to make His home in the heart of the church means that He is transfused into the center of the church's inner being. Through such a transfusion, the church is filled unto all the fullness of God. In this way the church is mingled with divinity and saturated with it. Therefore, the church is humanity mingled, saturated, and permeated with divinity.

In chapter four we see the church as the new man. The new man in chapter two is organically complete, but not functionally perfect. In order to be functionally perfect, the church as the new man must grow in life. The more the new man grows, the more he will be able to function. In Ephesians 4 we also see the daily walk of the new man. As we have pointed out, fallen mankind walks according to the vanity of the mind, but the walk of the church as the new man is in the spirit of the mind.

In Ephesians 5 we see another aspect of the church—the church as the Bride prepared for Christ. In one sense, the church is the new man who needs growth, function, and a proper daily living. In another sense, the church is the Bride who must be beautified in order to be presented to Christ at His coming. With the church as the Bride, the problem is not with ordinances, doctrine, or the old man.

The problem is with the spots and wrinkles, defects that are organic and that ruin the beauty of the church. In order to be free from such defects, the church must be sanctified, purified, nourished, and cherished by having the element of Christ wrought into her metabolically. This element will cause the spots and wrinkles to disappear, and it will beautify the Bride for her presentation to Christ. Eventually, through this process of metabolic transformation the church will become glorious.

THE BRIDE AND THE WARRIOR

In Ephesians 6 we see still another aspect of the church. In this chapter the church is not the Body, the building, the family, the kingdom, the new man, or the Bride. Here the church is God's warrior. The church should be not only the Body to express Christ, the dwelling place for God's habitation, and the new man for the fulfillment of God's economy; the church must also be a warrior, a soldier, to defeat God's enemy.

According to Revelation 19, the church is both the Bride who is presented to Christ and the warrior who fights with Him against God's enemy. At His coming again, the Lord Jesus firstly will meet His Bride. After receiving the Bride, Christ and the overcomers will enter into battle against the enemy. According to Revelation 19:11, the Lord will ride on a white horse, and the armies which are in heaven will follow Him on white horses, dressed in fine linen, white and pure (v. 14). Revelation 17:14 also refers to this: "These shall make war with the Lamb, and the Lamb shall overcome them, for He is Lord of lords and King of kings; and they who are with Him are called and chosen and faithful."

In Revelation 19:7 and 8 we see that the Bride is clothed in "fine linen, bright and pure." Then in verse 14 we see that the armies which follow the Lord into battle are "dressed in fine linen, white and pure." These verses indicate that the Bride's wedding garment will also be the uniform she wears as God's army to fight against His enemy. Therefore, to have the wedding garment is also to have the uniform.

In Ephesians 5 and 6 we see the church as the Bride and as the warrior. In Revelation 19 we also have these two aspects of the church. As the church, we are not only the Body, the dwelling place of God, the kingdom of God, the family of God, and the new man; we are also the Bride and the warrior. As the Bride, we must be beautiful, without spot or wrinkle, and be clothed in fine linen. As the warrior, we must be equipped to fight against God's enemy.

SPIRITUAL WARFARE—A MATTER OF THE BODY

In God's economy there is one army constituted of a corporate warrior. This means that the warrior in Ephesians 6 is a corporate entity. Only as a corporate entity, the Body, can we put on the whole armor of God. This is contrary to the concept held by many Christians that an individual believer is able to wear the entire armor. The armor in Ephesians 6 is not for Christians as individuals; it is for the church corporately as the Body. What this chapter reveals is not the believers fighting as individuals, but a corporate army fighting the battle for God's interests on earth.

Spiritual warfare is not an individual matter; it is a matter of the Body, a corporate entity to fight the battle against God's enemy. No soldier in a modern army would enter into battle by himself. Rather, he would fight as part of a well-trained and fully equipped army. After we have been formed corporately into an army, we shall be able to fight against God's enemy. God's strategy is to use the church as His army to fight against the enemy. Therefore, it is very dangerous to be isolated from the army. Only by remaining in the army will we have the necessary protection.

Years ago, the Lord's people regarded spiritual warfare as an individual matter. But through the years we have seen that it is altogether a matter of the church as God's corporate army. If you separate yourself from the church, you will be defeated. Satan's strategy is simply to isolate you from the church as God's army. It is crucial for us to realize that spiritual warfare is a Body matter. If we realize this and stay with the church, we shall be victorious. The battle is not for us as individual believers; it is for the church as God's army.

EMPOWERED IN THE LORD

As God's warrior, the church does not fight by her own strength. Ephesians 6:10 says, "For the rest, be empowered in the Lord and in the might of His strength." This verse indicates clearly that we should not fight in our own strength. On the contrary, we must be empowered in the Lord and in the might of His strength. The Greek word rendered "empowered" has the same root as the word power in 1:19. To deal with God's enemy, to fight against the evil forces of darkness, we need to be empowered with the greatness of the power that raised up Christ from the dead and seated Him in the heavens, far above all the evil spirits in the air. In the spiritual warfare against Satan and his evil kingdom, we can fight only in the Lord, not in ourselves. Whenever we are in ourselves, we are defeated.

PUTTING ON CHRIST AS THE ARMOR

According to Ephesians 6, the Lord with His might is the very armor that we put on for our protection. This means that we, as the Body, need to put on Christ Himself as our armor. In order to fight in the spiritual warfare, we must have Christ as the whole armor of God.

In 6:14-17 there are six aspects of Christ as armor: the girdle of truth, or reality; the breastplate of righteousness; the firm foundation of the gospel of peace (the shoes); the shield of faith; the helmet of salvation; and the sword of the Spirit. Therefore, the whole armor of God consists of the girdle, the breastplate, the shoes, the shield, the helmet, and the sword. The shield is for defense, whereas the sword is for offense. In fact, the sword is the only item of the armor that is for offensive warfare.

APPLYING THE ARMOR BY PRAYER

According to verse 18, we receive the helmet of salvation and the sword of the Spirit by means of all prayer and petition. Actually, prayer is the means by which we receive all the aspects of the whole armor of God. Do you know how to apply the girdle of reality? It is by praying in spirit. Prayer is also the way to apply the breastplate, the shoes, the shield, the helmet, and the sword.

PRAY-READING THE WORD

In Greek, the antecedent of "which" in verse 17 is the Spirit, not the sword. This indicates that the Spirit is the word of God. Both the Spirit and the word are Christ (2 Cor. 3:17; Rev. 19:13).

We need to receive the word of God by means of all prayer and petition. According to verses 17 and 18, we are to take the word of God by means of all prayer. These verses indicate that we may take the word by pray-reading, that is, by praying with the words of Scripture and over them, using the words of the Bible as our prayer to God. The term pray-reading is not found in the Bible. However, the fact of pray-reading is according to the Scriptures. Just as the Bible reveals the fact that God is triune, even though the word Trinity is not found in the Scriptures, so the Bible contains the fact of pray-reading, even though this term is not actually used.

I can testify that to pray-read the word is better, higher, richer, and fuller than simply to read it. Day by day I am watered, filled, satisfied, enlivened, strengthened, nourished, and cherished through pray-reading the word of God. Furthermore, by pray-reading I am sanctified, purified, and transformed. Although I certainly would not impose pray-reading on others, I would never give it up. It is too sweet, too good. Simply by praying over John 1:1, for example, I am nourished, filled, and satisfied in the Lord.

PRAYING AT EVERY TIME IN SPIRIT

As we receive the word by means of all prayer and petition, we should pray "at every time in spirit." The spirit in verse 18 is our regenerated spirit indwelt by the Spirit of God. Hence, this spirit is the mingled spirit, our spirit mingled with God's Spirit. Whenever we pray as a means of taking in the word, we need to be in spirit. The spirit is the proper organ for prayer. As we have pointed out many times, we can be in spirit simply by calling on the name of the Lord Jesus from deep within. When we call "O Lord Jesus," we turn from the vanity of the mind to the spirit of the mind. How sweet and enjoyable it is to call on the Lord Jesus in spirit!

By praying in spirit we apply Christ as the whole armor of God. As we take the word by praying in spirit, we spontaneously contact Christ as the life-giving Spirit. Immediately, our praying and reading become living, and we are empowered by Christ and covered with Him as our armor. Furthermore, we have the realization that we are in the Body and that Christ with all that He is and has is our portion. In this way we apply Him as the all-inclusive armor.

NOT FIGHTING BUT ENJOYING

When we are in the Body, we actually do not carry on the spiritual warfare; we simply enjoy it. Instead of struggling in the battle, the battle becomes an enjoyment. Because we pray in spirit to apply all the aspects of Christ as the armor, spiritual fighting becomes an enjoyment. We enjoy Christ as the reality that girds us and as the righteousness that covers and protects our conscience. Furthermore, we enjoy Him as the firm foundation of the gospel of peace and as our shield of faith. Christ Himself is faith to us. As Hebrews 12:2 says, He is the Author and Perfecter of faith. With Christ as our shield, we are defended from the flaming darts of the evil one. Moreover, we enjoy Christ as the helmet of salvation that covers our head, and also as the sword of the Spirit, which is the word of God. Psalm 23:5 says, "Thou preparest a table before me in the presence of mine enemies." This indicates that the battlefield is a place of feasting. We feast in the presence of the enemy, enjoying Christ as reality, righteousness, peace, faith, salvation, and as the living word of God. We enjoy Him and apply Him by praying in spirit.

THE KILLING POWER OF THE WORD

We have pointed out that by pray-reading we take the word of God into us. Usually when we speak of taking the word of God into us, we think of the word as nourishment. However, in Ephesians 6 the emphasis is not on the nourishing word, but on the killing word. The nourishing word is for our building up, whereas the killing word deals with the enemy. In this context, we should pray-read the word not mainly to receive nourishment, but primarily to experience the sword as the killing instrument. The more we pray-read the word, the more we should experience the killing power of the word.

THE ENEMY AND THE ADVERSARY

We have pointed out that the sword is the only aspect of the armor that is for offensive warfare; that is, it is the only item of God's armor used for attacking the enemy. Perhaps you are wondering what this has to do with our subjective experience of the killing power of the word. If we would understand this, we must see that in spiritual warfare we must deal not only with the objective enemy, but even the more with the subjective adversary. Satan is not only the enemy outside us; he is also the adversary inside us. Today we face a greater problem with the inward adversary than with the outward enemy. The attacks of the enemy from without are not as serious as those of the adversary from within. To deal with this inward adversary we need to experience the killing power of the word. Yes, the enemy is outside us, but his elements are within our very being. Because the enemy's elements are within us, we need the killing power of the word to be applied to our being subjectively. Since the enemy has injected himself into our being, what we need is for the killing power of the word to be applied to us to deal with the elements of the enemy within us.

If you consider your spiritual experience, you will realize that much of the enemy's attack upon you comes from within. Most of the flaming darts come not from the enemy without, but from the adversary within. If you go into seclusion, you will discover that flaming darts will attack you inwardly. By this we see that we must face the adversary as well as the enemy. In our experience we eventually come to realize that the most difficult foe is the self. The self is our worst enemy. Many times we are tempted, not by an objective enemy, but by the self, our own inner being.

SLAYING THE ADVERSARY BY PRAY-READING THE WORD

Because the self is the greatest enemy, we need to experience the killing power of God's word. As we pray-read, we are nourished on the one hand, but certain elements are killed on the other hand. Perhaps you are troubled by doubts, hatred, jealousy, pride, or selfishness. Do you realize that these things can be killed through pray-reading the word? The more we take in the word with its killing power, the more our pride and all the negative elements within us are put to death. By pray-reading, the inward adversary is slain. After a time of pray-reading the word, we may discover that the adversary who was attacking us has disappeared. In a very practical sense, he has been slain by the word we have taken into us.

Do not think that the battlefield for the spiritual warfare is outside us. The battlefield is within us; in particular it is in our mind. All the elements of the adversary can be found in the mind. The way to slay them is to pray-read the word. As we pray-read God's word, the elements of the adversary within our mind will be killed one by one. In this way we shall gain the victory.

A PRACTICAL WAY TO KILL THE NEGATIVE ELEMENTS

Christians today are often very vague or general about matters. They may talk about such things as oneness, holiness, love, or the Lord's coming. But much of the time they are not definite or specific. It is impossible to pin them down. The situation among us in the Lord's recovery must be different. We need to be definite and specific in our experience with the Lord. Many of us can testify that when we pray-read the word, we are pinned down by the Lord. For instance, a brother who is having a problem with his wife may pray-read Paul's word about husbands loving their wives. The more he pray-reads this verse, the more he senses that love for his wife is imparted into him in a practical way that swallows up the negative element of his problem.

As those who are in the Lord's recovery, we need to be practical. We should not simply have a lot of theories, but we need a way to put theory into practice. Pray-reading is a practical way to kill the negative elements within us. The more we take the word of God by means of all prayer in spirit, the more the negative things within us will be put to death. Thus, pray-reading is not only feasting; it is also a way of fighting. As we pray-read the word, the battle is raging as the negative elements in our being are slain. Eventually, the self, the worst foe of all, will be put to death. When the negative things in us are killed through pray-reading, the Lord is victorious. Because He is victorious, we are victorious also.

My concern in this message is not to present Ephesians 6 in a mere objective way. Instead, it is to help you experience Christ subjectively as all the aspects of the armor, especially as the sword of the Spirit. We have pointed out again and again that pray-reading is the way to kill the adversary within us. Every day and in every kind of situation, you should pray-read. Whenever you are troubled by something negative within you, take the word of God by means of prayer in spirit. As you do this, the negative element will be killed.

In Ephesians 5 the word is for nourishment that leads to the beautifying of the Bride. But in Ephesians 6 the word is for killing that enables the church as the corporate warrior to engage in spiritual warfare. Through the killing word, the adversary within us is slain. Sometimes we gain the victory over the enemy objectively, but we are defeated by the adversary subjectively. Although we may rejoice that the enemy outwardly is fleeing, we are still troubled by the adversary within us who remains. For this reason, we should be more concerned for the hidden adversary within us. Let us kill the adversary by pray-reading the word.

THE BLESSING OF BEING IN THE LORD'S RECOVERY

As we consider all these messages on the book of Ephesians, we need to thank the Lord that we are in His recovery. What a blessing it is to be in the Lord's recovery! Day by day, we enjoy inner satisfaction as we go forward under His blessing. The Lord will be victorious, He will gain all the ground within us, and He will prepare the way for His coming back.

About the Author

Witness Lee was born in 1905 in northern China and raised in a Christian family. At age 19 he was fully captured for Christ and immediately consecrated himself to preach the gospel for the rest of his life. Early in his service, he met Watchman Nee, a renowned preacher, teacher, and writer. Witness Lee labored together with Watchman Nee under his direction. In 1934 Watchman Nee entrusted Witness Lee with the responsibility for his publication operation, called the Shanghai Gospel Bookroom.

Prior to the Communist takeover in 1949, Witness Lee was sent by Watchman Nee and his other co-workers to Taiwan to ensure that the things delivered to them by the Lord would not be lost. Watchman Nee instructed Witness Lee to continue the former's publishing operation abroad as the Taiwan Gospel Bookroom, which has been publicly recognized as the publisher of Watchman Nee's works outside China. Witness Lee's work in Taiwan manifested the Lord's abundant blessing. From a mere 350 believers, newly fled from the mainland, the churches in Taiwan grew to 20,000 in five years.

In 1962 Witness Lee felt led of the Lord to come to the United States, and he began to minister in Los Angeles. During his 35 years of service in the U.S., he ministered in weekly meetings and weekend conferences, delivering several thousand spoken messages. Much of his speaking has since been published as over 400 titles. Many of these have been translated into over fourteen languages. He gave his last public conference in February 1997 at the age of 91.

He leaves behind a prolific presentation of the truth in the Bible. His major work, *Life-study of the Bible,* comprises over 25,000 pages of commentary on every book of the Bible from the perspective of the believers' enjoyment and experience of God's divine life in Christ through the Holy Spirit. Witness Lee was the chief editor of a new translation of the New Testament into Chinese called the Recovery Version and directed the translation of the same into English. The Recovery Version also appears in a number of other languages. He provided an extensive body of footnotes, outlines, and spiritual cross references. A radio broadcast of his messages can be heard on Christian radio stations in the United States. In 1965 Witness Lee founded Living Stream Ministry, a non-profit corporation, located in Anaheim, California, which officially presents his and Watchman Nee's ministry.

Witness Lee's ministry emphasizes the experience of Christ as life and the practical oneness of the believers as the Body of Christ. Stressing the importance of attending to both these matters, he led the churches under his care to grow in Christian life and function. He was unbending in his conviction that God's goal is not narrow sectarianism but the Body of Christ. In time, believers began to meet simply as the church in their localities in response to this conviction. In recent years a number of new churches have been raised up in Russia and in many European countries.

Other Books Published By
Living Stream Ministry

Titles by Witness Lee:

Abraham—Called by God	978-0-7363-0359-0
The Experience of Life	978-0-87083-417-2
The Knowledge of Life	978-0-87083-419-6
The Tree of Life	978-0-87083-300-7
The Economy of God	978-0-87083-415-8
The Divine Economy	978-0-87083-268-0
God's New Testament Economy	978-0-87083-199-7
The World Situation and God's Move	978-0-87083-092-1
Christ vs. Religion	978-0-87083-010-5
The All-inclusive Christ	978-0-87083-020-4
Gospel Outlines	978-0-87083-039-6
Character	978-0-87083-322-9
The Secret of Experiencing Christ	978-0-87083-227-7
The Life and Way for the Practice of the Church Life	978-0-87083-785-2
The Basic Revelation in the Holy Scriptures	978-0-87083-105-8
The Crucial Revelation of Life in the Scriptures	978-0-87083-372-4
The Spirit with Our Spirit	978-0-87083-798-2
Christ as the Reality	978-0-87083-047-1
The Central Line of the Divine Revelation	978-0-87083-960-3
The Full Knowledge of the Word of God	978-0-87083-289-5
Watchman Nee—A Seer of the Divine Revelation ...	978-0-87083-625-1

Titles by Watchman Nee:

How to Study the Bible	978-0-7363-0407-8
God's Overcomers	978-0-7363-0433-7
The New Covenant	978-0-7363-0088-9
The Spiritual Man • 3 volumes	978-0-7363-0269-2
Authority and Submission	978-0-7363-0185-5
The Overcoming Life	978-1-57593-817-2
The Glorious Church	978-0-87083-745-6
The Prayer Ministry of the Church	978-0-87083-860-6
The Breaking of the Outer Man and the Release ...	978-1-57593-955-1
The Mystery of Christ	978-1-57593-954-4
The God of Abraham, Isaac, and Jacob	978-0-87083-932-0
The Song of Songs	978-0-87083-872-9
The Gospel of God • 2 volumes	978-1-57593-953-7
The Normal Christian Church Life	978-0-87083-027-3
The Character of the Lord's Worker	978-1-57593-322-1
The Normal Christian Faith	978-0-87083-748-7
Watchman Nee's Testimony	978-0-87083-051-8

Complete Set, Vols. 1-3, Catalog No. 10-040-001
ISBN 978-0-7363-0962-2
9 780736 309622

10-035-001
ISBN 978-0-87083-149-2

9 780870 831492